# Why Do Donuts Have Holes?

# Why Do Donuts Have Holes?

## Fascinating Facts About What We Eat and Drink

## Don Voorhees

CITADEL PRESS
Kensington Publishing Corp.
www.kensingtonbooks.com

CITADEL PRESS BOOKS are published by

Kensington Publishing Corp.
850 Third Avenue
New York, NY 10022

All Kensington titles, imprints, and distributed lines are available at special quantity discounts for bulk purchases for sales promotions, premiums, fund-raising, educational, or institutional use. Special book excerpts or customized printings can also be created to fit specific needs. For details, write or phone the office of the Kensington special sales manager: Kensington Publishing Corp., 850 Third Avenue, New York, NY 10022, attn: Special Sales Department; phone 1-800-221-2647.

CITADEL PRESS and the Citadel logo are Reg. U.S. Pat. & TM Off.

First printing: October 2004

10  9  8  7  6  5  4  3  2  1

Printed in the United States of America

Library of Congress Control Number: 2004106013

ISBN 0-8065-2551-7

*To Mom, pork chops and scalloped potatoes,
and "real" macaroni and cheese.*

# Contents

1. A Brief History of Food   1
2. What's in a Name?   19
3. Moo Juice   27
4. On the Hoof   42
5. Feathered Friends   53
6. Chicken of the Sea   64
7. Apples and Oranges   72
8. Eat Your Greens   93
9. Amber Waves   107
10. Nuts!   121
11. Sweet Stuff   130
12. Junk Food   140
13. Saucy!   156
14. Cheers!   164
15. Thirst Quenchers   183
16. Eating Out   194
17. It's In There!   212
18. Kitchen Science   221
19. Kitchenware   227
20. Packaging   243
21. Chop Suey (Odds and Ends)   257

# Why Do Donuts Have Holes?

# 1

# A Brief History of Food

### What vegetables did prehistoric man eat?

Walk into any large supermarket today and you can pick from thousands of food products. We are truly blessed. Prehistoric humans were not so fortunate. They supplemented whatever meat they could find with a limited number of plant foods. Early Europeans probably ate wheat along with beans, cabbage, onions, peas, radishes, and turnips. These foods may have been flavored with mustard seed. The early Asians subsisted on a diet of bananas, coconuts, millet, rice, and wheat, flavored with ginger. The early Central American menu included avocados, beans, corn, squash, and tomatoes, seasoned with red pepper.

### Do beans and grains have a symbiotic relationship?

Beans were one of the first crops cultivated by humans. Archaeologists have found peas in Thailand dating back to 9750 B.C. and the peoples of Mexico and Peru were growing the common green bean, kidney beans, and lima beans as early as 7000 B.C. Lentils date to 6750 B.C. in the Middle East and soybeans to 2800 B.C. in China. Fortunately, all these civilizations also cultivated grain crops, such as as barley, corn, millet, rice, or wheat, and did not rely solely on legumes for their protein.

Beans are an incomplete source of protein, but happily they are complemented perfectly by grains, which also are incomplete

1

proteins. Beans and grains have a symbiotic nutritional relation-ship, forming a complete protein when eaten together. This bean-grain combination served as the foundation of most major early civilizations. Combinations of lentils and rice or chickpeas and couscous are good examples. The early Mesoamericans relied on a food triad, known as the "three sisters," of beans, corn, and squash.

Beans stored wonderfully for up to three years if kept dry. Soaking them for a few hours brought them back to life, making their proteins, enzymes, vitamins, and minerals available. There were hundreds of varieties and a multitude of ways of preparing them. They could be eaten raw, cooked, sprouted, ground into flour, made into tofu, or fermented into soy sauce or miso paste.

Beans not only have a protein content of around twenty per-cent and are high in carbohydrates and fiber, they are also very low in fat and contain no cholesterol. Their high fiber content may even lower your cholesterol.

### Why is it considered unlucky to have thirteen guests at dinner?

The most well known dinner with thirteen guests that turned out badly was the Last Supper, where the thirteenth guest—Judas—betrayed Christ. However, there is an even earlier dinner of note, with thirteen guests, that turned out badly. In Scandinavian mythology, there was a dinner of twelve gods at Valhalla that the god Loki crashed, making the number of guests thirteen. Loki later incited Hod, the blind god of winter, to kill another god at the dinner—Balder the Good. Ever since, the Norse have consid-ered dinner parties of thirteen to be unlucky.

### What do hot cross buns have to do with Christianity?

What food could be more Christian than hot cross buns? These small, sweet yeast buns with raisins or candied fruit are a staple of Christian Good Friday observations, although they were prob-ably not first created by Christians. In fact, they most likely pre-date Christ himself. It is believed that these round buns with a cross on top were made by the ancient Romans, Greeks, and

Britons. They saw the round bun as a representation of the sun and the four arms of the cross as symbolic of the four seasons and the four phases of the moon.

As Christianity evolved, hot cross buns became associated with Good Friday and were eaten at other times of the year to ward off bad luck. They became firmly linked with Christianity in the 1500s, when English monks would use leftover dough from the baking of their sacramental Good Friday breads to make little round buns with crosses on them for the poor.

### What new foods were first brought to Europe by the returning Crusaders?

Those knights of yore were pretty persistent about reclaiming Jerusalem from the Muslims and putting it into Christian hands. They never really fulfilled their goal, but not for lack of trying. Thousands of lives were lost on the many Crusades to the Middle East and not much good came out of them. However, each time the knights returned to Europe, they brought back some wonderful new food with them.

On the First Crusade, the soldiers ate sugar while besieging Acre, in 1104. In 1148, the Second bunch of Crusaders returned home with sugar, which was highly prized. It would go on to replace honey as the main food sweetener.

In 1191, on the Third Crusade, Richard the Lionhearted defeated the Muslim leader Saladin and was offered a sweet treat as a peace gesture. It was a fruit-flavored ice desert made with snow brought down from the mountains of Lebanon. Saladin called it *charbet*. When introduced to Italy, it was called *sorbetto*. The French called it *sorbet*.

The Fourth Crusade brought back the Damson plum from Damascus, in 1204. These crusaders also introduced rice and lemons and helped to popularize sugar even more.

Crescent rolls were created to honor Duke Leopold VI when he was departing on the Fifth Crusade and bakers in Vienna gave the Crusaders crescent-shaped rolls.

The Crusaders, at one time or another, were also responsible for introducing the spices cinnamon, cardamom, cloves, nutmeg, mace, coriander, cumin, and saffron to Europe.

### How did sugar start the American slave trade?

Sugar production was already big business in the West Indies by the early 1500s. It was the practice of the Spanish government to give explorers and others grants of land in the New World. Along with the land, the grants included whatever indigenous peoples happened to be living on that land. These grants were invariably turned into sugar plantations and the people into slave laborers. The Spanish weren't too bright when it came to managing their slave labor. They often simply worked people to death. By the time they realized the folly of this form of worker management, it was too late; their slave laborers were already running low. So they turned to Africa for a fresh supply of slaves. Many thousands of native peoples were enslaved and killed to satisfy the sweet tooth of the Old World.

### Who wrote the first cookbook?

The first printed book containing recipes, as well as tips on living well, was published in 1475. Titled *Concerning Honest Pleasure and Physical Well-Being*, it was written by the Vatican librarian, Plantina (Bartolomeo Sacchi). There were recipes for many dishes that we would find odd today, including peacock, hummingbird livers, and lark's tongues.

Plantina published an illustrated cookbook in 1570—*Cooking Secrets of Pope Pius V*—which contained the first known picture of a fork. The fork was still held in disdain in America as late as 1779, when John Adams was ridiculed for setting his table with forks after returning from his post as Minister to France.

### How did the Pilgrims really survive their first few winters?

We are all familiar with the story of Thanksgiving and how the "Indians" and Pilgrims shared in a feast of friendship. This one feast was not enough to sustain them for long. The Pilgrims really survived by accidentally coming across one of several emergency caches of food the Indians would store over the winter at various places. This pilfered food saw them through that first terrible winter.

One reason the Pilgrims had such a hard time those first few years is that they were not inclined to eat from the bounty of local foods available to them; they were too set in their culinary ways. Among the foods in the local natural larder were plentiful game, fish and shellfish, lobsters, mushrooms, cherries, strawberries, blueberries, huckleberries, blackberries, raspberries, elderberries, currants, grapes, cranberries, and nuts. Many died because of their stubbornness.

The Pilgrims were woefully unprepared for life in their new homeland. They had neither the inclination nor equipment to hunt or fish. One local Indian named Squanto had to show them how to catch eels with their hands, as they had no nets or appropriate fishing tackle. They did not know how to hunt, as hunting was reserved for the upper classes in England. Why they did not collect the bounty of the forests' plant life is less easy to explain.

In the south, the Cavaliers of Virginia actually did survive by the active support of the Native Americans, who gave them food, although they soon lived to regret the decision. The Virginians were smart enough to have brought pigs and chickens to raise. These animals were small and easily transportable, plus they were easy to keep and would eat just about anything. The hog was so successful in the colonies that pork became the most important meat for the next three centuries.

### What game bird was once so plentiful that it blackened the sky?

The passenger pigeon was an American bird that was so plentiful that its flocks would literally blacken the sky for miles at a stretch. One flock was estimated to have been a mile wide and 240 miles in length! They were the bison of the sky—seemingly infinite and inexhaustible. One estimate put their number at nine billion at the beginning of the eighteenth century. Like the bison, the myth was soon dispelled through man's overexploitation.

Passenger pigeons were hunted with guns and nets. During their migrations, some towns lived almost exclusively on them for weeks at a time. Farmers fed them to their pigs and they could be bought for a penny a piece. Up until the Civil War, their numbers did not seem to decrease much, but like the bison, the relentless hunting of the passenger pigeon decimated its population, until the last wild bird was killed in Ohio, in 1900. The last captive passenger pigeon died in 1914.

Man can accomplish great feats of destruction when he puts his mind to it. Thankfully, enough bison escaped the slaughter that wild herds could be reestablished in the West. Sadly, the same cannot be said of the passenger pigeon.

### What animal's nose was a delicacy for American colonists?

Early Americans ate a wide variety of native game, once they became accustomed to it. Bears, for instance were popular fare, as were elk, where they could be found. The moose was also eaten, with its nose being a highly prized delicacy. Another odd morsel favored by some was tail of beaver. Squirrels were widely enjoyed in the country, but turkeys and lobsters were held in low regard by many, as they were so common.

### What did seventeenth-century housewives do with table scraps?

Not much went into the garbage back then. Leftovers would not keep in warm weather. They were typically thrown back in the kettle to keep hot for the next meal, as were table scraps and any bones or vegetable materials not used. This catchall kettle provided a perpetual stew that was constantly changing in its content and always ready for a quick meal. Sometimes a brown bread might be suspended above the stew to cook in its steam.

### What was the only item of cookware available before the eighteenth century?

Before the invention of the oven, cooking was done in the fireplace. Up until the 1700s, about the only cookware the family kitchen had was a large iron kettle with three stout legs. Oftentimes it was set directly onto the fire or hot coals. Sometimes it was hung over the fire, suspended from a hook attached to an arm made of green wood, which would not burn.

The first advance in kitchen technology was the introduction of an iron arm that was hinged at one end so that the kettle could be swung in or out. Before this, the cook had to be fairly agile to reach into the kettle without getting burned or spilling its contents into the fire.

How did they adjust the cooking temperature, you may ask? We don't realize how lucky we are with our modern kitchen conveniences. If you want to bake bread at 350 degrees, you turn a knob until the oven reads 350. The housewife of 400 years ago had a rather complicated task to get the right cooking temperature for the food she was preparing.

The first key was selecting the right kind of wood to use in the fire. Different woods burn at different temperatures and at different speeds. Hickory and oak were preferred, as they burned more evenly and with a greater amount of heat than other common woods. Chestnut and hemlock were avoided as they tended to crackle and throw glowing embers into the kettle. Just starting the fire in the morning could be a challenge. There were no matches back then and the prudent housewife kept some coals hot overnight for this purpose; otherwise she might have to borrow a hot coal from a neighbor.

Another decision was whether to cook over flames or directly on hot coals. If the latter was preferred, she had to plan to start the fire early enough to have embers when she was ready to cook. To determine the temperature, cooks became skilled at holding their hand over the fire to determine how far above it the kettle should be placed. A chain could be put on the cooking arm hook and the kettle hung at the proper height. Cooking times could also be a little tricky: timers and watches may or may not have been available, sundials worked on sunny days, but on cloudy days and at night guesstimates were used.

One final obstacle the cooks of old faced was the lack of standardized measuring cups or spoons. Most people didn't have them and therefore the cookbooks of the time didn't mention any exact quantities or weights in recipes.

## How did dogs help seventeenth-century women cook?

The one other method of cooking available to the seventeenth-century woman, aside from the kettle, was the spit. As today, meat could be impaled on a rod and turned as it cooked over the fire. However, one could not stand around turning a spit all afternoon. This is where the dogs came in. It may sound bizarre, but some ingenious ladies attached the spit to a treadmill on which they put a dog. Fido had to do a little work for his dinner!

## Who invented pasties?

The tin mines of Cornwall have been worked for thousands of years and mining is a local tradition. By the Middle Ages, the inventive wives of the miners came up with a convenient all-in-one dish for their men to carry with them into the mine—the pasty. This clever baked-dough envelope is kind of like a calzone, containing a complete lunch meal. The original pasties were made with the meat in one end, vegetables in the middle, and fruits in the other end. By eating from the meat end, through the vegetable middle, and finishing with the fruit end, a three-course meal could be enjoyed. They were baked in the morning and tightly wrapped so that they could be enjoyed warm at lunchtime. They were also neat and easy to carry. Many clever wives baked their husbands' initials on one corner of the pasty to avoid any later confusion at lunch.

## What are "beefeaters"?

London's famed yeomen of the guard at the Tower of London are known as "beefeaters." They are easily recognizable by their colorful uniforms. It is said they got their name in 1669 from the grand duke of Tuscany Cosimo de' Medici, because their daily ration of beef was so high.

## What food was involved in the longest running interstate conflict?

The longest running conflict between two states was probably the Maryland-Virginia Oyster Wars. It may sound silly, but these two states battled, often with bloodshed, over the rights to catch oysters in the Potomac River and Bay. The conflict had its origins in 1632, when Charles I cut off the top of Virginia, creating Maryland, as a gift to his friend Lord Baltimore. It wasn't just the formation of Maryland that caused the friction, but where the king drew the boundary line. It was customary, when using a river to establish a border, to draw the line right down the middle. Charles, as a favor to Baltimore, gave Maryland the whole Potomac, right up to the high-tide line on the Virginia side. Hence all oysters and crabs in the river belonged to Maryland and many skirmishes broke out between the watermen of the two states. Things got so bad that in 1868, the Maryland Oyster Navy was formed to keep the peace. As recently as 1959, blood was spilled over this dispute. It took until 1962 for laws to be passed to bring the Oyster Wars to an end.

### When did Thanksgiving start?

President Abraham Lincoln made it official in 1863, proclaiming the last Thursday in November to be a national day set aside to commemorate that first Thanksgiving dinner in 1621, but Thanksgiving was already being observed in thirty out of thirty-two states. The chief instigator in the Thanksgiving movement was Sarah Josepha Hale, editor of *Godey's Lady's Book*. She had been campaigning for a national Thanksgiving day since 1846. Hale was influential in Lincoln's decision, as was the Civil War.

It was at the urging of Federated Department Stores executive Fred Lazarus that the date of observance was changed to the last Thursday in November. In 1939, the economy was sluggish and Lazarus convinced President Roosevelt that a longer Christmas shopping season would help to stimulate it. Roosevelt issued a proclamation prompting many states to change the date.

### Who figured out fluoride could prevent cavities?

One of the first people to put together the fact that fluoride was somehow good for the teeth was, predictably, a dentist. Frederick S. Motley, a dentist in Colorado Springs, Colorado noticed, in 1916, that his patients' teeth were discolored, but that they had very few cavities. He made the linkage between the city's drinking water, which had fluoride salt concentrations of two parts per million, with the reduced tooth decay.

The first city to intentionally fluoridate its drinking water was Grand Rapids, Michigan, in 1945. Plans were also made to fluoridate the water in Newburgh, New York, but there was intense political pressure from groups that didn't think the government should be messing with something as personal as their drinking water.

There are still many people and studies that suggest that fluoride in the drinking water does not prevent cavities. It is suggested that fluoride applied topically to the teeth, as in toothpastes or mouth rinses, may be effective. Fluoride in the bloodstream, as when consumed in drinking water, may do no good or may even be detrimental to the teeth. The Centers for Disease Control and Prevention, however, still recommend the fluoridation of drinking water to prevent cavities.

## How did dogs help bring about the iodization of salt?

David Marine is the father of iodized salt in America. In 1905, he moved from Baltimore, Maryland, to Cleveland, Ohio. To his dismay, he noticed that all the dogs in the town had goiter, as well as many of the people. He vowed to crusade for the iodization of table salt.

In 1916, physician E. C. Kendell and Marine ran a study of the effect of iodine on goiter. They tested schoolgirls in Akron, Ohio. The teens who were given 0.2 gram tablets of sodium iodide had a significantly lower rate of goiter incidence. As a result of their work, iodized salt started being offered for sale along with un-iodized salt.

## When were people first lectured about chewing their food?

Around the turn of the twentieth century, one Horace Fletcher preached to the masses about the virtue of chewing one's food thirty-two times per mouthful. Fletcher gained notoriety when his personal physician, Dr. Ernest Van Someren, reported in a paper to the British Medical Association that Fletcher had reduced his intake of protein and significantly increased his well-being, curing him of gout, headaches, frequent colds, boils on the neck and face, eczema on the toes, and loss of interest in life. The British prime minister, William E. Gladstone, an ardent supporter of over-masticating, was said to have prompted Fletcher's crusade.

In 1903, Fletcher wrote *The A.B.-Z. of Our Own Nutrition*, which began a fad of chewing each mouthful of food carefully thirty-two times. He believed that people eat too much because they eat too quickly. By chewing for so long, one would eat less. He also recommended not eating when you are angry or upset. His work was translated into several languages and thousands of people adopted his mastication techniques.

### What food company's sacks were used as clothes by poor Southern families?

In the early 1900s, the J. Allen Smith Company had a fabulously successful product that was sold from northern Florida to southern Virginia—White Lily Flour. Made exclusively from soft winter wheat, White Lily flour was lower in protein than other flour brands, making it perfect for baking biscuits, cakes, and pies. White Lily flour and cornmeal were so common that poor children in much of the South wore shirts and dresses made from their sacks.

### When did Americans start brushing their teeth?

Hard as it may be to believe, most Americans didn't brush their teeth prior to World War II. The habit was brought back with the GIs who were forced to do so while in the service. That's not to say that there weren't dentifrice products available before this. The first American patent on a toothbrush went to H. N. Wadsworth. Companies began mass-producing them around 1885. Early toothbrushes used hair from the necks of cold-weather pigs for bristles. DuPont introduced nylon bristles in 1938. The first electric toothbrush was sold in the U.S. by Squibb in 1960.

Toothpastes have been around in China since 500 B.C. Modern toothpastes were developed in the 1800s. They contained chalk and soap and didn't taste or smell all that great. In 1873, Colgate made the first good-smelling toothpaste, which they sold in a jar. Toothpaste wasn't put into a collapsible tube until Dr. Washington Sheffield of Connecticut did so in 1892.

## How did American housewives help win World War II?

World War II was a time of hard work and sacrifice. Even if she wasn't Rosie the Riveter, out in the factory building materiel for the war, the average American woman could still help the war effort at home. The main way was by conserving and cutting back on the use of certain products. The government maintained that if each family used one less tin can per week, there would be enough extra tin and steel to build five thousand more tanks or thirty-eight Liberty ships. So women washed and flattened their cans. They also saved their kitchen oils and turned them in to the local butcher for ration points. One jar of fat had enough glycerine in it to make a pound of black powder.

## Who came up with the idea for TV dinners?

Sometimes, necessity really *is* the mother of invention. At least that was the case with the invention of TV dinners. C. A. Swanson and Sons of Omaha, Nebraska, began selling frozen beef, chicken, and turkey pot pies in 1945. One day in 1953, Swanson's found itself with a bit of a problem—they had too many turkeys, which were sitting on railway cars. A thirty-one-year-old employee—Gerry Thomas—had an idea. He had seen airline foods being tested and was inspired to freeze the turkey meat and put it on aluminum trays with a vegetable and a brownie.

Since television was the hottest new technology of the time, they called the frozen meals TV dinners and designed the packaging to look like a TV screen. Thomas's superiors were quite skeptical at first, but after selling ten million dinners at ninety-eight cents in the first year, they came to appreciate the concept a little more. The "generous" company gave Thomas a $1,000 bonus for his new creation. Swanson's next introduced fried chicken TV dinners, followed by salisbury steak, and haddock. In the early 1960s, they took the "TV" part out of the name because too many people were eating in front of the TV. Turkey and fried chicken are still the best-sellers today.

Campbell Soup Company acquired control of Swanson's in 1955 and built their Swanson frozen food product line to sixty-five, by 1972. The introduction of frozen dinners radically changed the food industry and several competitors came on the market. Stouffers Lean Cuisine frozen dinners appeared on the market in 1981. Diet-conscious consumers helped this new line of frozen entrees capture one third of the market within three years.

Frozen dinners were not as quick to prepare in the old days as they are now. In the 1950s, a frozen pot pie needed about forty-five minutes to cook in a conventional oven. With microwave ovens, it can now be ready to eat in just five minutes.

If you are really into frozen meals, check out TheSingleMan's GuideToTVDinners@yarayara.com/tv. It's a site devoted to rating frozen entrees.

## How did baby food help free the Bay of Pigs prisoners in Cuba?

After President John F. Kennedy oversaw the Bay of Pigs debacle in Cuba, it was up to his Attorney General brother, Bobby, to arrange a ransom for the freedom of the captured soldiers. As part of the release deal, RFK solicited food donations from the Grocery Manufacturers of America. General Mills and H. J. Heinz gave $500,000 and $1,000,000 respectively, and Gerber contributed $910,000 worth of baby food. All went well, and Jack and Jackie had a homecoming for the prisoners at the Orange Bowl in Miami, on December 29, 1962.

## What ever happened to fondue?

Fondue is one of those sixties food fads that is making something of a comeback. There was a time, about thirty-five years ago, when it seemed like every home had a fondue set. But like the wok, and then the crock pot, this trendy item did not enjoy a long popularity and was soon stuck in the back of the cabinet and forgotten.

The word "fondue" comes from the French word for "melt"— *fondre*. It became a popular way to eat bread in eighteenth-century Switzerland. Cheese, white wine, and seasonings were melted into a central pot at the table and diners would dip bread into it. A dessert fondue had melted chocolate, cream, and sometimes liqueur, into which fruit was dipped.

The etiquette of fondue required that each person have their own color-coded fondue fork and that the fork never touch the lips. Another cute fondue tradition holds that if a male diner drops his bread into the pot, he must buy a bottle of wine. If a female does so, she must kiss the host.

## What is the oldest American supermarket chain?

A&P supermarkets began as the Great American Tea Company, at 31 Vesey Street in New York City. Two spice and tea merchants— George Huntington Hartford and George P. Gilman—decided in 1859 to start buying whole shiploads of Japanese and Chinese tea from ships in New York harbor and selling it through the mail. They then began buying tea in bulk directly from China and Japan. By purchasing tea in such quantity they were able to resell it at one-third the going rate of other merchants. For most of the 1800s, more tea than coffee was consumed in the United States and business prospered.

In 1861, they opened their first store, at the corner of Broadway and Grand Streets in New York City. Within four years the Great American Tea Company had six stores and began selling grocery items. Four years later, in 1870, they changed their name to the Great Atlantic & Pacific Tea Company to take advantage of the public fascination with the newly opened transcontinental railway. They increased business by offering more goods for sale, as well as making use of clever marketing gimmicks, such as running contests, having bands play on Saturdays, and putting cashiers in pagoda-style cages. Their storefronts were colored Chinese vermilion red with gold lettering to conjure up an image of the Orient from where their tea originated.

By 1876, A&P had 100 stores and became the nation's first major grocery chain. In the 1880s, A&P employed horse-drawn wagons to travel along 5,000 routes peddling their goods. By 1912, they had almost 500 stores, and by 1929, there were nearly 16,000 A&Ps with sales of more than $1 billion.

A&P did not begin opening supermarkets until 1937, as did other food store chains. The supermarket spelled the death of smaller food stores. For each supermarket opened, four or five smaller stores were closed.

Up until 1973, A&P was the largest American grocery chain. A&P started to lose its dominance in the dog-eat-dog supermarket world when they failed to realize that the future of the grocery game was in the suburbs. Instead of building big superstores in shopping malls, they stuck with their smaller stores in the cities. Thus began their decline. In 1975, A&P closed about 1200 stores and began building 160 new larger supermarkets. By 1979, they had closed about half of their 3500 stores. A controlling interest in the company was purchased by the Tengelmann Group, a family-owned German food retailer. They also failed to appreciate the superstore concept and opened A&P Plus stores that didn't carry as many products. One-stop shopping Americans stayed away in droves and the company's financial health continued to falter. In 1981, Tengelmann brought in English food retail whiz James Wood to try and save what was left of the grocery chain. Wood shut down many more stores, including half of the Plus stores and reopened them as Super Fresh. As a result, A&P dropped to the number five supermarket chain, with 1,055 stores, trailing Safeway, Kroger, Lucky, and American Stores. Today, there are "only" about 700 A&Ps in the U.S. and Ontario.

## What other grocery giants started out selling tea?

Another little tea shop that went on to become one of the largest grocery chains in the United States is Grand Union. The Grand Union Tea Company was begun by twenty-year-old Cyrus Jones in Scranton, Pennsylvania. At first he sold tea, coffee, spices, and food flavorings, sometimes door-to-door. He made $12,000 in his first year. Sales eventually would reach $1 billion.

Yet another early grocery store that had its roots in tea was B. H. Kroger Company, which was founded under the name Great Western Tea Company in 1883. It was begun by Cincinnati grocery salesman Bernard H. Kroger. In two years he had four stores and at its peak Kroger had 1,250 stores in twenty states. In 2001, sales topped $50 billion.

## What was the first true self-service grocery store?

Piggly Wiggly was the first true self-service grocery store. Before Piggly Wiggly was founded in Memphis, Tennessee, by Clarence Saunders, grocery-store shoppers had to present their orders to a clerk who would collect the goods from the store shelves. Saunders realized that this was a waste of time and manpower, and more important, prevented the shopper from making impulse buys that could really add to his profit. Self-serve was the way to go.

His competitors predicted failure, but Saunders opened this new kind of store on September 16, 1916, at 79 Jefferson Street, with shopping baskets and open shelves. Saunders began franchising his concept to hundreds of grocery retailers for the operation of Piggly Wiggly stores. The company went public, trading on the New York Stock Exchange, but Saunders lost control of the Piggly Wiggly Corporation after a series of stock transactions in the early 1920s.

Why did Saunders pick the odd name Piggly Wiggly? He never gave a good explanation. When asked, he simply replied, "So people will ask that very question." He wanted a name that would be talked about and remembered.

Piggly Wiggly first introduced many other shopping conveniences that we now take for granted, among them:

Checkout stands
Prices marked on all items in the store
Carrying a full line of nationally advertised brands
Refrigerator cases to keep produce fresh longer
Putting employees in uniforms

Today there are over six hundred Piggly Wiggly stores in sixteen states, all independently owned and operated, primarily in the Southeast.

## Who invented the shopping cart?

It's hard to imagine going to the supermarket and not using a cart, unless you only need a few items. In the days before the refrigerator caught on, women had to shop quite often for fresh food and tended not to buy too much at one time. One man got the idea into his head to change this.

On June 4, 1937, Sylvan Goldman, the owner of Humpty Dumpty stores in Oklahoma, noticed that people stopped adding items to their wicker shopping baskets when they got full or became too heavy. He figured if customers could carry more, they would buy more. Goldman fashioned a crude shopping cart from lawn chair frames to which he attached two shopping baskets and wheels. Shoppers' reception to the new convenience was less than enthusiastic. Men felt silly pushing a cart around the store, and women liked carrying their goods in a basket. To make people feel comfortable with the idea, Goldman had employees posing as shoppers wheel his carts around the markets. The rest, as they say, is history.

## When did bar code scanners first appear in supermarkets?

Two graduate students at Drexel University in Philadelphia—Bernard Silver and Norman Woodland—received the first patent for a barcode scanner in 1952. Bar codes were first used commercially in 1966, but Silver and Woodland realized that for the system to catch on across the country, there would have to be some sort of industry-wide standard set. In 1970, the Universal Grocery Products Identification Code was written by a company called Logicon Inc. This led to the Universal Product Code (UPC) still in use today. In 1974, the first UPC scanner was installed in Marsh's Supermarket in Troy, Ohio; it scanned a ten-pack of Wrigley's Juicy Fruit chewing gum.

Merchants were at first reluctant to invest in the equipment needed to operate the system, as they usually are with any new technology. Consumers lamented the elimination of individually marked prices and the cashier saying the price out loud as she rang up an order. What if the computer made a mistake? Once people got used to the speed, convenience, and accuracy of price scanning, few wished to go back to the old system.

# 2

# What's in a Name?

### Is French toast from France?

The French can't take credit for French toast. This is another American creation that somehow got associated with the French. There are a couple of different theories about how this fried bread dipped in an egg-milk mixture came by its name. One is that it was invented at a roadside tavern near Albany, New York, in 1724, by a guy named Joseph French. Another version is that the name comes from the French-speaking cajun cooks in Louisiana who made the dish *pain perdu*, or "lost bread," from day-old bread. Either way, people have been soaking stale pieces of bread in various liquids and frying them for centuries.

### What is a Po' Boy?

For those of you who don't know, a Po' Boy, or Poor Boy, is a sandwich that was born in New Orleans around 1895. Some credit a local coffee stall owner named Mme. Bégué with its invention. She is said to have taken a French bread, sliced it in half, slathered it with butter, and filled it with different ingredients. Legend says its name comes from the pleas of hungry black youths of the time who would say, "Please give a sandwich to a poor (po') boy."

Another tale of later origin credits a New Orleans streetcar strike with helping to give birth to the "poor boy" name. In 1929, New Orleans Public Service planned to replace their streetcars with buses. Big deal, right? Well, streetcars required conductors and buses didn't. The streetcar workers went on strike and things got ugly. Many strikers were killed and injured. Bennie and Clovis Martin, former streetcar workers, offered free sandwiches to "any poor boy," or union member, who came into their French Market restaurant.

Today, the Po' Boy has such fillings as ham, roast beef, oysters, bacon, cheese, tomato, lettuce, and so on, with gravy, Tabasco, and Creole mustard.

### Who invented the club sandwich?

As with many of these "Who created the first?" questions, there are different versions of the story of the club sandwich. The more interesting one is that it was first made at the Sarasota Club in Sarasota Springs, New York. The club was purchased by sportsman Richard Canfield, in 1894, and turned into a casino. The club's kitchen is said to have made the first sandwich with three layers of white toast filled with sliced turkey, lettuce, tomato, and mayonnaise. Others claim the sandwich first appeared on railway club cars.

### Who invented the Reuben sandwich?

A guy named Reuben, right? Yes, but the dispute is over which one. Many say that the Reuben was first created at Reuben's Delicatessen in New York, in 1914. Arnold Reuben is said to have made a Reuben Special, consisting of meat, cheese, cole slaw, and Russian dressing on buttered toasted rye bread for Annette Seelos, one of Charlie Chaplin's leading ladies.

Others, especially those in Nebraska, maintain that a wholesale grocer named Reuben Kolakofsky did so during a poker game at the Blackstone Hotel, in Omaha, in 1925. The hotel's owner liked it so much that he put it on the menu and named it in Reuben's honor. Take your pick.

### How did Tombstone Pizza get its name?

Ron Simek owned a tavern in Medford, Wisconsin. His bar was named The Tombstone Tap because it happened to be across the street from a graveyard. In 1962, he and his brother began selling frozen pizza to the bar's patrons. They became popular and the brothers went into the frozen pizza business. They put a cactus silhouetted by a setting sun on their packaging to give the feel of the western desert (a nicer image than a graveyard). Kraft bought the business in 1986 and it became the top-selling frozen pizza brand.

## What American city is named for garlic?

The Windy City, of course. Chicago got its name from the Indian word for the wild garlic that grew around Lake Michigan— "chicagaoua." Garlic was also around for thousands of years in the Old World. The workers who built the pyramids were fed garlic. A member of the lily family, garlic has been used as a medicine for almost every ailment imaginable. It is related to the onion, chives, shallots, and leeks.

California is the leading producer of garlic. The town of Gilroy is known as "The Garlic Capital of the World." Some people can't get enough garlic. There are a few all-garlic restaurants where you can order everything from garlic cheesecake to garlic ice cream.

## Why are the elite known as the "upper crust"?

Before 1900, ninety-five percent of flour was sold for household baking. In most places, you couldn't pop down to the local bakery for bread. Wealthy homes had cooks who would do the family baking. As the modern oven didn't appear until the end of the nineteenth century, baking was done in the fireplace and the resultant bread often had a sooty bottom. The blackened bottoms of bread were given to the household staff, the more desirable upper crust was reserved for the lord and lady of the house.

The word "lord" is derived from the Anglo-Saxon *hlaford*, meaning "loaf ward." It was the male head of the house who furnished his charges with bread. Likewise, "lady," is from the Anglo-Saxon *hlaefdige*, meaning "loaf kneader," or she who makes the bread to be supplied by the lord.

## What do the words "cream" and "Christ" have in common?

Unhomogenized milk that is left to stand will separate into two layers—a relatively fat-free skimmed milk on the bottom and fat-rich cream layer on top. It is this high percentage of fat (oil) that gives cream its name. The words "cream" and "Christ" both derive from the Greek *chriein*, meaning "to anoint." Since ancient times, oil has been used to anoint the chosen.

## Who coined the term "comfort food"?

We all have our own comfort foods. These are foods that give us a deep-down sense of well-being. They are often foods that we enjoyed as children and still take comfort in as adults. While comfort foods have always been around, the term "comfort food" didn't appear in print until it was first used in describing grits in a 1977 article in the *Washington Post Magazine*. The term caught on and now comfort foods can be almost anything from potatoes to bread and macaroni and cheese.

## Did the Japanese invent tempura?

Of course not; that wouldn't be interesting. Today we associate this specialty dish of batter-dipped, deep-fried pieces of fish or vegetables with the Japanese; however, tempura was actually introduced to Japan by Jesuit missionaries, in 1585. The word "tempura" comes from the Portuguese *temporras*, which means "Friday," the day when deep-fried fish was eaten.

## How did the Battle of Hastings change the culinary language of the English?

Wars usually aren't good for much, but they certainly help to introduce new cultures to conquered territories. Such was the case with the Norman invasion of England. In 1066, William the Conqueror defeated the English at the Battle of Hastings. One of the lasting results of this conquest was the introduction of new food words into the ever-evolving English language. French words such as *boeuf*, *mouton*, *porc*, *poularde*, and *veau*

became the English words "beef," "mutton," "pork," "poultry,"
and "veal."

## How did the Dutch influence our culinary language?

Back in the 1600s, the Dutch held sway in the areas that were to
become New Jersey and New York, and their people and culture
remained long after the English had displaced them politically.
Remnants of America's Dutch past can still be found in some of
our common food terminology. (Don't confuse the real Dutch
with the Pennsylvania "Dutch," who were actually Germans with
the word "Deutsch" somehow twisted into "Dutch.")

The word "cookie" was derived from the Dutch *koekje*, which
was short for *olykoek*, meaning "oil cake." The Dutch word for
"cabbage" is *cool* and the Dutch word for "salad" is *sla*, hence the
modern cole slaw. Our word "cruller" comes from the Dutch
*krullen*, meaning "to curl." "Pancake" comes from the Dutch *pan-
nekoeken*. Two other Dutch foods that are still popular are waffles
and dumplings.

## What is the origin of the word "teetotaler"?

A teetotaler is someone who abstains from alcohol. The term was
first noted in the records of the Temperance Society in Laings-
burg, Michigan, in the 1830s. The Society made its members take
one of two pledges. The Old Pledge (O.P.) allowed its adherents
to drink in moderation. Those taking the T. Pledge were required
to totally abstain and were known as "T-Totalers."

## What dessert was created for Queen Victoria's Diamond Jubilee?

On June 22, 1897, Great Britain's Queen Victoria celebrated her
Diamond Jubilee, commemorating sixty years on the throne.
There was a huge week-long celebration. One reminder we still
have with us today of the gala event is cherries jubilee. This flaming dessert of cherries, sugar, and brandy served over ice cream
was created just for the jubilee by Auguste Escoffier, chef at
London's Carleton House.

### Who is Suzette and why does she have a crêpe dessert named for her?

One of our more impressive desserts is crêpes suzette. It consists of crepes in an orange-butter sauce that are doused with orange liqueur and set aflame. If the story is to be believed, crêpes suzette were first concocted in 1895, at a party given by the Prince of Wales at the Café de Paris in Monte Carlo. A young waiter at the affair, one Henri Charpentier, made very thin pancakes over which he poured a liqueur sauce. They accidentally caught fire and wowed the gathering. One guest had a daughter named Suzette and he named the dish for her.

Don't believe that story? Another version puts the origin of the dish in 1667. French chef Jean Rédoux may have created crêpes to honor Suzette, Princesse de Carignan.

### Who created Bananas Foster?

Bananas Foster is another flaming dessert. This crowd pleaser was created at Brennan's Restaurant in New Orleans, in 1951, for one of their best customers—Richard Foster. In this dish, bananas are cut lengthwise, sautéed in rum, brown sugar, and banana liqueur, and served over vanilla ice cream, flambé-style. One reason bananas were used in the dish was that New Orleans was a major port of entry for bananas being shipped into the country from Central and South America. *Holiday Magazine* asked owner Owen Brennan to create a new dish for an article they were doing on the restaurant. Brennan challenged his chef Paul Blangé to come up with a dish that would help promote bananas and impress the magazine. It has since become their signature dish. Brennan's flames 35,000 pounds of bananas a year to satisfy demand for Bananas Foster.

### What dish's name means "chamber pot"?

One of our favorite Italian dishes has a name with a most amusing origin. The Italian word *lasagna* comes from the Roman word *lasania*, meaning "a cooking pot," which in turn is from *lasanum*, the Latin word for "chamber pot." The word lasagna came to mean the food cooked in such a pot—flat sheets of pasta with meat, sauce, and cheese—and later to the pasta itself.

### How did Post Toasties get their name?

Originally, the Postum Company named its cornflake cereal, introduced in 1906, Elijah's Manna. American clergymen protested the name as sacrilegious and England denied the company a trademark. Company founder, C.W. Post, was forced to quickly recall the product and rename it Post Toasties.

### How did Ding Dongs get their name?

The original Hostess Ding Dongs came out in 1967 and were so named because of the ringing bells featured in early commercials for the product. However, they were only marketed as Ding Dongs in the Midwest and West. To avoid possible confusion with other products, they were called King Dons in the East and Big Wheels elsewhere. Hostess later got its marketing act together and sold them everywhere as Ding Dongs, with King Ding Dong appearing on the box in 1970.

### How did some other common foods come by their names?

*Kaiser roll.* The kaiser roll, also called a Vienna roll, is a crisp round roll often topped with poppy seeds. It is said to have been named in honor of Hapsburg emperor, Kaiser Franz Josef.

*Chicken Tetrazzini.* This dish of cooked spaghetti and strips of chicken with a sherry-Parmesan cheese cream sauce is said to have been named after famed Italian opera singer Luisa Tetrazzini (1871–1940), by an American chef in the early 1900s. It can also be made with turkey.

*Fettuccine Alfredo.* Yes, fettuccine Alfredo was created by a guy named Alfredo. In the 1920s, Roman restaurateur Alfredo di Lelio first whipped up this rich fettuccine in a cream, butter, and Parmesan cheese sauce.

*Steak Diane.* This is an impressive flaming dish. It was popular in the 1960s and was probably first created at the legendary Hollywood restaurant, the Brown Derby. Originally, the dish used venison, and its name is a reference to Diana, goddess of the hunt. It was made with thinly sliced tenderloin and prepared tableside using brandy to provide the flame.

# 3

# Moo Juice

### What is milk?

Milk is the nourishment female mammals produce to feed their young. In this respect, it is akin to the mother's blood, which nourishes the young in the womb. Almost all milks contain water, protein, fat, minerals, vitamins, and milk sugar (lactose).

### Why is milk white?

The ingredient that makes milk white is called casein. This is the milk protein that is rich in calcium and is therefore white in color. There is also cream in milk that has fat, which is white in color. This is why low-fat and skim milks are not as white as whole milk. Substances that reflect all wavelengths of light appear white in color. To be another color, an object must absorb some wavelengths of light and reflect other wavelengths. The grass is green, for instance, because it absorbs all wavelengths of light, except green, which it reflects. The molecules in cream and casein reflect no colors, and in the absence of color, things appear white.

### When did people start drinking milk from animals?

Drinking milk is taken for granted today, but thousands of years ago there were no domesticated animals and someone had to be the first to say, "Hey, I think I'll try to get some milk out of that goat." It wasn't until the first mammals became domesticated that it was practical to try and obtain their milk on a regular basis. No one knows who first domesticated dairy animals, but we do know that sheep were domesticated first, around 11,000 years ago, followed by goats, around 9,500 years ago. The larger, more ornery cattle weren't tamed until 8,500 years ago.

Ancient Greeks and Romans wanted milk in order to make cheese. They weren't big on milk and butter consumption. These foods would have quickly spoiled in their Mediterranean climate. They preferred olives as their source of oil. Conversely, the peoples of northern Europe were milk drinkers and therefore were considered barbarians by the Greeks. Curiously, the animal milk that most closely approximates that of human milk is that of the female ass. It is said that Nero's wife, Poppea, always traveled with 500 female asses so that she still could enjoy milk baths when away from home. (Sounds like she was a bit of an ass.)

Getting the milk out of an animal and processing it (milking, churning, and making cheese) had always been hard work, most suited for women. Our word "dairy," is from the Middle English *dey-ery*, with the word *dey*, meaning "woman servant."

### When did dairying come to North America?

Before the Europeans descended upon the New World, foods like yogurt and cheese were unknown to native populations. Cows first came to America with the Jamestown settlers, in 1611, and they were in the Plymouth colony by 1624. Due to the high loss of life when Pilgrims voyaged to the New World, it became English law that each ship would carry one cow for every five passengers. Farm families began drinking fresh cow's milk early on, but the poor city folk rarely enjoyed that luxury. What little milk came their way was usually contaminated with bacteria and watered down. While the invention of milking machines and automatic churners increased the amount of milk and butter produced, it took the advent of refrigeration and efficient transportation to make wholesome milk widely available.

### Do cows like cornflakes?

People love milk on their cornflakes. It turns out, cows love eating cornflakes while making milk. The average cow produces about eight gallons of milk a day, or 2,305 gallons a year. That's enough for 128 people to have a glassful every day. To produce this much milk, a cow needs to drink at least sixteen gallons of water a day (two gallons of water for every gallon of milk).

Cows also have to eat a lot to produce milk at these high levels. An average cow may eat up to eight times a day. Its diet is called Total Mixed Ration, or TMR. This TMR is a combination of hay, corn, barley, field grasses, and cotton seed. A cow will eat up to eighty pounds of TMR a day, at a cost of $3.50. Another part of the cow diet is bakery by-products. Extra breakfast cereal from the large manufacturers does not go to waste. It is packed in large bins and sold to farmers every two weeks to feed to their dairy cows. Cows love cereal. (They also love leftover potato chips.)

So the next time you are enjoying a bowl of cornflakes and milk, just think—the cow that produced your milk actually ate cornflakes to help make the milk on your cornflakes!

## How long will a cow produce milk?

The production of milk by a cow is triggered by hormones released at about the time a calf is to be born. If the cow is milked regularly, she will produce for about ten months. The cow is usually allowed to go dry for a couple months before being inseminated again. After a gestation period of around 282 days, she will begin giving milk again. When the calf is born, it only gets to suckle at mom for a few days. The farmer wants all the milk for himself. The first fluid the cow secretes is colostrum, which is clear and nutrient-rich. After that, milk is produced and the little calf is put on a formula of reconstituted and soy milks. Once he starts milking a cow, the farmer will do so two or three times a day to keep her producing at full capacity.

The average cow will give twelve thousand pounds of milk a year, or about one thousand four hundred gallons. The milk production record for a single cow was a whopping 55,600 pounds in one year. Today's milking machines make milking a cow much easier than in the old days. Back when cows were hand-milked, it took 350 squirts to get a gallon. As you would probably guess, Wisconsin is the leading milk-producing state.

### At what temperature is milk when it leaves the cow?

When milk is inside the cow, it is 101°F. As soon as it is milked, it is reduced to between thirty-eight and forty degrees. Within two days, milk moves from cow to store. All milk is marked with a sell by date. This indicates when it must be purchased by, not its expiration date. Milk, when stored at forty degrees, will be good for five to seven days after the sell-by date. Milk should not be frozen, as this will destabilize its protein, and particles may appear floating in the milk.

### What is the difference between cow's milk and mother's milk?

Different animals make different kinds of milk, depending on the needs of their offspring. The faster a young animal must grow, the more protein and minerals the mother's milk will contain. A calf, for instance, will double in weight in fifty days, so cow's milk is rich in protein and minerals. On the other hand, a human baby takes one hundred days to double in weight and a woman's breast milk contains only about one-third of the protein and minerals as that of cow's milk.

Because there is less protein, mother's milk is more easily digestible than cow's milk. And what protein there is, curdles less in the stomach. The processes of pasteurization, homogenization, and cooking all help to make cow's milk more digestible.

Another important difference between breast and cow's milk is the presence of the "bifidus factor." This is a property of breast milk that promotes the growth of beneficial bacteria, particularly *Lactobacillus bifidus*, in an infant's digestive tract. This bacterium produces lactic acid, which serves to inhibit the growth of harmful bacteria. Mother's milk additionally contains various antibodies against coliform bacteria, polio, and salmonella.

### How is breast milk better than formula?

We all know that most experts recommend that infants drink breast milk rather than formula. The World Health Organization and UNICEF both advise breast-feeding for up to two years or more. Studies have indicated that breast-fed babies suffer less from diarrhea, urinary tract infections, pneumonia, vomiting, asthma, earaches, allergies, cot death, viral and bacterial infections, cancer, learning disabilities, and psychological problems. (And it's free!)

Breast milk contains many helpful molecules, including antibodies like immunoglobulin A, that babies don't produce in the first few weeks of life. When the mother is exposed to pathogens in her environment, her milk produces highly specific antibodies to fight these pathogens. These are then passed to the baby to help it fight off the microorganisms it is most likely to encounter. These antibodies also ignore the beneficial bacteria found in the gut, which crowd out harmful bacteria.

## Why is skim milk green?

Did you ever notice that sometimes your skim milk looks kind of greenish? It's not from the grass that the cow ate. Skim milk has most of its fat content removed. As mentioned previously, one of the reasons whole milk is so white is because of its fat. Riboflavin, which remains in skim milk, has a greenish color that it can impart to milks with most of their fats removed.

With the increase of the public's awareness of fat intake and good health, the combined sales of skim and low-fat milk exceeded that of whole milk for the first time in 1988.

## Why is milk so perishable?

Milk is pasteurized to kill the bacteria, right? So then why is it so perishable? This is because even the best milk still contains millions of bacteria. Given the opportunity, these little guys will quickly reproduce in your milk and spoil it. This is why we must keep milk refrigerated constantly. Ideally, milk should be stored at slightly above the freezing point; however, this is impractical, as our refrigerators must store other foods and we don't set the temperature this low.

Keeping milk cold is not the only key to maintaining it at top quality. Exposure to light can adversely affect the flavor of milk. Normal daylight carries electrical energy that can change the structure of the fat in your milk. Such a reaction, known as "autoxidation," can give milk a metallic, oily, or fishy taste and smell. Exposure to direct sunlight can cause something called "sunlight flavor," a chemical reaction between the riboflavin and an amino acid, called methionine, which will give the milk a flavor somewhat like cabbage. Happily, most of us keep our milk in a dark refrigerator, so this is rarely a problem.

### Is one percent milk ninety-nine percent fat free?

Low-fat milks are the result of the milk being centrifuged to remove some of the fat globules before the homogenization process. Whole milk is not centrifuged. While one percent milk does contain only one percent fat, it is not ninety-nine percent fat free. This is because whole milk only contains four percent fat. As such, one percent milk is really seventy-five percent fat free.

### What woman is responsible for pasteurizing milk?

We all know that Louis Pasteur came up with the idea of pasteurization. Putting the principle into practice was up to others. As was usual with any new innovation, Americans were resistant to change. It took the efforts of bacteriologist Alice Evans, and nine long years, for Americans to accept pasteurized milk. In 1917, she showed that the bacterium that causes Bang's disease (contagious abortion) in cattle could be passed along to humans through unpasteurized milk, causing undulant fever, or brucellosis. Both the dairy industry and the medical profession spurned her pleas for safer milk. It wasn't until the late 1920s that it started to become mandatory to pasteurize milk.

### Who first sold homogenized milk?

The first person to successfully sell homogenized milk in America was Arthur G. Weigold of the Torrington Creamery, in Torrington, Connecticut. In 1919, he offered it on his home delivery route, but housewives were reluctant to accept this newfangled milk. They were used to seeing the cream at the top of the bottle. So Torrington approached restaurants and convinced them to give it a try. Their customers seemed to prefer its taste, consistency, and digestibility.

It took quite a while for it to really catch on though. At the start of World War II, only about one-third of milk was homogenized; ten years later, over two-thirds was; and by 1960, almost all milk was homogenized.

## What is lactose intolerance?

Lactose intolerance is the inability to digest significant amounts of lactose, the predominant sugar in milk. Lactose, which contains about fifty percent of the calories found in milk, is a disaccharide, composed of one glucose unit and one galactose unit. No other food contains lactose. In fact, the only other place it is found in nature, outside of mammals' milk, is in the flower of the *Forsythia* and some rare tropical plants. No other mammal, save humans, drinks milk after being weaned.

Like any multiunit sugar, lactose must be broken down in the intestine if it is to be absorbed into the body. The enzyme that breaks down lactose is lactase. Our levels of lactase are at their highest just after we are born. The level slowly decreases during the first three years of life.

If lactase is not present to break down the lactose in the small intestine, the sugar will travel to the colon intact, and can be fermented there by bacteria that will give off carbon dioxide, producing discomfort. Sugar in the colon can also promote water retention and diarrhea. This is not as bad as it sounds. Most intolerant individuals can consume a limited quantity of dairy products without significant problems. A pint of milk should not cause any trouble but will add needed nutrients to the diet. Fermented dairy products like cheese and yogurt have very little lactose and can be freely enjoyed by all.

If lactose intolerance is a problem for you, try one of the lactase enzyme capsules available on the market, or lactose-free milk, which tastes a little sweeter than regular milk because its lactose has been broken down into simple sugars.

## What's wrong with people who have lactose intolerance?

Nothing. Actually, you are kind of odd if you *don't* have some lactose intolerance. The fact of the matter is, the vast majority of the world's population is lactose intolerant. We just assume that lactose intolerance is abnormal, because ninety percent of white Americans have no lactose digestion problems. Neither do most people of northern European background. It wasn't until the late 1960s that this fact came to light. That's when researchers noticed that seventy percent of African-Americans are lactose intolerant; most Hispanics and Asians are as well. Up until that time, well-meaning but ignorant U.S. relief agencies were sending powdered milk to famine-struck parts of the world, where it could not be digested.

For most of human history, once you were weaned you didn't drink milk again, so you didn't need lactase anymore. With the advent of dairying, late in our history, this changed.

## Why do we only drink eggnog at Christmas?

Before the age of refrigeration, foods like milk and eggs had to be consumed or cooked in short order to prevent them from spoiling. In the Middle Ages, it was common for Europeans to add alcoholic beverages such as brandy, wine, or ale to milk and egg drinks to preserve them. One such hot, spicy English drink is "posset." These drinks came to America as early as 1607, when Captain John Smith noted that the settlers were making "eggnog." Americans, however, replaced the ale or wine with rum, which was from the Caribbean and thus much cheaper. Hot eggnog became a winter drink that eventually fell out of favor, except on Christmas.

There are a couple of theories as to how eggnog came by its name. The "egg" part is obvious, but what is "nog"? Some sources say "nog" is an old slang word for rum or rum drinks. It is also an old British slang for strong ale. The word eggnog may also derive from the word "noggin," a wooden cup used in taverns in days gone by. An egg drink in such a cup would have been called an "egg noggin." (These things aren't always cut and dried.)

Anyway, today eggnog appears in the supermarkets around

the end of October and is commonly served cold with spices and rum. Eggnog is made from homogenized milk or cream and must contain at least one percent egg-yolk solids by weight.

### What is buttermilk?

Butter is made by churning cream until it reaches a semi-solid state; buttermilk is the liquid left over after the butter is churned. In days gone by, this liquid was sold as buttermilk. Nowadays, it is made commercially by adding special bacteria to non-fat or low-fat milk; this thickens the milk and gives it a tangy flavor.

### What dairy product's name was inspired by the Waldorf-Astoria?

This is an easy one, right? Hotel Bar butter appeared in the same year—1931—that the Waldorf-Astoria Hotel opened on Park Avenue. Its packaging showed the New York skyline with hotels, including the swanky new Waldorf.

### Why is butter salted?

If you read the section on preserving meats, you can guess why. Salt was initially added to butter for its antibacterial properties. This was of paramount importance in the days before refrigeration. Today, the practice is continued because people are used to salted butter and it enhances its flavor.

### What is clarified butter?

Butter is composed of water, protein solids, and fat. When we clarify butter, we remove the water and protein solids, leaving the butterfat. The pure fat can be used to sauté foods at a higher temperature than whole butter, because the protein solids tend to smoke and burn and the water keeps the temperature down. Protein solids will begin to burn at about 250°F, whereas clarified butter is good up to about 350°F. Clarified butter will also store longer than whole butter. Bacteria like proteins but not pure oils.

To clarify butter, slowly heat it at a low temperature. It will separate out into three distinct layers—a casein (protein) froth, which contains the buttery flavor, on top, the yellow oil in the middle, and the watery milk solids at the bottom. Skim off the froth layer, then ladle out the oil.

## What makes one ice cream better than another?

Some ice creams are made better than others. And just as with other products, the reason boils down to money.

There are federal standards that must be met by all ice cream manufacturers. There must be a minimum of ten percent milkfat and twenty percent total milk solids, and up to 0.5 percent stabilizers, and 0.2 percent emulsifiers are allowed. Ice cream makers are also permitted to double the volume of their product by adding air to the ice cream.

The two most important factors when it comes to quality are the amounts of fat and air in the ice cream. Super premium brands have at least sixteen percent fat, while average brands have around twelve percent. Cheap brands may be up to fifty percent air, which makes the ice cream lighter and fluffier. By law, a gallon of ice cream must weigh at least 4.5 pounds. Premium brands will weigh much more, as they have less added air. One way to judge the quality of an ice cream is to compare its weight to another brand. Cheaper isn't cheaper if you are buying fifty percent air.

Whether premium or the cheap stuff, we Americans eat 1.6 billion gallons of ice cream a year, or roughly twenty-three quarts per person. Reportedly, ninety-eight percent of American households buy ice cream, with Sunday sales the highest. The people who eat the most ice cream, according to surveys, are those over forty-five years of age, living in Portland, Seattle, and St. Louis.

## Why doesn't ice cream freeze solid?

As its name implies, ice cream should be at least a little creamy. But why doesn't it freeze into a solid block in the freezer? To understand this, we must look at the makeup of ice cream.

Ice cream is a frozen foam. At freezer temperatures, it does not freeze solid because not all of its liquid content actually freezes. It is the presence of the dissolved sugars in ice cream that lowers the freezing point of some of the liquid. The other portions of ice cream are solid globules of milk fat and frozen crystals of water. The fat globules give the ice cream richness, creaminess, and body. The ice crystals stabilize the ice cream by trapping the other components in their crystalline latticework structure. These components are surrounded by air cells of varying sizes, depending on the quality of the ice cream. The air cells are needed to make the ice cream lighter and soft enough to scoop. Typically, air cells are on the order of 0.1 millimeters in diameter.

## What causes an ice cream headache?

We've all had that intense migraine-like headache that occurs sometimes when we drink a super-cold Slurpee or milk shake too fast. The intense pain can occur in different parts of the head. Some people get it right behind the eye, others near the temples. Regardless, the pain will usually subside in less than thirty seconds.

The pain is caused by dilation of the blood vessels in the head. This may be caused by a nerve center located above the roof of the mouth. Research has found that the ice cream headache is triggered when something cold touches the roof of the mouth near this nerve center. To avoid this "brain freeze" in the future, try not slurping your Slurpee up onto the roof of your mouth. This may be tough on a hot summer day, though.

## Who invented the ice cream soda?

In 1874, Robert N. Green was demonstrating a soda fountain at the semicentennial celebration of Philadelphia's Franklin Institute, by making a soda, sweet cream, and syrup drink. When he ran out of cream, he tried using ice cream. He immediately experienced one hundred times the demand for his new creation than he had for his old one. The ice cream soda was born.

## Who invented the banana split?

Some great food inventions don't make their creators rich or even famous. This was the case for the maker of the first banana split. Its creator was David Strickler, a pharmacy apprentice in Latrobe, Pennsylvania. On a trip to Atlantic City, New Jersey, in 1904, he watched a soda jerk and had his revelation. On his return to Latrobe, he split a banana in half and topped it with three scoops of ice cream, chocolate syrup, marshmallow, nuts, whipped cream, and a cherry and sold it for a dime. Other soda jerks seized upon the idea, using three scoops of different flavored ice creams, usually vanilla, chocolate, and strawberry, topped with chocolate, strawberry, pineapple, nuts, whipped cream, and a cherry, but no marshmallow. Strickler bought the pharmacy and went on making his banana splits until he retired in 1956.

### When was pre-sliced cheese introduced?

Pre-sliced bread came on the market in 1928, but it took another eighteen years for the cheese industry to follow suit. It wasn't until 1947 that Kraft Foods test-marketed Kraft Singles in Detroit supermarkets. At first glance the processed cheese did not appear to be sliced and consumers were wary, but Singles slowly came to gain the public's acceptance. In 1965, Kraft determined how to individually wrap each slice of cheese.

### Who was Monterey Jack?

Cheddar is an English cheese that originated in the village of Cheddar, in Somerset. It ranges in flavor from sharp to mild and in color from orange to white. Ninety percent of the cheese sold in America is of the cheddar type. America has come up with its own versions of this classic—Colby and Monterey Jack.

Colby is a mild, whole-milk cheddar cheese that is more open in texture (because of its tiny holes) and is softer. It was first made by a Vermont dairyman named Alfred Crowley in 1824. His family continued to make the cheese for over 170 years. Colby is named after a town in Wisconsin.

Monterey Jack is another American cheddar. It is so named because it originated in Monterey, California. This creamy white cheese was first marketed to grocers by local dairyman David Jacks—hence the name. This type of cheese was not invented by Jacks but goes all the way back to the semisoft Italian cheeses that fed Caesar's armies. It was introduced to Spain and then to Mexico and was brought to California by Franciscan monks in the 1700s. It can be made from whole, partly skimmed, or skimmed cow's milk. Unaged, it has a semisoft texture, creamy color, and a mild, almost bland flavor. Aged Jack bears a close resemblance to cheddar with its dry, firm texture, yellow color, and sharper taste.

### What is Emmenthaler cheese?

Whether you realize it or not, you have most likely eaten Emmenthaler cheese. That's the name of the cheese introduced to the United States in 1850 by Swiss immigrant Adam Blumer. He didn't invent this cheese. From the Emmenthal Valley in the canton of Bern, it had been around since the 1400s. Yes, this is the cheese we call Swiss.

### Have the holes sizes in Swiss cheese gotten smaller?

Have you noticed that the holes in your Swiss cheese have gotten smaller? Well, they did—and the Swiss aren't too happy about it. The USDA changed the regulations on the size of the "eyes" (holes) in domestically produced Swiss cheese. The old minimum size of $^{11}\!/_{16}$ inch is now the maximum size. The new minimum size is $^3\!/_8$ inch. Basically, eye size was cut in half. (You probably didn't know the federal government cared about such things, but your tax dollars have to go somewhere.) Cheeses that don't meet the new standard—and that will be most traditionally produced Emmenthalers (Swiss cheese made in Switzerland)—may not be given the USDA "A" grade.

   The reason given for the change is that large-holed cheese tends to crumble in the high-speed slicing machines used by big commercial food service operations. The real reason may be that the American cheese industry, which makes Swiss with smaller holes already, wanted their "Swiss" to qualify for the "A" grade instead of the "B" grade and thus allow them to charge more money for it. The Swiss call the new regulations crazy and apparently are quite upset about them.

### So why does Swiss cheese have holes anyway?

The holes in Swiss cheese are due to carbon dioxide gas bubbles produced by bacteria during fermentation (aging). The longer the fermentation, the larger the holes. True Emmenthaler from Switzerland comes from small village dairies and is aged for at least one hundred days. Most American Swiss is made in factories and is aged only sixty days. The Swiss contend that their longer aging gives their cheese not only bigger holes, but a softer more aromatic product with a richer, nuttier flavor.

All cheese is made with the help of bacteria. These "starter organisms," which are added to milk, determine the type of cheese that is produced. In the case of Swiss cheese, the bacteria *Streptococcus thermophilus* and various members of the *Lactobaccilus* species start the process by giving off lactic acid. This mixture is then put in a warm room and the bacteria *Propionibacterium shermanii* begins to grow on the lactic acid, producing propionic acid and carbon dioxide gas. As the carbon dioxide gas expands, it forms the bubbles that give Swiss cheese its holes. The propionic acid gives Swiss cheese its distinctive flavor.

The size of the holes is controlled by adjusting different bacterial growth factors, such acidity, temperature, and length of curing time. By refrigerating the cheese sooner, the cheesemaker ensures that smaller holes will develop.

Ohio is the top Swiss cheese–producing state, making 64 million pounds a year.

### Where did the expression "big cheese" come from?

The term "big cheese" for someone important or high up in a company, like the term "big wheel," is derived from the cheese-making industry. In days gone by, cheeses used to be made in huge wheels (some still are), from which smaller wedges were cut out and sold. Only wealthy people could afford to buy the whole wheel of cheese.

Americans eat about a half pound of cheese a week. It takes ten pounds of milk to make one pound of cheese.

### What is Cheez Whiz?

Cheez Whiz was first marketed by Kraft in 1953 to simplify the making of Welsh rarebit. It is a processed cheese sauce that contains cheese, water, whey, sodium phosphate, milk fat, skim milk, salt, Worcestershire sauce, mustard flour, lactic and sorbic acids, and coloring (don't forget the coloring!). This stuff was very stable and came in a jar. Kraft's original intention of having housewives use it on Welsh rarebit was a bit shortsighted. Women soon came up with well over 1,000 culinary uses for Cheez Whiz, including cheese dogs, macaroni and cheese, cheese and crackers, cheese over vegetables, and so on.

### Why does cheese smell like feet?

As with the making of yogurt, the process of making cheese is one of controlling spoilage, or fermentation. In the case of yogurt, the time in which the bacteria are allowed to act is short, and only the lactose (sugar) in the milk is broken down into lactic acid. In the case of cheeses, the "spoilage" is allowed to continue long enough so that the milk fats and proteins are also broken down, producing some rather odoriferous by-products. These same smelly by-products are given off by the microbes that inhabit the dark, damp areas of our body, especially the feet. Hence the expression "toe cheese."

If cheese smells like feet, and we think foot odor is offensive, why do we like cheese? Actually, there are people who can't stand the smell of cheese. The smell and taste of cheese is an acquired attraction. There is a part of our primordial brain that gives us an aversion to the smell of spoiled foods. Evolutionarily, this would have been very useful. However, when we started spoiling (fermenting) foods on purpose, our brains had to overcome the foul odors these foods sometimes emit. Unfortunately, some people's brains can't manage to do that.

# 4

# On the Hoof

### Who were the first Americans to raise cattle?

Believe it or not, it was the Pueblo. Even though cattle were not a native animal, they nevertheless made their way to the Pueblo people when Spanish explorer Francisco Coronado showed up one day, in 1540, with a bunch of livestock. Not only did Coronado bring cattle, he also introduced hogs, sheep, and horses, all of which the Pueblo raised. Cattle would arrive in Texas later in the 1500s, where they would escape from the conquistadors. These wild bovine would become the famed Texas longhorn.

### How did the longhorn almost become extinct?

In the old days, cattle were usually raised quite far from their ultimate destination—the slaughterhouse. It was this fact that created the great icon of the American West—the cowboy. The cattle had to be "driven" from their feeding grounds to either the slaughterhouse, in the early days, or the railhead, when the railroads reached that far. A typical drive involved several thousand head and maybe twelve to fifteen cowboys. Some drives took three months to complete and only covered seven or eight miles a day. It is estimated that between 1865 and 1880, some ten million cattle were driven north.

Longhorns were ideal specimens for this type of operation because they were very tough and held up better to the rigors of the drive than did other breeds of cattle. However, the drawback was that their meat was less tender and not as tasty. Other breeds were later introduced. Herefords were brought over from Europe and longhorns fell out of favor—so much so that they were eventually totally abandoned. By 1927, longhorns, symbols of Texas pride, had dwindled in number to only about two hundred animals. Happily, the breed was saved and today there are about 250,000.

## How are cattle bred?

Bulls are kind of like stallions. When one is found with all the desirable traits a breeder is looking for, its sperm can become quite valuable. Champion racehorses are put out to stud at the end of their racing careers. The sperm of champion bulls is collected so that the best meat-producing animal possible can be bred.

How does one collect bull sperm? It's not pretty, but here is the process: The bull must first be stimulated; then it is presented with a steer (castrated male) to mount. (This is to prevent accidental penetration and, thus, loss of sperm.) As the bull attempts to mount the steer, some poor technician has to run over to the bull with a container and put it directly over the bull's penis and get him to ejaculate into it. The whole procedure happens in the blink of an eye, about two seconds. Not a job for everyone!

A good bull can earn his owner up to $150,000 in sperm alone and he will end up fathering 100,000 offspring from his collected sperm. Apparently, the size of a bull's testicles is very important. At one year of age, if a bull's testicles measure less than thirty centimeters around, he is shipped off to be slaughtered. This is the fate of ninety-five to ninety-nine percent of bulls. The big boys are spared and can expect regular servicing, as it were.

Today, cattle breeding is a high-tech business. Computers are used to analyze every match according to numerous traits to determine the best outcome.

## Who is the biggest user of baking soda?

No, it's not Entenmann's or some other huge baking company. It's the cattle industry. There are close to seven hundred major cattle feedlots in the United States. These are places where roughly three quarters of domestically raised cattle are brought to be fattened up, or "finished," before being slaughtered. Here they enjoy a diet of corn, hay, and supplements—sometimes including growth hormones—and can eat up to 25–30 pounds of grain a day. However, there is a problem with this fattening diet: a cow's stomach is designed to digest grass, not grain. As a result, many of the poor creatures get indigestion. To keep them happy and their appetites healthy, feedlots give the cattle baking soda (sodium bicarbonate). Believe it or not, one half of all the baking soda sold in the United States goes to help ease the indigestion problems of cattle.

### What is the biggest ranch in the U.S.?

Wild cattle roamed Texas by the millions in the early nineteenth century. All one had to do was catch them and brand them. In the early days of the cattle industry, before the 1880s and the intro-duction of barbed wire, there were no fences keeping one's cattle herd from wandering around at will. In order to keep them dis-tinguished from another cattleman's stock, branding a logo on the creatures back left hip was crucial. Cattlemen had their own brands and there were even official brand guidebooks one could refer to when in doubt.

The King Ranch in southern Texas is the biggest ranch in the continental United States. Richard King originally purchased 15,500 acres in 1853. King added more acreage; the ranch reached a size of 1.25 million acres at the time of his death in 1885. Today, King Ranch is about 825,000 acres, or thirteen hundred square miles—bigger than the state of Rhode Island!

### How did Hawaii come to have one of the biggest ranches in the United States?

It's a daring story of adventure and romance. In 1809, a nineteen-year-old named John Palmer Parker jumped ship in the Sand-wich Islands (Hawaii). The Massachusetts native lived on the islands for seventeen years before marrying a granddaughter of the Hawaiian monarch Kamehameha and providing hides and meat to the royal family. He started a ranch with wild cattle that were put ashore on the island by George Vancouver from his ship

*Discovery,* in 1793. Parker Ranch started as a small piece of land near the base of Mauna Kea volcano and eventually grew to encompass over five hundred thousand acres and over fifty thousand heads of cattle, making it one of the largest privately owned ranches in the United States.

## How are animals slaughtered?

It's not nice to think about, but any meat that you eat comes from some poor animal that somebody had to kill first. Slaughterhouses try to kill animals in the least traumatic way possible. This is not due to any altruistic feelings on the part of slaughterhouse owners but just good business. It has been found that a traumatic death can make the animals contract their muscles and can cause internal bleeding, thus making the meat less desirable at market.

Larger animals are usually killed with something called a bolt gun. This "gun" has a retractable steel bolt that fires into the animals skull and then retracts back into the gun so it can be used to kill the next animal in line. Many chickens are stunned in an electrified bath before having their heads cut off with a spinning blade. Others are suffocated with carbon dioxide or simply have their necks broken.

By killing an animal with a sharp blow to the head or electrocuting them, less trauma results. So concerned are the slaughterhouses about trauma, that there have been studies to determine the best kind of electrical current with which to stun the animals. Normal house current is made of curvy sine waves and produces more trauma than does a square wave with a high frequency.

## How old are the animals we eat when they are slaughtered?

The meats that we enjoy at our tables, for the most part, did not come from animals that led long, happy lives. Since younger meat is more tender, and the growers like as quick a turnaround on their investment as possible, food animals don't live long. A young calf used for veal never sees the end of its third month. Other calves are killed anywhere from three to twenty-four months after birth. Steers are allowed to live to the ancient age of about three years. Lambs are slaughtered in less than fourteen months; pigs at around six months. The fowl fare no better, with broiler chickens getting axed at five to seven weeks, roasters at nine to twelve weeks, game hens at five to seven weeks, young turkeys in under fifteen months, mature turkeys at over fifteen months, and ducks in under four months.

Each year ninety-seven million hogs, thirty-five million cattle, eight billion chickens and turkeys, three million sheep and lambs, and one million calves are slaughtered in the United States.

### Is raw meat really bloody?

Blood contains hemoglobin, which is a red, iron-containing protein that carries oxygen from the lungs to the muscles. The red color of your chunk of raw beef is not due to blood or hemoglobin, but because of myoglobin, another oxygen-carrying protein.

Myoglobin also contains iron and has a red pigment. The oxygen carried by myoglobin is stored in the muscle tissue for use at a moment's notice. This way, muscles always have an emergency oxygen reserve at the ready. Some animals have more need of stored oxygen (myoglobin) in their muscles than others. Different levels of myoglobin give animal muscles varying colorations; for instance, the slow, fat pig has whiter meat than the cow. Fish have whiter muscles still. However, the tuna, which is a strong migratory swimmer, has red meat. The same holds true for chicken and turkey muscle color. The little-used breast meat is very white, while the more exercised leg muscles are darker.

### Why is ground beef bright red on the outside and purple on the inside?

Myoglobin is the reason. Fresh-cut meat is naturally purple-red in color, due to myoglobin. When the myoglobin at the meat's surface comes into contact with the oxygen in the air, it turns into oxymyoglobin, which is bright red in color. The meat away from the surface retains its purplish, oxygen-deprived coloration. The plastics that meats are wrapped in at the supermarket are not

totally airtight. The stores intentionally use air-permeable membranes for wrappings, like polyvinyl chloride and low-density
polyethylene, to ensure the attractive bright red meat color that
we have come to associate with freshness.

### What gives meat its grain?

Meat is the muscle tissue of an animal. Muscles are composed of
fibers that run the length of the muscle. These fibers are joined
together into bundles by thin sheets of connective tissue. The
bundles make up a muscle and are attached to bones. It's the
directional orientation of the fibers within the muscle that gives
meat its grain. Meat is easier to cut or chew in the direction of the
grain, as opposed to across it. In order to make the chewing of
tougher meats easier, you should cut them across the grain so
that you can chew them with the grain.

### Why is aged beef more tender?

Meat starts to become more tender after it has been slaughtered.
As such, many meats are aged for two weeks to a month in
climate-controlled rooms at about 36°F. Others meats can be aged
faster, at 68°F, for a couple of days. Aged meat costs more than
unaged meat. The reason? Aging takes time, and time is money.
While there are other ways to tenderize meat, aging is the only
method that also improves the flavor.

### How long do meats last in the refrigerator?

For centuries, people have been using the cold to keep meats
fresh. Before the invention of refrigeration, meat would be stored
underground with harvested ice that was used to keep it cold.
Today, we take our refrigerator/freezers for granted. Obviously,
freezing is the best way to store fresh meat for a long period of
time. At freezer temperatures of about 0°F, all microbial activity
ceases, as the water required for metabolism is frozen solid.
Frozen meats will keep for six months to a year.

The refrigerator doesn't stop biological activities, it just slows
them down, so spoilage just marches along at a slower pace. But

not *that* slow. A piece of chicken with a relatively low bacterial count will explode with up to ten thousand times more bacteria in as little as six days when it is stored in the refrigerator at 40°F! Fish can go bad even faster, as their microbes are already used to the cold (having lived in the cold water).

### Why is it safe to eat rare roast beef but not rare hamburger?

You may think you know the answer to this one, but maybe not. Beef roasts and steaks can be eaten rare because any bacteria present will be found only on the surface of the meat. The high cooking temperatures reached on the surface of roasts and steak kill any bacteria very quickly. Hamburger, however, is ground-up beef, and any surface bacteria from the pieces of beef are mixed throughout the product. So make sure to cook your hamburgers to at least 160°F.

### Why shouldn't a woman eat a steak well done?

A recent study has shown that women who eat steak, hamburger, and bacon very well done are over 4½ times more likely to get breast cancer than those women who eat these meats cooked rare or medium. According to scientists at the Lawrence Livermore National Lab in Livermore, California, compounds called hetero-cyclic amines (HAs) form in overcooked meats. In animal studies, HAs are shown to cause cancer. To lower the chance of HA formation, try eating meats in roasts or stews, which retain moisture. It is when meat dries out that HAs tend to form. If you grill, try marinating the meat first. Marinating chicken before grilling will greatly reduce HAs. On the other hand, you still want to cook meat past the rare to medium-rare range to prevent any chance of bacterial illness. There seems to be a fine line in degree of doneness if you want a perfectly health-conscious meat.

### Why is meat next to the bone the juiciest?

Many people prefer the meat next to the bone when eating a steak. This is because it is usually juicier and more tender than the rest of the meat. One reason for the juiciness is that the bone doesn't get as hot as the surrounding meat and it cooks slower, making the meat next to it a little rarer. Another reason is that there are a lot of connective tissues and tendons that fasten the meat to the bone, which contain collagen protein. This protein turns into gelatin when cooked. Gelatin is soft and very watery, adding to the juiciness and tenderness of the meat by the bone. Ribs and chops have the further advantage of being very fatty near the bone, adding even more flavor and moisture.

### Is there another name for this steak?

Walking down the meat aisle at your local supermarket can be a little confusing. There are many different names for steaks, and sometimes the same cut of beef has two or three different names. The following is a short list of meat cuts and other names:

| | | |
|---|---|---|
| Short loin | T-bone steak | porterhouse |
| | tenderloin steak | filet mignon* |
| | | fillet steak |
| | | chateaubriand |
| | top loin steak | strip steak |
| | (bone in) | sirloin strip steak |
| | | club steak |
| | | shell steak |
| | | Delmonico steak |
| | top loin steak | New York strip steak |
| | (boneless) | strip steak |
| | | Kansas City steak |
| Rib | rib-eye steak | Delmonico steak |
| Flank | flank steak | London broil |
| Sirloin | sirloin steak | |
| | top sirloin steak | London broil |
| Round | round tip steak | beef sirloin tip |
| | top round steak | top round London broil |

*The term filet mignon first appeared in print in O. Henry's 1906 book *The Four Million*. It derives from the French *filet* (boneless meat) and *mignon* (small, dainty).

## What company is the world's largest supplier of beef and pork?

Have you ever heard of IBP Fresh Meats? Maybe not, but you have probably eaten some of their meats. Headquartered in Dakota Dunes, South Dakota, IBP Fresh Meats is part of the Tyson family (the world's largest chicken supplier) and is the world's largest processor and marketer of beef and pork products. Formerly Iowa Beef Processors, IBP has twenty production sites in North America as well as in Russia, China, and throughout the world.

## How did Richard Nixon contribute to the success of Hamburger Helper?

What child of the early 1970s doesn't remember Hamburger Helper? Tricky Dick didn't mean to boost sales of this meat-extender product, but that's just what happened when he lifted the price controls on beef. Meat prices went up and to economize, many thrifty homemakers bought Hamburger Helper. (Many still do.) Sales were so high in the first two years that the company had a hard time keeping up with the demand. In 1977, Hamburger Helper introduced the "Helping Hand" cartoon character to further increase sales. He stuck around until he was canned in the 1990s. However, the little guy found employment with the company again in 2001. Hamburger Helper was followed by Chicken Helper and Tuna Helper.

## Are pigs skinnier than they used to be?

Commercial pigs are grown much leaner today than they were years ago. Between the 1950s and 1983, pigs became fifty percent leaner. Since 1983, they have become thirty-one percent leaner, still. Farmers started breeding more muscular pigs when they realized consumers were becoming more fat conscious. Pigs used to average about 300 pounds when they went to market. Now, through careful feeding, they go to market at 240 pounds. Once they reach this weight, pigs will put on a disproportionate amount of fat rather than muscle. As a result of these new production practices, a three-ounce serving of pork loin has about the same fat content of a chicken thigh, and only 180 calories.

Not all pigs are on a diet, though. The waste from Ben and Jerry's Ice Cream plant in Vermont is fed to local pigs. It is said that they don't really care for Mint Oreo.

### What is Canadian bacon?

Traditional bacon is pork that comes from the side of the pig. It has a high fat content, at least one-half to two-thirds of its total weight. Known as "back bacon" in Canada, Canadian bacon isn't really bacon. It is taken from the lean, tender eye of boneless pork loin located in the middle of the back (hence the name "back" bacon). Being precooked, it shrinks less than regular bacon when fried, which helps make up for its higher cost. In Europe, bacon mostly comes from the thigh or shoulder meat.

### How did the expression "pork barrel politics" arise?

We Americans use the expression "pork barrel politics" to denote politicians who use political clout to obtain government projects or appropriations, yielding rich patronage benefits for their districts or themselves. This political larder, as it were, is named after the old American reliance on salt pork as a food source.

When North America was first colonized by Europeans, wild game was quite plentiful and meat made up a large part of the Colonial diet. By comparison, Europeans of the time ate a paltry amount of fresh meat of any kind and relied heavily on bread. As the colonies grew, so did the establishment of the raising of livestock. Our ready access to fresh meat was to change with the urbanization of the country in the 1800s. While country folk still enjoyed fresh game and livestock, city dwellers were more likely to eat salt-cured meats, especially pork. Salt pork, which was stored in barrels, became a staple food in America. From this reliance on salt pork came the expressions "pork barrel politics" and "scraping the bottom of the barrel."

Americans have always loved their meat. In the 1830s and 1840s, Americans ate more meat per person than they did in 1980.

By the 1870s, with the introduction of transcontinental railroads and refrigerated railcars, fresh cattle meat from the West was made available to the populous East Coast cities.

## How common is trichinosis?

For decades people lived in fear of getting trichinosis from under-cooked pork. It was feared that pork cooked to less than a 185-degree final temperature allowed Trichinella worms to survive and grow in your body. Thus, most of us grew up on tough, dry pork chops. About ten years ago, scientists had a revelation of sorts—the dreaded trichinae are actually killed at 135 degrees. So if you cook your pork to about 155 degrees, you will be perfectly safe and can enjoy a nice, juicy chop.

# 5

# Feathered Friends

*When did our modern chicken appear on the culinary scene?*

There are many varieties of chicken. The breeding of what have come to be our modern varieties of chickens began in earnest in the mid-1800s. It was then that a particularly well-suited breed of chicken arrived in England by way of China. Known as the Cochin, this bird set off a breeding frenzy, which was to result in hundreds of new breeds. By the turn of the twentieth century, the white leghorn had established itself as the best egg layer of the lot. Birds derived from the Cornish had the best meat production. As a result of the intense breeding and selection process, just a few varieties of chicken dominate U.S. production today. The average American eats about eighty pounds of chicken a year.

*Why do chickens have their beaks removed?*

The raising of chickens for egg or meat production is big business. Today, large egg farms may have flocks of up to one million birds. Before World War II, the average egg production flock was just a few hundred hens. Gone are the backyard chicken coops of the past. Chickens are mass-produced in factorylike settings. The hens no longer sit on their eggs as they did in the henhouse days. By removing the eggs right away, the hen will continue laying, as there is no need to stop and incubate her clutch. In the egg production business, male chicks are not needed. Hatcheries will quickly cull the male chicks and dispose of them.

The hens are housed in incredibly cramped quarters to prevent any unnecessary movement that would take energy away from the laying process. They live in wire cages devoid of comfort. When an egg is laid, it rolls down the sloped floor of the cage onto a conveyor belt that whisks it away. Artificial lighting is supplied to avoid the slowdown in egg laying that occurs during the shorter daylight hours of winter. The hens are also given vaccines and antibiotics to prevent diseases that could quickly sweep through the "factory" and decimate thousands of birds.

Another management practice that protects the birds is called debeaking. Chickens can become cannibalistic. To keep the hens from pecking at one another, parts of their beak are cut off and cauterized.

## Who's the king of the chicken world?

Tyson Foods had its beginnings when founder John Tyson ran out of gas in Springdale, Arkansas, and decided to stay. He used his truck to haul fruit from the local orchards and then turned to trucking chickens. When he found that the growers didn't have enough poultry to keep him busy all the time, he began hatching chicks for the growers to raise. He eventually bought a chicken farm, feed mill, and growing houses and his became the first company in the poultry business to run the entire show from top to bottom. Tyson is now the largest purveyor of chickens in the world.

One of Tyson's main rivals—Perdue Farms—also had humble beginnings. In 1920, Arthur Perdue, an ex-railroad employee in Salisbury, Maryland, bought fifty leghorn chickens for fifty dollars. He built a backyard coop and set out to sell eggs. (It's amazing how many large corporations started in somebody's basement or backyard.) The company grew into the fourth-largest poultry seller in the country.

## What fast-food item had a special chicken bred to meet demand?

When McDonald's started test-marketing Chicken McNuggets in 1980, they had no idea how popular they would become. Upon their introduction in Knoxville, Tennessee, it was immediately apparent that McDonald's had another winner. So great was demand for McNuggets that their original chicken supplier could not provide enough meat. Tyson stepped in and bred a new bird designed just to make McNuggets. The new chicken, dubbed "Mr. McDonald's," was twice as big as the normal broiler. Since the bird had more meat, there was less de-boning to do; the beauty of Chicken McNuggets is that they have no bones.

### Why have they bred bald chickens?

It can get pretty hot in the Middle East. This means that chicken farmers need a way to keep their charges cool. Instead of using cooling systems, an Israeli researcher decided it would be easier and cheaper to raise featherless chickens. Avigdor Cahaner of Hebrew University did just that. By crossbreeding normal chickens with those that have a gene that makes them partly bald, he came up with a completely bald chicken. These normal-sized, featherless birds are also less fatty. The lack of feathers not only makes them more suitable for raising in hot climates, it also eliminates the need for the water and electricity required to pluck them. The only negative to these chickens is their somewhat hideous appearance.

### Are turkeys from Turkey?

This would make too much sense. Turkeys originated in the New World and were brought to Spain in 1523. The primary large birds eaten in Europe at this time were peacocks and swans, along with herons, cranes, storks, cormorants, and egrets. The turkey was actually called a peacock (*gallopavo*) in Spain after it first arrived. Turkeys may have acquired the name they are known by when they were introduced to England. One story has it that the turkey got its name because its arrival in England coincided with that of the guinea fowl from Africa, which was sold by Turkish traders, known as "turkey merchants." Whatever the story, turkey had displaced swans and peacocks on the European dinner table within a hundred years.

## Why are turkeys so cheap around Thanksgiving?

If you ever shopped for a turkey just before Thanksgiving, you probably noticed that they are extremely cheap or are even given away by the supermarket if you purchase a certain dollar amount of other goods at the store. The reason? The stores are willing to pay full price for the birds, and take a loss on them, if they can get customers to buy enough other goods at full price. Merchants call this a "loss leader."

Turkey's popularity has been increasing recently. Between 1979 and 2001, the consumption of turkey shot from 9.9 pounds per capita to almost eighteen pounds. One reason is that you don't have to buy a whole turkey anymore; the parts are now sold separately. Tom turkeys are usually the ones cut up for parts; hens are sold whole.

Sometimes you end up with too many turkeys and must freeze one or more. The turkey industry says there is no difference between fresh and frozen turkey in taste or nutrition. However, some cooks believe that freezing reduces the moisture content of the bird, as some meat cells rupture and lose their liquid. About seventy-five percent of us buy frozen turkeys for Thanksgiving; the rest buy fresh. Thirty-two percent of the 270,000,000 turkeys grown in the United States each year are sold at Thanksgiving.

## How do they separate the tom turkey chicks from the hen chicks?

The sexing of newly hatched turkey chicks—also known as poults—is not as easy as you may think. Birds do not have visible sex organs and poults don't have any obvious defining sexual characteristics. So how do they tell the hens from the toms? Only very highly trained specialists seem to be able to do the job. They are predominately Asians, who have been taught the art from a young age. These turkey sex experts quickly feel the poults and separate the males from the females. They can sex up to one thousand birds an hour and make between $60,000 to $70,000 a year. (Chicks are likewise separated by chicken sexers.)

The chicks only weigh about one-tenth of a pound when they hatch but reach twenty pounds by the time they are twenty weeks old. One oddity of commercial turkeys is that the tom actually grows too large to inseminate the hen. Therefore, pro-creation is achieved entirely through artificial insemination.

## Do all turkeys gobble? (And other turkey facts.)

Only the male tom turkey gobbles. The female simply makes a kind of clicking sound. Neither male nor female domesticated turkeys can fly; this wouldn't be practical to the farmer. How-ever, their wild cousins can take flight for short distances with speeds of up to 55 miles per hour. They can also run quite fast, reaching 20 miles per hour.

The Israelis are the turkey-eating champs with a per capita consumption of nearly thirty pounds. The United States comes in at a distant second at eighteen pounds.

We humans like to eat turkey occasionally and so do our pets. Thirteen percent of turkey goes into pet food.

More people prefer white meat to dark meat. This is good since a bird is seventy percent white meat and thirty percent dark meat. The dark meat is moister (fattier) and has more calories.

Minnesota and North Carolina are the leading turkey-producing states, raising about forty-four million birds a year each.

The wild turkey is the state bird of Oklahoma.

## Why do commercial turkeys have white feathers?

Commercially raised turkeys are white, unlike their wild cousins. The reason they are bred with white feathers is so that their skin is not discolored by feather pigment. In case you were wonder-ing, an adult turkey has three thousand five hundred feathers and the eggs are tan with brown speckles.

## What made Butterball turkeys different?

Before the 1950s, turkeys had tough, dark meat and a lot of pin feathers. Through a breeding program, Swift-Eckrich Company developed a more tender bird with a larger breast that had its feathers removed in a hot water bath. The company debuted their new turkey, dubbed "Butterball," in 1954.

### What's that red flap of skin on top of a turkey's head?

There is some interesting terminology associated with turkey anatomy: that long, red fleshy growth at the base of the beak that hangs down over the the neck is called the "snood"; the pink or red fleshy growth on the top of the head and neck is the "caruncle"; the "wattle" is the bright red appendage on the neck.

### How do pop-up timers work?

Pop-up turkey timers are one of the greatest cooking conveniences ever created—and one of the simplest. What easier way could there be to tell if your turkey is done than to look at this little plastic thing that's been shoved into your bird? Gone are the days of continually opening the oven door to check an old-fashioned thermometer. But how does this wondrous device work?

There are four components to a pop-up timer. The barrel holds the plunger (stem). Under the plunger is a spring and a firing mechanism. The firing mechanism is made of a material that will melt at a very specific temperature. When it does, it activates the spring, which in turn pushes up the plunger out of the barrel. For turkey, the firing mechanism is designed to melt at 180°F and is accurate to within 2 degrees.

### What came first, the chicken or the egg?

Eggs have been around much longer than birds. In fact, the birds are believed to be evolutionary descendants of the egg-laying dinosaurs. The modern chicken (*Gallus domesticus*) is of very recent origin, having been domesticated around five thousand years ago from the jungle fowl of Southeast Asia.

The chicken's early popularity was not just culinary. The cocks were raised extensively for fighting. The hens were just kept around to make more cocks. The "sport" of cockfighting is very old and was widespread in the ancient world. By the time of the Roman Empire, the eating of eggs had become quite common.

If the question is, "Which came first, the chicken or the chicken egg?" then the answer is a little trickier.

## How does a chicken make an egg?

Similar to humans, female chickens are born with thousands of immature eggs in their ovaries. When the hen is ready to start laying, these ova will mature one at a time. If two ova mature at the same time, a double-yolked egg will be produced. When the ova mature in the ovary, the accumulation of yolk material begins. The yolk is made up of proteins and fats that are made in the hen's liver. This process takes a few weeks. When complete, the large yolk, with the tiny egg cell attached, will be released into the upper oviduct at ovulation.

If the hen had been inseminated, the egg will meet the sperm here and be fertilized. Then the egg and yolk travel into the next part of the oviduct—the magnus—where the albumen, or egg white, will be laid down in four layers around the yolk. The word "albumen" derives from the Latin *albus*, meaning "white." The first albumen layer forms the "chalazae," which are the cords that attach the yolk to the shell and keep it nicely centered. A little farther down the oviduct, the yolk and albumen are enclosed in two tough, thin membranes that serve as a barrier to bacteria. They are attached to each other all around, except for an air pocket between them at one end. This is the air space you find at the wide end of a hard-boiled egg. Its purpose is to give the hatching chick its first breath of air while pecking through the shell. The next step in egg formation is called "plumping." Water and salts are pumped into the albumen from the walls of the oviduct, increasing its size.

The yolk and albumen now enter the uterus, where the shell is laid down. This step of the process takes about fourteen hours. A shell gland secretes calcium carbonate and the egg is formed. The calcium for the shell comes from the calcium found in the hen's bone structure. The shell is an effective physical barrier to the outside world, but it is not completely impermeable. Some gas exchange through the shell is necessary to keep the living embryo inside alive. The egg "breathes" oxygen in and carbon dioxide out. To retard the loss of water, the shell receives a final waxy coating.

## How long does it take a chicken to produce an egg?

A chicken is a type of bird that is known as an "indeterminate" egg layer. While some birds will lay a set number of eggs, most, like chickens, will keep laying until they accumulate a certain number in their nests. By removing the eggs as they are laid, chicken farmers can keep the poor hens laying eggs indefinitely, in a vain effort to reach their number.

In the United States there are about 240 million hens laying approximately 5.5 billion eggs a year. That's a lot of eggs! A hen can lay an egg every twenty-four to twenty-six hours, and begins to start a new egg a mere thirty minutes after laying one. Today's hens can lay an average of 250 to 300 eggs per year. (And a year is about the useful life of an egg hen.) This is up from 151 in 1945. The increase is due to improvements in breeding, housing, and nutrition.

## Can a chicken egg have a clear yolk?

Americans prefer egg yolks that are gold or lemon yellow colored. The diet of the hen is key to yolk color. Yellow-orange plant pigments (called xanthophylls) found in chicken feed are deposited into the yolk, imparting its familiar color. Hens fed a mash of yellow corn and alfalfa meal lay medium-yellow eggs, while those eating wheat or barley produce lighter-colored yolks. Bright yellow marigold petals can be added to the feed to enhance yolk, as well as skin, color. It is possible to produce a nearly clear egg yolk by feeding the hen a colorless diet, like white cornmeal, although not many of us would buy such an unusual egg!

No matter what their diet, it takes about 4½ pounds of feed for a hen to produce a dozen eggs.

## Why do eggs sometimes have a red spot on the yolk?

About one in a hundred chicken eggs you crack open will have a red spot on the yolk. Many people find the spot to be disgusting and discard the egg. Your mother probably told you that there was a red spot because the egg had been fertilized. This is a common misconception.

These red spots are known as "meat spots." They are caused by a rupture of a blood vessel on the yolk surface during egg formation. Electronic candling reveals most red-spotted eggs, but some slip through the process. Actually, the red spot is an indication that the egg is fresh. In older eggs, the yolk takes up water from the albumen and dilutes the spot. In any event, red-spotted eggs are chemically and nutritionally good to eat. If the spot bothers you, it can be removed with the tip of a knife.

Many of you worry about bacteria in eggs and cook them thoroughly. These fears may be unfounded. The USDA reports that only one egg in twenty thousand contains harmful bacteria. You'd have to eat an awful lot of eggs to get a bad one.

## Why do some hard-boiled eggs have a greenish ring around the yolk?

The word "yolk" comes from the Old English word for "yellow." We expect our yolks to be yellow, but sometimes there is a greenish ring around hard-cooked egg yolks. This is due to sulfur and iron compounds reacting at the yolk surface.

Yolks are high in iron content, while albumen contains sulfur. When heated, the iron and sulfur react to form ferrous sulfide. Either overcooking or a high amount of iron in the cooking water can cause this to occur. While the green hue may be unappealing to some, the eggs taste normal and produce no ill effects. To decrease the chance of this happening, place the boiled eggs in cold water immediately after boiling, to prevent overcooking, and peel right away.

If you don't like the look of greenish eggs, don't cook a duck egg. The yolk turns reddish orange and the white turns blue.

One additional bit of hard-boiled-egg trivia: How can you tell if an egg is hard boiled or raw? You don't have to crack it open or shake it; just spin it. A cooked egg will spin like a top.

## Do you have to refrigerate eggs?

When we think of farm-fresh eggs, many of us have a picture in our minds of the idyllic country kitchen table with a basket of fresh eggs, like something out of *Martha Stewart Living*. It's a nice little fantasy but could be detrimental to your health. Refrigerated eggs will be fresher after one week than eggs kept at room temperature will be after one day. This is why egg cartons have dates that indicate what day they were packed. Starting with January 1 as day one and ending with December 31 as day 365, these numbers represent the consecutive days of the year. Eggs may be kept, refrigerated, for four or five weeks after this date.

While in the fridge, eggs should be stored in their carton, as they can pick up aromas and flavors from other foods if placed in those little egg-cup holders on the door of some refrigerators. An egg shell has up to 17,000 pores on its surface. These pores allow moisture and carbon dioxide out, and air in to form the air cell at the end of the egg. They also permit unwanted flavors and aromas to filter into the egg.

One easy way to gauge egg freshness is to put it into a bowl of cold water. An egg has an air cell at its wide end. At the time the egg is laid, this space is one-eighth-inch deep and the size of a dime. Over time it gets larger and larger. When placed in water, the big air cell of an older egg will cause the wide end to rise above the narrow end. A fresh egg will probably sink.

### Why do brown eggs cost more than white eggs?

Chickens with white feathers and white earlobes (yes, chickens have earlobes) lay white eggs. Breeds with red feathers and red earlobes lay brown eggs. Breeds that lay brown eggs include the Rhode Island Red, New Hampshire, and Plymouth Rock. Most Americans prefer white eggs, but in certain regions, such as New England, consumers like brown eggs. Birds that lay brown eggs are larger breeds; they eat more food and lay larger eggs. That's why brown eggs cost more. There are two breeds of chickens that lay bluish or greenish eggs—Ameraucana and Araucana—but you can't buy them at the supermarket.

The Rhode Island Red was bred by a sea captain in Little Compton, Rhode Island, in 1824. It was the result of crossbreeding several domestic types of chickens and wild fowl from Southeast Asia. New Englanders have eaten brown eggs since, as their color was a sign that they were probably locally laid and, therefore, fresh.

## Why is it so difficult to peel a hard-boiled egg?

Hard-boiled eggs are one of the easiest foods to cook but one of the most difficult to open. One reason for this difficulty has to do with the pH of the egg white. As we discussed previously, the pH of the albumen is lower in a really fresh egg than in one that has been in the fridge a few days. The lower the pH, the more tightly the albumen will stick to the outer membrane inside the shell. Eggs should peel more easily as they get older because their pH goes up. Adding salt to your cooking water may help alleviate the problem.

# 6

# Chicken of the Sea

*Are Maine lobsters* **(Homarus americanus)** *only found in Maine?*

Maine is world famous for its Maine lobsters, but they can be found all along the East Coast, from Newfoundland down to North Carolina. There are even lobstermen in New York City. They trap what are known locally as "Long Island Lobsters," because they are taken from the waters of the Long Island Sound, off City Island, in the Bronx. These lobsters are smaller, browner, and not as sweet as Maine lobsters. Other lobsters are found in other parts of the world—spiny, or rock lobsters, for example. They don't have the large edible claws of the Maine lobster, and they are caught for their tail meat.

Maine has the strictest laws of any state regarding the harvesting of lobsters. It takes seven years for a lobster to reach the state's minimum size for harvesting about 1¼ pounds. The maximum size allowed is about three to four pounds. Lobster size is measured with a special carapace (body) gauge. Maine supplies about ninety percent of the American lobster harvest.

*Are there any poisonous parts of a lobster?*

Not really, but you may want to avoid the tomalley—a light greenish substance found inside the body. While not necessarily poisonous, it is the lobster's liver and pancreas, and may accumulate toxins it filters from the seawater.

Other colorful parts of a lobster are the red balls sometimes found on the tail, which are called "coral." If you find coral on your lobster, you have a female; the red balls are her eggs. You may not want to eat the lobster roe, but some people find it very tasty.

### Do lobsters have blood?

They do, but it's clear when they are alive. It's not until you boil them that you see the blood. When heated, lobster blood coagulates and turns white. This is the white globby substance you often find on home-cooked lobster meat, especially near the claws, and quite often floating in the boiled water. It may look unappealing but is quite harmless.

### Why do lobsters turn bright red when cooked?

Maine lobsters are kind of greenish brown when they are alive. Pop them into a pot of boiling water, and like magic, they turn a beautiful brilliant red. The live lobster has many different color pigments (chromatophores) in its shell (carapace). However, when cooked, all the pigments are masked except for astaxanthin, which is a red background pigment in its shell color.

To tell if your lobster was alive when it was boiled, check to see that its tail is tightly curled under the body. When stretched out straight, it should spring back into place. If not, the poor guy was dead before he hit the water.

### Which crabs do we eat, the male or female?

Trick question! We eat both, but they are sold in different forms. Male blue claws are bigger than their female counterparts and they are sold whole. The smaller females are usually canned.

How do you tell the two apart? Look at the bottom side of the crab (use caution if they are still alive!). A mature male crab, called a "jimmie," will have an "apron"; this is a flap that covers much of the abdomen and is shaped like a little Eiffel Tower. The apron on a mature female looks more like the dome on the U.S. Capitol. Immature females look like a combination of the two—the Capitol dome with an Eiffel Tower top.

## What are softshell crabs?

Crabs and lobsters are crustaceans. As such, their bodies are covered with a hard exoskeleton. Because their outer covering is rigid and does not grow along with the crab, it must be shed and a bigger one regrown periodically, much like a snake must do with its skin. The process of shedding is called molting. It takes the crab between one and three days to grow a new shell. During this time it is known as a softshell crab. As the term implies, its body is very soft and the crab is very susceptible to hungry predators. For this reason, softshell crabs hide until their new armor has formed. While in hiding, they are very hard for crabbers to catch. Happily for softshell crab lovers out there, an experienced crabber can tell when he catches crabs that will soon be molting. These crabs, called "peelers," are set aside in a special tank until they do.

America has more kinds of crabs than any other country. The American blue crab industry started on the Chesapeake in the early 1600s.

## Why is caviar salty?

Caviar is fish roe. "True" caviar comes from sturgeon. There are three types of caviar: beluga, osetra, and sevruga. Beluga caviar is considered top quality. It comes from the beluga sturgeon that inhabits the waters in the Caspian Sea, between Russia and Iran. Beluga caviar has large eggs that range in color from silver-gray to black. The medium-sized brownish gray to gray osetra caviar is next in quality, followed by the small, gray roe of the sevruga. Other species of fish, including whitefish, lumpfish, and salmon, are sources of much cheaper caviar.

Caviar is loaded with anywhere from eight to twenty-five percent fat, which makes it very perishable. As caviar is rarely served fresh, it must be preserved for later sale and consumption. It is preserved with salt. This is fine, but some fussy caviar connoisseurs claim that a metal spoon will react with the salt in the caviar, giving it a slightly metallic taste. Since caviar is so expensive, nothing should interfere with its enjoyment. Thus, these folks won't use steel or silver spoons. Spoons made out of gold or mother-of-pearl, which do not react with salt, tradition-ally have been used. Caviar eaters on a budget, if there is such a thing, can always use a plastic spoon.

## How did lobster Thermidor acquire its odd name?

Lobster Thermidor is a dish consisting of chopped lobster tail meat in a béchamel sauce that is flavored with wine, shallots, tar-ragon, and mustard. The lobster mix is put back into the tail and baked with some Parmesan cheese. If the dish sounds French, that's because it is. It is said to have been created on January 24, 1894, in Paris, at a restaurant named Chez Maire, to commemo-rate the opening of the Victorien Sardou play *Thermidor*, at the Comédie-Française. The play, which was named after one of the months on the French republican calendar, was not kind to the French Revolution and was not performed again for three decades. The dish named in its honor fared much better.

## Why does fish cook so much faster than meat?

If you have much kitchen experience, you probably know that fish cooks much faster than meat, and it is softer, drier, and flakier too. Did you ever wonder why? It has to do with the kind of environment they live in and the kind of muscles they have.

Unlike land animals that have big bundles of muscle fibers designed for slow movement, fish have shorter, thinner muscle fibers, designed for quick movements. These thinner fibers are more readily broken down when cooked. They are also easier to separate when chewing. This is one reason we see raw fish dishes, like sashimi, and not many raw meat dishes (except for steak tartare, which must be ground up to make it soft enough to eat uncooked.)

Fish meat is drier and flakier than red meat because it doesn't have much connective tissue. Living in water, fish muscles aren't exposed to as much gravity and don't need to be connected as firmly to their skeleton. This is why fish don't need all the big bones and gristly cartilage found in land animals. Less connective tissue means less collagen (mentioned previously) and therefore less gelatin and moisture when cooked. Less cartilage makes for softer meat. In addition, fish are cold-blooded; that makes their meat drier because cold-blooded creatures have less fat than warm-blooded ones. Less fat equals less moisture.

## So how do you know when your fish is cooked?

As with red meat, if you overcook fish it will become drier and tougher. However, there is quite a range of doneness with a meat such as beef. With fish, when it's done, it's done, and the cooking time is much shorter. Your fish will be done when it loses its translucent color and turns white. Generally, you need only cook a piece of fish for eight to ten minutes per inch of thickness.

## Why do we squeeze lemons on fish?

Another difference between fish and other meats is that fish will spoil much more quickly. Just plucked from the sea, extremely fresh fish doesn't really have a "fishy" smell. But in short order, it acquires one. This doesn't mean it's not good to eat though. A little fishiness is okay.

Bacteria and enzymes do their dirty work of decomposing a fish once it is no longer alive. They produce smelly chemicals like ammonia, sulfurous compounds, and amines. An acid, like lemon juice, can help to neutralize the odors given off by the amines and ammonia. Plus, lemon juice has a pleasing aroma and adds a little zing to the fish flavor.

Another thing that makes fish stink in a hurry is its unsaturated fat content; this is higher than that of land animals, which have more saturated fats. These unsaturated fats are converted into fatty acids, which cause the fish to turn rancid.

The reason seafood is stored in ice immediately after being caught is to retard the bacterial decomposition. Since fish live in the cold seas, their decomposition bacteria can begin to work at a much lower temperature than will the bacteria that decompose warm-blooded land animals. Ice is better than your refrigerator for storing fresh fish. Whereas your refrigerator is probably kept at about 40°F, ice never gets above the freezing mark, and, happily, ice will not give you a frozen block of fish as your freezer will.

## What fish is worth $50,000?

Atlantic bluefin tuna goes for about $50 a pound. These suckers can weigh in at over a thousand pounds. Do the math. But why is this tuna so expensive? You can thank sashimi's recent rise in popularity. A few decades ago, Atlantic bluefin was considered a garbage fish, selling for about a penny a pound and used for cat food. How times have changed.

## What is mahi-mahi?

Mahi-mahi is a Hawaiian word for dolphin. Don't be shocked though; mahi-mahi is not the marine mammal dolphin but the fish we call dolphin. Also called dorado or dolphinfish, restaurants prefer to call this dolphin by its Hawaiian name to avoid any confusion. Many people would be distressed to think that they were eating a marine mammal (never mind that they eat plenty of land mammals). Mahi-mahi is found in warm waters around the world. It has firm, sweet flesh and can range in weight from three to forty-five pounds. Japan catches more than half of the mahi-mahi harvest.

## How did missing sardines create the canned tuna industry?

Canned tuna was unknown a century ago. It wasn't until 1903 that a fish packer in San Pedro, California, began canning white albacore after the Pacific sardine he normally canned didn't show up. It was not unusual for the sardines to disappear, as it was natural for them to run in unpredictable cycles. Canner Alfred P. Halfhill had a plan, though. He experimented with canning albacore tuna. When he cooked it under pressure with steam, Halfhill found that the flesh turned white and took on a flavor more like chicken than fish. Within ten years, nine other tuna canners were in operation and canned tuna went on to become an American staple. At first, only albacore was canned. Soon, bluefin and yellowfin tuna, as well as the smaller skipjack, were canned as "light meat" tuna; "white meat" albacore tuna was considered a specialty.

We now eat about a billion pounds of some kind of tuna every year, although much of it is now packed in easy-open pouches. In case you were wondering, it takes two pounds of raw tuna to get one pound of canned tuna.

### What is "fancy" tuna?

In 1926, Roy P. Harper of Van Camp Sea Food came up with a way of selling more yellowfin tuna, a fish that can be packed year-round but was looked down upon because it did not have the nice white meat of the more expensive albacore. By packing yellowfin in solid pieces rather than flakes, and calling it "fancy," he opened up a new market for this previously unappreciated fish. Calling his brands Chicken of the Sea and White Star didn't hurt sales either.

### Shouldn't it be called Mr. Paul's Kitchen?

There is no Mrs. Paul, but there was a Mr. John Paul. In 1946 he founded Mrs. Paul's Kitchen with Philadelphia entrepreneur Edward Piszek. Piszek worked at Campbell Soup Company for five years and earned a degree in business administration at the University of Pennsylvania night school. Paul, a short-order cook, and Piszek, each came up with $450 to start their frozen seafood business. The company's first offering was frozen deviled crabs, which sold at fifty-nine cents for a six-ounce package.

### What event greatly reduced the consumption of fish in England?

There have been a few culinary turning points in English history, some of which involved invasion, exploration, or disease. This one involved religion. In 1534, Henry VIII broke with the Roman Catholic Church when the annulment of his marriage to Catherine of Aragon was voided and he was excommunicated. Even after the Anglican schism, the English continued to observe Lent and meatless Fridays, but the consumption of fish still decreased, to the detriment of the fishing and shipbuilding industries. Parliament was subsequently forced to establish a new fish day, on Saturdays, in addition to Fridays, in 1548. This was intended to help the shipbuilding industry and thereby increase the fishing fleet, giving the Royal Navy more seafaring men to draw on as recruits. In 1563 Parliament enacted another law, also making Wednesdays meatless, again hoping to strengthen the navy and drive down the price of meat. Violations of the new law were punishable by three months in prison or a fine of three pounds. Observance was low and did not last long.

Another effect of the break with Rome was the disbanding of monasteries, the main makers of wine in England, effectively killing English wine production.

The French were also sticklers when it came to Lent. The government felt compelled to enforce the Catholic rules of Lent. In the seventeenth century, French police would raid homes during Lent and give any forbidden foods they found to hospitals. In 1659 they even went so far as to raid a Paris monastery and arrest twelve monks for eating meat and drinking wine during Lent.

In more modern times, up until 1966, the Vatican forbade American Catholics from eating meat on Fridays.

# 7

# Apples and Oranges

### Why are fruits sweet?

The short answer is propagation. Fruits contain seeds that need to be dispersed. The best way to have them dispersed is by animals, since plants don't move around much. Like humans, other animals like sweets. Many plants have evolved sweet fruits to entice animals to eat them; seeds are then spread around to new areas in the animal droppings. The plants are "smart" enough to make their fruits sour until the seeds within are fully mature. This way they are not dispersed until they are ready. The plants also make their seeds bitter or even poisonous (such as apple and peach) so they are not chewed up and destroyed.

### What is the sweetest fruit?

Of all the fruits, the fig is the sweetest. It has a sugar content of fifty-five percent. Oddly, the fig tree doesn't have any flowers—not ones that you can see, anyway. The blossoms are contained inside the fruit.

The fig trade is very ancient, going back to at least 6000 B.C. The Egyptians imported it from Asia Minor. It was a staple of their diet, as well as the diet of the Romans and Greeks. The word "sycophant" derives from the early trading of figs. The root words of sycophant are *sykon*, meaning "fig," and *phainein*, meaning "to show." It is believed that the word originates with the old Greek fig trade. Apparently there was some concern in those days about the smuggling of figs. Those who informed the authorities about fig smugglers earned the name *sycophant*, or "one who shows the fig." "Showing the fig" is now an obscene gesture in some Mediterranean countries, involving showing one's thumb.

Figs were brought to America by Franciscan monks in 1770. The first commercial fig crop was grown in California, in 1885, but it ended in failure when the immature fruits fell off the tree. Growers had no success until they finally heeded the advice of third century B.C. Greek botanist Theophrastus, who recommended "caprification"—planting one wild fig tree (or capri) with every one hundred cultivated fig trees. *Blastophaga* wasps that live in the wild figs help to set the fruit. By 1900, figs were successfully harvested in California.

### When were Americans afraid of fruit?

Unless you are on some kooky fad diet, most of us consider fresh fruits to be a healthful part of a balanced diet. This was not the case in early America. In the first half of the 1800s, many people believed that fruit was dangerous and that it caused cholera epidemics. Young children were thought to be particularly susceptible. Some cities even banned the sale of fruit during epidemics.

### More of this fruit is eaten every day than any other fruit, what is it?

No way you guessed this one. It's mangoes! Cultivated in India for over four thousand years, the mango is known as the "apple of the tropics." More fresh mangoes are eaten every day than any other fruit. You may be surprised to learn that the mango is a relative of the cashew and pistachio. Like these two plants, the sap of the mango contains oils that are skin irritants. The cashew shell has similar irritants and cashews are actually poisonous until roasted.

### What is the most popular fruit in America?

Did you know that the banana (*Musa sapientia*) is classified as a berry? And a banana tree is not a tree but a giant herb. These "berries" are the most popular fruit in the United States. The average American eats about twenty-eight pounds of bananas a year.

The banana originated in Malaya and India and was brought to Africa by the Arabs in the seventh century. The Spanish brought bananas to the New World in 1516, where they were known as "Indian figs." The first banana appeared in America in 1690, but it didn't go over too well. It took some two hundred years before they became widely available in the United States; this was because of transportation and refrigeration problems. The first full shipment of bananas—sent from Kingston, Jamaica—didn't arrive in Boston until 1871, after a two-week sea voyage. Many Americans tasted their first banana at the Philadelphia Fair of 1876, where they were sold wrapped in foil for ten cents each. The advent of refrigerated ships and railway cars spread the banana across the nation.

Bananas are loaded with carbohydrates. When green, they are mostly starch. Natural enzymes convert this starch into sugar as they ripen. A nice yellow banana has twenty percent assimilable sugars by weight.

One notable fact about the banana is that its peel makes drugs like dopamine, norepinephrine, and serotonin. This was not lost on the "Now" generation of the 1960s. People smoked banana peels in the hopes of getting a high. It never really caught on, though, or banana would probably be illegal today.

One odd banana is the "Ice Cream Banana." It is blue before ripening and turning yellow, and tastes something like vanilla custard with a marshmallow texture. There are also red bananas, which ripen to a dark reddish purple color with a pink fruit inside. Perfect for Valentine's Day.

### What popular cartoonist created Miss Chiquita?

The same artist who draws *Hagar the Horrible* created the Campbell Soup Kids and Miss Chiquita Banana. The artist is Dik Browne, and in 1944 he came up with Miss Chiquita Banana in the first "branding" of a banana. The first woman to play Miss Chiquita was Patty Clayton, also in 1944. She was the goodwill ambassador of the brand, teaching consumers about the nutritional value of bananas and how to ripen them. Elsa Miranda (not related to Carmen Miranda) acted as Miss Chiquita in 1945 and 1946.

Miss Chiquita first appeared on banana labels in 1963. She was depicted as a banana character until 1987, when Pink Panther cartoonist Oscar Grillo transformed her into the present-day human figure.

## What is the most cultivated fruit in the world?

While the mango is the most popular eating fruit, far more acreage is devoted to the cultivation of the grape. There are thousands of varieties of grapes being grown on some twenty-five million acres worldwide. Most of these are European wine grapes (*Vitis vinifera*). The Thompson seedless grape is a member of this group and is sold as a table grape and is used to make California raisins. A small portion are the American Concord grape (*Vitis labrusca*), which is used in jellies, juice, and East Coast wines. Most wine grapes have a high acidity and are not suitable for eating.

Owing to its magical ability to turn into wine, the grape has been cultivated for about eight thousand years. The Old World grapes are native to Asia Minor and were probably first grown in the region between the Black and Caspian Seas, near northern Iran. Grapes were improved by the Romans and Greeks. It was the Romans who first brought grapes and winemaking to France during their conquests.

## Why did Mr. Thompson have grapes named after him?

The name Thompson will forever be associated with seedless green grapes; however, their namesake had nothing to do with breeding them. The Thompson seedless grape was named to honor William Thompson, of Yuba City, California, in 1876. The Horticultural Society of Marysville, California, erroneously credited Thompson with developing the grape because he had shown these grapes at the Marysville Fair. The Society was ignorant of the fact that Thompson bought some cuttings of this grape variety four years earlier from a nursery in Rochester, New York and that these grapes, also known as sultana, had been grown since ancient times in the Middle East. Nevertheless, Thompson seed-less grapes are the best-selling table grapes in America and are the most common grapes used in raisin production.

Table grapes were first planted in California in 1839, by a William Wolfskill, somewhere near present-day Los Angeles. Americans did not take to eating dark red varieties until the 1980s, although our European cousins had been enjoying them since long before that. The average American eats eight pounds of grapes a year. One quarter of these are imported from Chile, when grapes are not in season in the U.S. California alone grows some 300,000 tons of grapes annually on some 700,000 acres. This is about ninety-seven percent of domestic production. Grapes are the most valuable fruit crop in the United States, followed by apples, oranges, and strawberries.

### How did the American grape save the French wine industry?

The French have always looked down on the American grape—*Vitis labrusca*—as an inferior cousin to the European grape—*Vitis vinifera*. The American grape comes in several varieties and is well suited to the North American climate. Early colonists tried to make wine from wild grapes but failed; the grapes had a low sugar content and didn't ferment well. They also tried to grow European grapes with little success. During the Revolutionary War, some wild grapes were domesticated and U.S. wine produc-tion began. Better varieties of *Vitis labrusca* were later found. Ephrain Bull discovered the most dominant variety today near Concord, Massachusetts, in 1849, and it bears the name of the town. He began selling cuttings from the parent vine for $5 a piece and the Concord grape was soon growing throughout the country.

The prestigious French wine industry suffered a catastrophe between 1860 and 1880. A foreign insect pest—*Phylloxera vastatrix*—was inadvertently brought to France on some infected grape root-stock imported from the United States. This root-boring insect slowly decimated the vineyards of France. The poor French had no choice but to condescend to grafting their grapevines onto Ameri-can grape rootstock, which had a natural resistance to this pest.

## What does Kaopectate have to do with jams and jellies?

Pectin is a naturally occurring water-soluble, gelatinlike substance found in various ripe fruits and vegetables; it is known for its thickening properties. Its ability to thicken is utilized in the making of jams, jellies, and preserves. It is added to certain fruits that don't have enough pectin to "jell" on their own. While pectin is used to advantage in the culinary world, its thickening properties have not been lost on the pharmaceutical industry. One of the first antidiarrheals—Kaopectate—is made from pectin. Its name is a combination of its two main ingredients—kaolin (clay) and pectin.

## What is the difference between jam and jelly?

Jellies are made from fruit juice, sugar, and sometimes pectin. Jam is a mixture of cooked whole fruit that becomes formless, sugar, and sometimes pectin. Preserves are whole or cut up fruits that are cooked in a thick sugar syrup and usually pectin; chunks of the fruit are present after cooking. Marmalades are citrus preserves. Preserves and jams must contain at least forty-five percent fruit; no artificial colors or flavors are permitted.

## What food do we eat that is covered in shellac?

America's favorite fruit—the Red Delicious apple—is a thing of beauty. It's almost perfect in shape, color, and shine. Freshly harvested apples have a naturally occurring waxy coating that protects them from drying out. When apples are washed to remove dust and chemical residue, about half of this waxy coating is lost. Apple growers replace this lost wax with a natural, non-petroleum-based coating, such as carnauba wax or shellac. Both are approved by the Food and Drug Administration (FDA) and have been used on a variety of produce for decades. According to FDA rules, retailers must note which fruits and vegetables are coated. As many as twenty-one other produce items may be found on the list. Excessive heat or moisture may cause the wax to turn whitish. Don't fear, this is normal.

## Who was Granny Smith?

The modern domesticated apple (*Malus domestica*) originated from the wild apples (*Malus sieversii*) in the mountains of present-day Kazakhstan. These wild apples still grow quite prolifically and can reach heights of sixty feet.

Each of our familiar modern apple varieties came from a single unique tree that was propagated by grafting. For instance:

The Golden Delicious came from one original tree in Clay County, West Virginia, that lived into the 1950s.

The Red Delicious was found on an Iowa farm.

The McIntosh, which would become the main variety grown in New England, was propagated from a seedling found by Canadian Allan McIntosh on his Ontario orchard in the late 1700s.

The Jonathan was found in the Hudson Valley of New York and cannot grow outside certain geographical areas.

The Baldwin apple is named for Continental army officer Laomo Baldwin, who found it growing in Wilmington, Massachusetts, in 1777.

The Cortland apple was created in 1915, when a Ben Davis and a McIntosh were crossed in upstate New York.

The Newton pippin was named in 1666 and commemorated the famed apple that fell on the head of Sir Isaac Newton and got him to thinking about the force of gravity, which changed the course of physics forever.

The Granny Smith was discovered by a Mrs. Maria (or Mary) Smith in Australia. In 1868 she found this new variety growing in her garden. It had started from the seed of a French crabapple she had discarded. Granny Smiths were originally sold in America, starting in 1960 as a summer apple, since U.S.-grown apples are scarce at this time of year. They were initially imported from New Zealand because of a quarantine on the importation of Australian apples at the time. They were then imported from South Africa and France until orchards were established in California.

## Why did Johnny Appleseed plant so many trees?

Up until Prohibition, more apples went into cider than were eaten in the United States. Hard cider was easy to make. In fact, it was hard to avoid making. Before refrigeration, any sweet apple cider would quickly turn hard. This fact did not escape people's attention, and hard cider became the American drink of choice once John Chapman's (Johnny Appleseed's) orchards began to bear fruit across the frontier. Many folks bought seedlings from Johnny, but not for eating, because only grafted apple trees bear sweet, tasty fruit. Trees planted from seed bear any of a wide assortment of odd-shaped, -colored, and -tasting apples. The reason for the apple's popularity was for its cider.

Before the apple tree became so widespread on the frontier, corn liquor, or "white lightning," was the frontiersman's drink of choice. Hard cider was easier to make, it was safer, and it tasted better. If allowed to ferment for a few weeks, cider turned into a drink with about half the alcoholic content of wine. If a harder drink was desired, they would distill it into brandy or freeze it to make Applejack, or "Jersey lightning." The freezing process (see ice wine question) removes water and concentrates the alcohol. William Laird began distilling Applejack in 1698, in Monmouth County, New Jersey. His descendants began commercial production in 1780. Laird & Company's distillery, in Scobeyville, New Jersey, is recognized as the oldest operating distillery in the country.

Most homesteads had apple orchards. As local water supplies were not always safe or reliable, cider was often the everyday drink of choice, even for children.

## Why did New York ban street apple sellers during the Depression?

The International Apple Shippers Association found a good way of selling their surplus apples during the Depression—give them on credit to the thousands of unemployed men to sell on the streets of New York. It was a good idea and it worked. However, it may have worked too well. By the end of 1930, there were more than 6,000 apple peddlers on the streets of the Big Apple, as well as thousands of others in cities across the country. Kind of like the squeegee guys from the 1980s, although not as messy, the apple peddlers became an annoyance to city officials and New York kicked them off the streets by early 1931.

## Who is the Bartlett pear named for?

The Bartlett pear originated from trees grown by an English schoolmaster named John Stair in 1769. The pear came to be known as Stairs pear in England. It was planted in a Massachusetts orchard in 1770 and forgotten. By some accounts, it was rediscovered there by Enoch Bartlett in 1817. He was a Massachusetts farmer who bought an orchard of Stairs pears that had been planted in 1798 by Thomas Brewer of Roxbury, Massachusetts. Bartlett began distributing his pears in 1848, and his name became attached to them.

Today, over ninety percent of the American pear crop is grown in northern California, Oregon, and Washington. More than half are Bartletts.

## Where did the grapefruit originate?

All of our present-day citrus fruits originated on the Indian subcontinent, and in China and Japan, except for the grapefruit (*Citrus paradisi*). The first citrus fruit to make it to the Western world was the citron, a small, bitter fruit brought back by Alexander the Great. It wasn't until the Middle Ages that the lemon found its way to Europe. It took the orange another two hundred years to do so. At first, Europeans didn't know what to do with these exotic plants and they grew them as horticultural curiosities.

The grapefruit, however, just appeared one day in the Caribbean, during the late eighteenth century. It was probably the result of crossbreeding between an orange and a pomelo (*Citrus maxima*), which was a large citrus fruit that was brought to the New World from Southeast Asia in the 1600s. The new fruit was called "grapefruit" because it grows in clusters, somewhat like grapes. The first grapefruit trees were planted by Frenchman Count Odette Philippe in 1823, somewhere around Tampa Bay, Florida. Later plant breeding improved the fruit's sweetness. Today, Florida grows more grapefruit than the rest of the world combined.

The Ruby Red grapefruit was a chance mutation that was discovered on a McAllen, Texas, farm, in 1929. The Texas Red Grapefruit is now the state fruit of Texas. A newer red-fleshed, thin-skinned, seedless grapefruit was developed and released in 1987. Called "Flame," over four million of these trees have been planted in Florida, making it the most widely planted grapefruit today.

## Is grapefruit juice dangerous to drink if you are taking medication?

Many prescription medications can be affected by grapefruit juice. It can reduce the production of a certain enzyme in the intestine that is involved in the metabolism of certain drugs. Grapefruit juice can even cause you to inadvertently overdose on some medications when taking them at the prescribed dosage, as it can increase the concentration of these drugs by three or four times in your bloodstream. It is best to read all labeling that comes with your medicines or ask your pharmacist before drinking grapefruit juice.

## Why are oranges orange?

Oranges (*Citrus sinensis*) only turn orange when they are exposed to cold weather while still on the tree. In the tropics, they stay green. One reason California oranges have such a nice bright orange color, compared to Florida oranges, is because the nights get much cooler.

Originally from Malaysia, the sweet orange was brought to Europe from the East by the Portuguese in 1529. In parts of Italy and the Balkans they were called "portugals," and still are in some areas. It came to Florida, either with Ponce de Leon in 1513 or Hernando de Soto in 1586. The Spanish planted citrus seeds wherever they went ashore. This was to maintain a steady source of future fruit to prevent their sailors from getting scurvy. These first oranges were not the sweet variety that we enjoy today but were likely bitter oranges, like the wild oranges found in Florida today. The sweet orange had yet to make its debut.

## Why do California oranges have such thick skins?

It's easy to distinguish a California orange from a Florida orange. Because of California's dry climate, their oranges need a thicker peel to prevent moisture loss. Florida's moist climate produces larger, juicier, thinner-skinned oranges. Since Florida's oranges are so juicy, they are primarily used in juice.

The Valencia orange was grown by American horticulturist Edmund Hart and his two brothers, in Federal Point, Florida, in the late 1860s. Originally called the Hart Late, or Tardiff, the Valencia was introduced in 1867 from Spain and went on to be the leading late-season orange variety in Florida and California. Their peak season is May through July. They have seeds, thin skins, and can be a bit difficult to peel. As such, they tend to be used for juice. Most of our juice oranges come from Florida or South America. Brazil is the leading grower of oranges.

The first seedless orange trees were imported from Bahia, Brazil, to Washington, D.C., in 1871, by USDA horticulturist William Saunders. The twelve trees he received would propagate all first growths of this variety, known as the Washington navel. Jonathan and Eliza Tibbetts would propagate navel oranges from two of these trees—the first seedless, winter-ripening oranges in America. They were called "navel" oranges because the blossom end resembles a human navel. Navels are large, sweet oranges for eating, with thick skins that peel off easily and sections that separate readily. Navel oranges found in the supermarket during the summer months probably come from Australia.

The father of the commercial orange business in Florida was James Armstrong Harris, who started with 525 acres of wild oranges on the shore of Orange Lake, in 1870, which he converted to sweet oranges. Hart shipped his orange crop north to New York by steamer and later introduced the North to grapefruits.

### When did orange juice come in a can?

Before the advent of frozen orange juice concentrate, sales of frozen orange juice and orange juice in a can (yuck!) were flat and Florida growers were starting to cut down orange groves to plant avocado trees. Orange juice was first condensed and frozen in 1948, by the Vacuum Foods Company (later Minute Maid

Corporation). Like any new product, bringing it to the public's attention was half the battle in making it a success.

Crooner Bing Crosby had a lot to do with the success of frozen concentrated orange juice. When an investor offered a glass to his golf partner, Bing, in 1950, the singer loved it. He bought twenty thousand shares in the company and put his name and talent to work promoting the new product, doing a daily fifteen-minute radio show hawking frozen concentrated orange juice. Along with Bing's efforts and a favorable piece in the June 1950 *Reader's Digest*, sales of Florida orange juice shot up to four times their previous level.

In 1973, Minute Maid introduced the first chilled, ready-to-drink orange juice.

### What famed orange variety saved the Florida orange industry?

Indian River oranges are quite well-known, and with good reason. They are a locally developed variety that saved the Florida orange growers—twice. On February 8, 1835, there was a freeze that wiped out all of the orange groves in Florida, except one. A grower named Douglas Dummett had a grove on the Indian River that for some reason endured through the brunt of the freeze. His oranges were particularly hardy and did not die. The buds from these Indian River orange trees were used to reestablish the groves in the rest of the state. Another similar freeze occurred, in 1895, and again the Indian River grove was spared. For a second time its buds came to the rescue.

Indian River oranges are still held in high esteem. They are one of the sweetest varieties and only oranges from this area are allowed to be stamped with the coveted "Indian River" name.

### What part of the orange has the most vitamin C?

Orange juice is a great source of vitamin C, but the juice of an orange only contains twenty-five percent of its total vitamin C content. Much of the vitamin C is concentrated in the peel and the albedo (the white membrane under the peel).

## What city is the tangerine named for?

Tangerines (*Citrus reticulata*) are a loose-skinned mandarin species that originated in China. The first ones came to Europe around 1805 and were grown in the Mediterranean region. It is possible that they came to southern Spain from Tangier, Morocco, in the Middle Ages—hence their name. Tangerines were first grown commercially in Florida by Colonel George l. Darcy, at Buena Vista. For a century, the Darcy tangerine, as it is known, was the most popular American tangerine.

## What produce is picked green and ripened during shipping?

Certain kinds of produce are so easily damaged when shipped that they are picked green and artificially ripened en route to market. Tomatoes come immediately to mind. A ripe tomato is a delicate thing of beauty. It could never withstand the rigorous handling of the harvesting and transport process. This is unfortunate, because artificially ripened tomatoes are a pathetic excuse for vine-ripened gems. Other kinds of produce that are picked green, like bananas and oranges, ripen nicely during transport. Green oranges actually don't ripen any more after picking, but they develop their lovely orange color.

The idea of chemically ripening produce after harvest started in the early 1900s. It was observed that bunches of green bananas stored next to oranges ripened faster than other bunches picked at the same time. California orange growers noticed their green fruit ripened faster when stored near a kerosene stove. It was apparent that stoves and fruit gave off some kind of gas that promoted ripening. Later studies revealed that gas to be ethylene. Today, it is ethylene gas that is used to ripen shipped produce.

## Why are limes green?

Lemons (*Citrus limon*) and limes (*Citrus aurantifolia*) are very closely related. Both come from evergreen tropical trees in the Rue family. Today's cultivated lemons are thought to be the result of a cross between a lime and a citron—a large (six to nine inches long) yellow, lumpy citrus fruit that looks like a huge lemon. Both are natives of Southeast Asia.

There are two main types of limes. The one you are probably most familiar with is the Persian (or Tahiti) lime. It is the large, lemon-shaped, green lime that is found in every supermarket. Persian limes were hybridized in the early twentieth century. They are picked while slightly immature and still green. They turn yellow when fully ripe and can be easily confused with lemons.

Key limes are smaller and rounder, with a thinner skin, and are more aromatic and flavorful than are Persian limes. They are found primarily in Florida and are also yellowish when ripe. Key limes are the predominant type outside the U.S.

## What native American fruit is also known as "bounceberry"?

When it comes to fruit, native North Americans didn't have a wide selection to choose from. Of all the fruits available to us in our modern supermarkets, only three are native to North America— the Concord grape, the blueberry, and the cranberry. Of the three, the cranberry is probably the least appreciated.

Cranberries are also known as "bounceberries" because they bounce when ripe. This bouncing effect is used to sort the ripe cranberries from the immature ones after harvesting. The name "cranberry" is a derivation of the other moniker the berry goes by—"craneberry." Early settlers noticed that the shrub's pale pink blossoms resembled the head of a sandhill crane and took to calling them craneberries.

Cranberries were very important to the diet of Native Americans. They used them to make cakes called "pemmican"—a high-protein combination of crushed cranberries, dried deer meat, and melted fat. These cakes had excellent storage properties and were taken on long journeys. The Native Americans also used cranberries as a dye and to treat wounds. A good source of vitamin C, the Pilgrims and whaling captains took to eating cranberries to avoid scurvy.

The first white man to aggressively cultivate the cranberry was Captain Henry Hall, of Dennis, Massachusetts. In 1817 he noticed that wild cranberries in his bog grew better when sand blew over them. He started transplanting his cranberries and spreading the sand himself. Others took note of his cultivation practices and copied him. Soon the number of cranberry growers increased wherever the proper growing conditions could be found—an acidic peat soil, adequate fresh water, sand, and an April to November growing season. Such naturally occurring environments allow wild cranberries to grow from the Carolinas to the Canadian maritime provinces.

Growers must maintain four acres of supporting land (wetlands, uplands, ditches, flumes, and ponds) for every acre of cranberry bog. In winter, bogs are flooded to protect the plants from ground frost. The bogs are drained in spring and the water is used for irrigation. In the fall, the bogs are flooded again to facilitate the cranberry harvest. Cranberries have little air pockets in the center and float nicely. This allows growers to shake the berries loose from the vine and corral the floating berries onto conveyors, which load them on trucks.

Undamaged vines will survive indefinitely. Some vines on Cape Cod are over 150 years old. The major cranberry growing states are Massachusetts, New Jersey, Wisconsin, Washington, and Oregon.

Cranberry juice was first enjoyed by early American settlers in 1683. Cranberry sauce didn't debut in its familiar canned "log" form until 1912, when the Cape Cod Cannery Company introduced Ocean Spray Cranberry Sauce. Eighty-six-million cans of the stuff are sold during cranberry sauce season—September through December.

### Why is cranberry juice good for a urinary tract infection?

Recent studies have shown that cranberry juice can prevent urinary tract infections. It may also help prevent gum disease and ulcers. Many people erroneously believe it is the acidity of cranberry juice that is responsible for its antibacterial properties. Recent studies have demonstrated that it is the pigments that give cranberries their beautiful deep red color—proanthocyanidins—that are actually responsible for its beneficial properties. These compounds create an environment so slippery that bacteria can't stick to it or to one another, be it in the urinary tract, the stomach, or the mouth.

Cranberries are also loaded with antioxidants, such as flavonoids, that can lower your risk of heart disease and certain types of cancer. One-third of all cranberries are made into juice.

## Why are blueberries blue?

There aren't many true blue foods, but blueberries are one. Their color is derived from the high content of the plant pigment anthocyanin (from the Greek words *antho*, meaning "plant" and *cyanin*, meaning "blue"). This pigment is water soluble and imparts a blue or very intense red color to the berries. Young blueberries are green. As they mature, they become translucent. Then as anthocyanin develops, they become light purple and then dark purple. Anthocyanins have another interesting property: early colonists made paint from blueberries. By boiling blueberry skins in milk, with indigo and sage blossoms, shades of blue and gray were created. The blue woodwork in Shaker houses was colored with blueberry paint.

## When did the cultivation of the blueberry begin?

Unlike raspberries, blackberries, and strawberries, the blueberry is a true berry (as is the cranberry, grape, and currant). Blueberries are native to North America and northern Europe and can be found growing wild there. While wild blueberries have been enjoyed for millennia, the commercial production of blueberries did not begin until around 1910, when a New Jersey cranberry grower, working with a United States Department of Agriculture scientist, bred the first plump seedless variety. New Jersey still has a thriving blueberry industry, but Maine leads the nation in production.

## Can blueberries make you younger?

Recent USDA studies show that blueberries take first place, out of forty fruits and vegetables analyzed, for antioxidant activity. This means that eating blueberries can fight aging, heart disease, and cancer. Scientists credit anthocyanins with some of these healthful antioxidant benefits. Antioxidants help the body block the effects of harmful oxygen molecules called free radicals. An animal study showed that supplementing the diet for eight weeks with blueberry extract improved two major age-related concerns—loss of memory and loss of coordination. Abundant antioxidants may reduce inflammation, a process that can impair brain tissue as people age.

Please pass the blueberries!

## How can you tell if a watermelon is ripe?

One oft-mentioned way is to thump it. What it is supposed to sound like is not clear. Good luck figuring out melon ripeness by picking them up and thumping them at the market. A better way to find a ripe watermelon (*Citrullus vulgaris*) is to examine the end where it was joined to the vine. A clean break between the fruit and the vine means it stayed on the vine long enough to achieve its full ripeness. (Watermelons do not ripen after picking.) A vine that was cut off, leaving a protruding nub still attached, indicates that this may not have been the case.

In any event, you may be interested to know that the watermelon is native to southern Africa and was eaten in Egypt by 4000 B.C. Slaves from Africa brought it to the Americas. The self-proclaimed "Watermelon Capital of the World" is Cordele, Georgia.

## How do they grow seedless watermelons?

Spitting out the seeds is half the fun of eating watermelon on a summer picnic. However, many people don't care for this practice and are loathe to swallow them. Hence the demand for seedless watermelons. But if they don't produce seeds, how do they grow them? They mess with their chromosomes, that's how.

The first seedless watermelon was created in 1939. By crossing a diploid watermelon plant (having the normal two sets of chromosomes) with a tetraploid plant (having four sets of chromosomes), a fruit with triploid seeds (three sets of chromosomes) will result. Seeds from this fruit will produce a watermelon that has very few seeds, although there may be some empty white seed coats. Aside from being seedless, these melons have a firmer flesh because the usual softening around the seeds does not take place.

How do they get tetraploid plants? They treat unpollinated flowers with colchicine, a poisonous alkaloid derived from the autumn crocus (*Colchicum autumnale*), that inhibits mitosis.

## Is the strawberry a fruit?

The strawberry (*Fragaria*) is what we call a "false fruit." The large, red, fleshy "berry" is not a fruit; but actually is composed of plant tissue derived from the base of the flower, instead of from an ovary, which true fruits are. The tiny black "seeds" on the surface of the "berry" are the actual fruits of the strawberry. They are called "achenes," and they each enclose a tiny seed. It may be splitting hairs, but now you know.

The strawberry is one of the few fruits native to the Americas, although it also occurs naturally in Europe and Asia. The two American species are bigger and made a big impression on the first white settlers on the East Coast. The larger New World strawberries, one from Virginia and another from the west coast of South America, were brought back to France in the 1700s and were eventually bred into the commercial strawberries available today.

Like the strawberry, blackberries (*Rubus*) and raspberries (*Rubus*) are not single fruits. Each little seed-containing section of the berries is an individual fruit. Raspberries are also native to North America.

## What is a "cling" peach?

Peaches are native to China and came to the West via Persia, hence its species name *persica*. Like the apricot, cherry, and plum, peaches (*Prunus*) belong to the rose family and are "stone" fruits, meaning that they have a large central seed, or pit (the stone), surrounded by the fleshy fruit. While hundreds of varieties have evolved over the centuries, all peaches fall into one of two categories—cling or freestone.

In cling peaches, the stone or pit adheres tightly to the fruit; in freestone peaches the stone is easily removed. Cling peaches tend to have nicer coloration. They are also firmer and thus less likely to bruise during harvesting, processing, and shipping. As a consequence, freestone peaches are hard to find today. One reason you can't find a decent peach at the supermarket is because they are picked early and stored cold for a couple of weeks, resulting in a hard, dry fruit. You can help to ripen peaches further by placing them in a paper bag with an apple for a couple of days. The apple will give off a natural ripening agent—ethylene gas.

The peach is the state fruit of Georgia and South Carolina, and the state flower of Delaware. Johnston, South Carolina, claims to be the "Peach Capital of the World." It was readily accepted by Native Americans when introduced here. In fact, they liked it so much that the peach spread across the country faster than the settlers did. Hence, many whites settling "new" territory were surprised to find that Native Americans already had well-established peach orchards.

### Is a nectarine really a peach?

Yes; nectarines are peaches that have no fuzz and are a little smaller. Nectarine trees arise spontaneously from mutations in peach orchards. For no apparent reason, a peach pit will some-times grow into a nectarine tree. Conversely, a nectarine pit can grow into a peach tree. Bud mutations can cause a peach to grow on a nectarine tree or a nectarine to grow on a peach tree. Some trees even produce fruits that are partly fuzzy and partly smooth. Go figure.

### What fruit was once known as "alligator pear"?

In 1833, the avocado, known as the "alligator pear," was brought to southern Florida by horticulturist Henry Perrine. He planted Mexican varieties on his property south of Miami. Commercial avocado production began in Florida in 1901, outside Miami. By 1965, Dade County had some 6,800 acres devoted to avocados. Southern Florida now grows the West Indian varieties, which are tropical and can grow nowhere else in the United States. In 1871, R. B. Ord started the commercial planting of Mexican avocados in California, near Santa Barbara, and the state still grows this variety.

## What's the best way to store an avocado?

Leave it on the tree. Avocados (*Persea americana*) don't ripen unless they are picked. This is the reverse of other fruits and vegetables, such as the tomato and orange, which do not ripen *after* picking. It is believed that the leaves on the tree release some kind of hormone that prevents the fruit from ripening. When picked, the avocado is cut off from the inhibitor and the production of ethylene causes ripening to begin. Avocados are frequently left on the tree for up to seven months, as a way to store them until needed.

Central Americans have been enjoying avocados for some seven thousand years. For many of these peoples, the avocado was a major source of fat. In fact, an avocado is twenty percent fat. Most other fruits have a fat content of around one percent. Avocados are also high in minerals and B vitamins.

## Why aren't there any plums in plum pudding?

There are hundreds of varieties of plums. They come in a wide range of colors, from green to yellow, red, purple, and indigo blue. The modern plum was brought to California from Japan in 1870. Called a Chinese plum, it would become the basis of our modern plum industry.

Plums are a wonderful-tasting fruit, but they are not to be found in plum pudding. Its ingredients include suet, flour, raisins, currants, nuts, sugar, and spices. It is boiled or steamed and usually served warm, flamed with rum or brandy, and accompanied with hard sauce and topped with a sprig of holly. There may or may not have been plums in early plum pudding. The word "plum" was used centuries ago for many dried fruits, such as prunes, raisins, and currants, all of which were found in plum puddings at various times.

Plum pudding isn't even a "pudding," not as Americans consider it anyway. In the United States puddings are soft, creamy, sweet desserts. In England, a "pudding" is any dessert served after a meal.

Also known as Christmas pudding, plum pudding is a must-have at English Christmas dinners. Tradition has it that small silver charms were baked into the pudding, each with its own meaning to the person who got it in his or her dish. A silver coin meant wealth for the coming year; a tiny wishbone brought good luck; a ring meant marriage within a year; and a silver thimble or button indicated the finder would remain a spinster or bachelor. By the Victorian era, only the silver coin remained, although you can still buy these charms in England to add to your Christmas pudding. It is also traditional for everyone who lives in a house to simultaneously hold the wooden mixing spoon and help stir the batter and make a wish.

Plum pudding started out in the fourteenth century as a porridge called "frumenty" that was made of boiled beef, mutton, raisins, currants, prunes, wines, and spices. It was eaten like a soup. By 1595, it had evolved into plum pudding, having been thickened with eggs, bread crumbs, and dried fruit, and made more flavorful with the addition of ales and spirits. It had become so widely enjoyed that in 1664, the Puritans banned it as a "lewd custom" and "unfit for God-fearing people." Then, King George I took a liking to it and reintroduced it to the Christmas feast in 1714. Plum pudding reached its present form by Victorian times.

There is said to be a great deal of Christian symbolism in Christmas pudding. Superstition holds that it should have thirteen ingredients to represent Christ and the disciples, and that it should be stirred from east to west in honor of the Three Wise Men. Flaming the dish before serving symbolizes Christ's passion and the sprig of holly on top represents his crown of thorns.

# 8

# Eat Your Greens

*What common wildflower is an escaped garden vegetable?*

If you are into backyard nature, perhaps you are familiar with the wildflower called Queen Anne's lace. It is a lovely plant with a white, flat-topped, lacy flower. Apart from its beauty, many people consider this biennial plant to be a troublesome weed. One reason for its troublesomeness is that it is not a naturally occurring species. It is actually a descendant of the common garden carrot that escaped cultivation by the colonists. Its leaves look like those of your garden carrot and it has a white taproot that is similar to that of a carrot in taste and smell.

The carrot has only been widely used in America since World War I. Europeans have been keen on them since the Middle Ages. Originally cultivated in Afghanistan in the seventh century, the early carrot came in varieties ranging from white to red, purple, and black, depending on the anthocyanin pigments they contained. A light yellow variety, lacking in anthocyanin, was popular in the 1500s. It wasn't until the 1600s that the Dutch bred the now-familiar carotene-rich orange carrot and the French developed the elongated shape.

*What are baby carrots?*

Big carrots are still around, but these newer "baby" carrots are quite popular. The name, however, is somewhat misleading. They are not young carrots or even miniature carrots. Baby carrots come from full-sized carrots that have been whittled down in size into those smooth, shiny, small orange things found in all the arkets nowadays. The appeal of baby carrots is that they are already peeled and snack-sized.

## Why do we call corn "corn"?

This may sound like a stupid question, but we North Americans are the only people in the world who use the word "corn" just for corn (*Zea mays*). Native Americans referred to what we call corn as "maize." When Columbus brought corn back to Europe, they called it "Indian corn" or maize. The word "corn" was, and still is, a generic term for any grain in Europe.

The domestication of corn began around forty-five hundred years ago in Central America and by the time Columbus arrived there were already some seven hundred varieties. Columbus and his crew didn't care much for maize, even though they took some with them to eat on their return journey to Spain.

Sweet corn (*Zea mays saccharata*) was not discovered by the white man until 1779, when Continental army officer Richard Bagnal chanced upon some that was growing near the Susquehanna River. Sweet corn does not convert its sugar to starch as quickly as other types of corn. The first sweet corn was probably the result of a natural mutation. It had been found and was cultivated by the Iroquois long before Bagnal happened upon it. However, it was he who collected the seeds and took them home to Plymouth, Massachusetts, where he began growing it. While Bagnal and his neighbors appreciated sweet corn, the rest of the country didn't know about it for many decades and it took the rest of the world well over a century to begin cultivating it.

## Who eats the most corn?

Our neighbors to the south in Mexico consume some four hundred pounds of corn per person per year. We Americans down about 140 pounds a year. India eats a measly fifteen pounds. How can we possibly eat so much corn? It's not like we eat corn on the cob every day. However, corn, in its different forms, is found in over three thousand food products on the supermarket shelves. Livestock love corn, too. Well over half of the U.S. corn harvested goes into animal feed.

If you ever find yourself in Mitchell, South Dakota ("Corn Capital of the World"), check out the Corn Palace. It's a big building with minarets and onion-shaped domes that bears a slight resemblance to the Kremlin. Each year it is decorated entirely in mosaics made up of corn kernels, grains, and grasses from around the state. The craftsmanship is phenomenal. Not only is it the world's biggest corn palace, it's also the world's biggest bird feeder. Each winter birds and squirrels feast on the building's facade.

Here's another bit of corn trivia: the first machine that stripped the kernels from the cob was invented in 1875.

## What is pellagra?

Have you ever heard of pellagra? It isn't talked about much anymore, but up until 1937, when scientists figured out what caused it, pellagra was a debilitating disease worldwide. Its symptoms included dementia, diarrhea, and dermatitis. The disease was widespread, including the poor rural areas of the southern United States. Curiously, it was not a problem in Mexico or Central America. Finally, they figured out why.

Pellagra is the result of a niacin deficiency. The reason Mexico didn't suffer from it was due to the country's heavy reliance on masa flour and tortillas. Because of the lime processing, masa flour is rich in available niacin. The corn that formed the staple of the poor South was not.

## Why is freshness in corn on the cob so important?

If you have ever eaten just-picked corn on the cob, you know there is nothing like it. This is because corn loses much of its freshness soon after being harvested. The problem with vegetables and fruits is that they keep on going about the business of respiration after being picked. Their cells are still carrying out their biological function even though they no longer receive water or nutrients from the plant. As a result, vegetables like corn and peas can lose more than forty percent of their water and sugar content within a few hours of picking. In the case of corn, the sugars that make sweet corn so delicious are converted to starch, leaving the kernels that are less sugary and more chewy. Other vegetables, such as asparagus and broccoli, convert their sugars into fibers that make them much tougher.

## What is baby corn?

Unlike baby carrots, baby corn really are immature ears of corn. Popular in Chinese dishes and at salad bars, these miniature ears of corn are picked by hand as soon as the silks emerge from the ear tips, when the ears are between 1¾ and 4 inches long. Most of our baby corn is grown in Asia, particularly Thailand, because it is too labor intensive to grow in the U.S.

## What vegetable did the French think was the cause of leprosy?

The Incas have been eating potatoes for five thousand years. It was the Spaniards who brought potatoes to Europe in the 1500s. The English and Irish had no problems accepting them, and by the early 1600s they had adopted the potato as a staple crop. One story has it that potatoes first came to Ireland when wreckage of the Spanish Armada washed them ashore. The potato was a godsend for the Irish. It was one nourishing crop that could grow well in their poor soil and harvesting it took no special tools—even bare hands would suffice.

But up until 1780, the French thought potatoes caused leprosy and were afraid of them. They were so afraid of potatoes that Burgundy banned growing them in 1618. It was an agronomist named Antoine-Augustin Parmentier who helped the potato gain acceptance in France. He had eaten them while a prisoner of the Prussians during the Seven Years War and suffered no ill effects. Parmentier had a field of potatoes planted and posted guards around it to raise the public's curiosity. At night, when the guards left, people would sneak into the field and steal potatoes, thinking that they must be something very special to be kept under guard. Parmentier also got Louis XVI to wear a potato flower and serve potatoes at his court. This convinced the aristocracy to eat them. It wasn't long before the common people were emulating the aristocracy.

For many years, the potato remained a food of the poor: it was easy to grow and cheap. Its trip to America was rather circuitous. The potato was not brought directly from the Andes to the American colonies, but with Irish immigrants, in 1719. The first large planting in America was near Londonderry, New Hampshire. However, many Americans thought they were poisonous for quite some time. Those who risked eating potatoes boiled them to remove the toxins. The later flood of Irish to America during the potato famine was due to the fact that all the potato plants in Europe originated from just two plants that were first brought there by the Spaniards. It was this lack of genetic diversity that made the Irish potato crop so susceptible to the potato blight in the 1800s.

## What are the most popular vegetables in America?

Potatoes and lettuce. Each year we eat about 145 pounds of potatoes per person, up from 115 in 1980. Potatoes are sold in the following forms:

| | |
|---|---|
| Frozen | 35 percent |
| Fresh | 26 percent |
| Dehydrated | 11 percent |
| Chips | 10 percent |
| Canned | 1 percent |

(The rest are used in potato starch and flour.)

Worldwide, potatoes are the fourth most important source of food, after wheat, rice, and corn. The United States alone grows some forty-eight billion pounds a year.

## Are lima beans poisonous?

It is fairly common knowledge that the pits of apricots, peaches, and plums, as well as the seeds of apples and pears, contain cyanogens—chemicals that are converted into hydrogen cyanide when the plant tissue is damaged. This is generally not a problem. People do not break open and eat peach pits and the odd apple seed is not dangerous enough to cause any harm. Deliberately eating quantities of these fruit seeds and pits can, however, be injurious or even deadly.

A lesser known fact is that lima beans also contain cyanogens. The United States limits the varieties of lima beans sold here to the ones with the lowest cyanogen content. In countries like Burma and Java, the cyanogen content of lima beans sold can be from twenty to thirty times higher than that allowed in most Western countries. You need not worry, though. By boiling the beans, the hydrogen cyanide gas is evaporated. Just don't cover the pot during cooking.

## What vegetable can give you red urine?

Beets! We have been eating beets since prehistory. Native from western Europe clear across to India, these underground vegetables were likely scratched from the earth by our ancestors millennia ago. Today, we eat the deep red "root" and we also enjoy the leaves in salads.

A beet is partly root and partly hypocotyl (swollen stem). The most characteristic thing about beets is their intense red color, which is the result of a pigment called betacyanin. Most of us can metabolize betacyanin and pass it normally through our bodies. The ability to metabolize it, however, is controlled by a recessive gene. Those people with two recessive genes cannot metabolize this red pigment, and it leaves the body in urine, which becomes bright red.

To buy fresh beets, look for greens that are crisp and bright. The greens should be cut off before storing, however, as they can draw nutrients and moisture away from the bulb. Leave about an inch of the stem attached, to prevent loss of nutrients and color during cooking.

Aside from the familiar garden beet, there is also the white sugar beet, which is the source of much of the world's sugar (along with sugar cane), and Swiss chard, or the spinach beet.

## What dish helped popularize carrots in America?

One dish that helped popularize carrots in America is carrot cake. Carrots have a rather high sugar content. During the Middle

Ages they were used as a sugar substitute and they are still used to help sweeten carrot cake. When baked in carrot cake, you don't taste carrots, just their sweetness and moisture. During the 1920s, carrot cake with cream cheese frosting became an American favorite and carrot sales took off.

You may not realize it, but members of the carrot family include anise, caraway, coriander, cumin, dill, fennel, and parsley.

### What is a choke?

An artichoke is a flower bud of a plant closely related to the thistle. A native of the Mediterranean region, it has been enjoyed since ancient times. The choke—that hairy thing near the vegetable's heart that is always cut out and discarded—is an immature seed. The first artichokes came to the United States with settlers to Louisiana in the nineteenth century. Italian immigrants started growing them commercially in Half Moon Bay, California, around the turn of the twentieth century.

Marilyn Monroe was crowned the first "Queen of Artichokes" in 1947, in Castroville, California—"Artichoke Capital of the World." Almost all of the U.S. artichoke crop comes from the mid-coastal region of California. If you really like artichokes, try cynar, an artichoke-flavored aperitif from Italy.

### What was the first vegetable to be sold frozen?

Spinach, which is native to Southwest Asia. Cookbooks in the 1800s recommended boiling spinach for twenty-five minutes to remove its toxins.

Spinach wasn't the only vegetable or fruit in the old days to be boiled until it became mush. Up until as recently as World War I, many people thought that fresh produce contained toxins that had to be boiled away. The lack of refrigeration before this time resulted in some fruits and vegetables reaching the home somewhat past their prime. Because of this, canned or preserved goods accounted for a much greater percentage of the diet from the Civil War to World War I. The introduction of frozen vegetables broadened the diet of most Americans.

Early on, frozen foods were considered a luxury. They didn't really catch on in a big way until World War II, when the Japanese cut off America's main sources of tin. The tin that was available was needed for the troops, so frozen foods filled the void.

### What vegetable became a favorite of kids because of a cartoon?

Sorry Bugs, it's not the carrot. It was spinach, thanks to Popeye. After the introduction of Popeye the sailor in the syndicated comic strip "Thimble Theater," in 1929, spinach sales rose by about a third. Kids later rated it as their third favorite food, behind turkey and ice cream. (Kids must have been a little weird back then.) Popeye found his prodigious strength by eating canfuls of spinach while exclaiming "I'm strong to the finish, 'cause I eats me spinach." Grammar notwithstanding, Popeye inadvertently did more for the sales of a vegetable than any other cartoon character. To express their gratitude, spinach growers commissioned a statue of Popeye, which was erected in Crystal City, Texas, in 1937.

### What members of the daisy family do we eat?

Daisies are part of the second largest plant family—the Compositae—which contains some twenty thousand species, including daisies, dandelions, chicory, artichokes, sunflowers, lettuce, and endive.

Lettuce (*Lactuca*) has been grown since about 3000 B.C. and probably came to the New World around the time of Columbus. Its genus name is from the Latin for "milk," due to the milky latex sap that is exuded when the growing plant's leaf stems are broken. This is a trait that lettuce shares with the dandelion. One curious thing about this sap is that it acts as a mild sedative in some varieties of lettuce. For this reason, the ancient Greeks served it at the end of the meal.

### How did iceberg lettuce get to be so popular?

With all the kinds of lettuce now available, why is it that iceberg lettuce is still so dominant? There are many kinds of lettuce with much more flavor and character than iceberg, but this bland old favorite continues to be very popular. It was first introduced commercially by W. Altee Burpee Company in 1894. Between the years 1920 and 1935, the sales of iceberg lettuce tripled. The reason for this lettuce's great popularity was one of simple economics. Growers and shippers found that this firm-headed lettuce was easier to ship and arrived at stores less damaged. We were thus trained to like iceberg, and we still do. During the 1920s it was shipped from California covered in crushed ice; that's how it came to be called iceberg lettuce. It is a type of crisp-head lettuce.

Lettuce, of all types, is the second most popular vegetable in America. We consume roughly thirty pounds of it per person each year. That is five times the amount we ate one hundred years ago, before refrigeration. Lettuce is one vegetable that must be eaten fresh; it can't be frozen, dried, or pickled.

## Why is Belgian endive white?

Endive is related to chicory. Both are in the genus *Cichorium*. The three types of endive are Belgian, curly, and escarole. They are all more bitter than lettuce. Belgian endive is white because it is grown without light. This is a labor-intensive operation that is called "blanching" and it's why Belgian endive is so pricey. In 1848, the chief gardener of the Belgian Horticultural Society accidentally grew it in the basement. This type of endive produced a cluster of pale leaves when grown in the dark. A little experimentation showed that if earth was pressed around them, the leaves would fold to form a hard white cone with a fresh, tart flavor.

## Who opened the first salad bar?

Today we take salad bars for granted. Many restaurants feature them, and they are a great way to pig out on healthful food in an economic way. They haven't been around for all that long, though. In 1971, Rich Melman began the Lettuce Entertain You concept at R. J. Grunts, a singles bar/restaurant located at 2056 Lincoln Park West in Chicago. R. J. Grunts and the famous salad bar are still in operation, as are countless imitators.

### Which vegetables came to the New World with the slaves?

Okra, black-eyed peas, peanuts, and watermelon all came to the New World with the slaves in the eighteenth century. Some say they hid okra seeds in their hair and planted it in the West Indies in 1674. Okra has been popular in the American South ever since. We use the unripe pods (capsules) as a vegetable. They give off a mucilaginous substance when cooked that is used to thicken soups and stews like gumbo.

### What do broccoli, Brussels sprouts, cabbage, cauliflower, kale, and kohlrabi all have in common?

Believe it or not, they are all varieties of the same species of plant—*Brassica oleracea*. Something else all of these plants have in common is the ability to grow in cool climates. This is why they are popular in the cuisine of Eastern European countries. One such dish is "sauerkraut," which is German for "sour cabbage." Curiously, sauerkraut did not originate in Germany or Eastern Europe. The workers building the Great Wall of China ate a similar dish some twenty-five hundred years ago. It was the Tartars who brought the recipe to Europe.

How can all of these plants be the same species? Cabbage is the large terminal bud; Brussels sprouts are lateral buds on the main stem and were developed around the fifth century; kohlrabi is a swollen stem; cauliflower is the white unopened flower florets; and broccoli is the green flower head.

### Which came first—broccoli or cauliflower?

No one seems to know which came first. Both are the edible flower heads of the cabbage. Cauliflowers are white because growers fold the plant's leaves up over the young flower head to keep it from photosynthesizing. The cauliflower was known in Europe by the 1500s, probably arriving via Cyprus. Broccoli first appeared in Italy and became accepted as a food in the 1600s. Broccoli was present in the colonies before the Revolution (Thomas Jefferson grew it), but no one seemed to notice. It wasn't until the Italian immigrants of the 1920s brought broccoli with them to California that it was grown in any quantity. Most Americans, however, didn't take to broccoli until the late 1940s.

## What is the national plant of the Welsh?

The leek (*Allium porrum*). Why the leek? Well, the legend goes that when Cadwallader, the last Briton king, defeated the Saxons in 640 A.D., the Welsh stuck leeks in their hats to distinguish themselves from the enemy during battle. Ever since, the leek has been a symbol of national pride. Each year on March 1—St. David's Day—Welshmen wear leeks to commemorate Cadwallader's victory. They also have a meal of *cawl* (leek broth) on this day.

Nero is said to have eaten leeks with oil to improve his singing voice. Italian-Americans who live in leek-growing areas enjoy leek and olive oil sandwiches when the leeks are harvested. As their genus name—*Allium*—implies, leeks are members of the onion family; however, their taste is much more sweet and subtle, allowing them to be more easily enjoyed raw.

The best-known leek dish is probably vichyssoise. This potato-leek soup is served cold. It may surprise you to learn that vichyssoise was created in the United States, not in France, though its inventor, chef Louis Diat of New York's Ritz-Carlton Hotel, was French. In 1910, he whipped up this cold soup as a refreshing dish for a summer's day. It is said he was inspired by boyhood memories of adding milk to hot soup to cool it down.

## What favorite vegetable is a member of the lily family?

The answer is asparagus. Its spears grow from a crown that is planted about a foot deep in sandy soils. Under good conditions, the spears can grow up to ten inches a day! This means that during the short six to seven week spring harvest period, asparagus pickers are kept quite busy. Spears that aren't picked are allowed to grow into the large ferns, which produce red berries and make the nutrients necessary for the next year's crop. The asparagus is a perennial plant that will produce spears for about fifteen years. The larger a spear's diameter, the higher its quality is considered to be.

The Romans were so fond of asparagus that it was served as an appetizer at any important dinner. The seventeenth-century English knew it as "sparrow grass," and it was called "grass" for hundreds of years after.

## What vegetable's name means "large pearl"?

Onions go back in recorded history to at least ancient Egypt and eventually made their way into Rome, where they were called *unio*, a Latin word meaning "large pearl." In Middle English it became *oinyon*.

## Who eats radishes for breakfast?

The radish is a root. The word "radish" comes from the Latin *radix*, meaning "root." Before they learned of olive oil, the Egyptians used radish oil. Most radishes have a little zip to them. We primarily eat them in salads, but some people enjoy them at breakfast. The Pennsylvania Dutch used to, and the Japanese still do.

## What is Green Giant named for?

We all know the big green leafy giant who is the spokesplant for Green Giant foods. How did the company come up with the name Green Giant?

It all started with a new variety of green peas that the Minnesota Valley Canning Company tried to sell in 1925. The Prince of Wales peas, which were brought over from Europe, were larger and more wrinkled than the peas Americans were used to, but they were very sweet and more tender. The public didn't know this, however, because they couldn't get past the fact that the peas weren't too attractive. As a marketing ploy, the company named the peas "Green Giants" and pushed them hard, creating a giant wearing a bearskin and carrying a club as their advertising symbol. But customers still remained wary. Then, in 1935, Leo Burnett, a Chicago advertising copywriter, colored the giant green, replaced the bearskin with leaves, and had him say "Ho Ho Ho" in a jolly voice. The ad campaign took off. It was so successful that by 1950, the company was the largest American canner of corn and peas and Minnesota Valley Canning Com-

pany renamed itself Green Giant Company. In 1958, they introduced Green Giant canned beans.

### What New World vegetables have been cultivated for more than nine thousand years?

The cucurbits, or squash and pumpkin. All of the members of the
genus *Cucurbita* are natives of the New World. The winter squash
varieties are hard and store well, and include acorn, butternut,
Hubbard, and spaghetti squash. Summer squashes are picked
when they are immature. They are soft and most cannot be kept
long. They include the yellow crookneck and green zucchini.

### What's so "cool" about a cucumber?

We've all heard the expression, "Cool as a cucumber." But are
cucumbers (*Cucumis*) really all that cool? Actually, yes. The inside
of a cucumber can be twenty degrees cooler than the outside air.
Cucumbers are about ninety-five percent water and have little in
the way of nutritional value. They were cultivated about ten
thousand years ago and came to the Americas with Columbus.

One odd thing about cucumbers: if you are allergic to pollen or
aspirin they can cause your mouth to itch.

### How did the pickle get its name?

In the 1300s there was a Dutch fisherman named William Beukelz
who was well known for pickling fish. English-speaking people
mispronounced his last name when referring to the way he preserved his catch, and the word "pickle" was born.

### How many warts do you like on your pickles?

If you are an average American, you like seven warts per square
inch on your pickles. (Yes, there has been research done on this
critical issue!) Pickle Packers International, Inc. cites this as the
perfect degree of wartiness for the American palate and eye
appeal. Europeans, it is reported, don't like any warts on their
pickles. They also claim that good pickles should have a "crunch"
that is audible from ten paces. Do yours?

## Why do we call chiles "peppers"?

Black and white pepper (*Piper nigrum*), or true pepper, is a spice that has no relation whatsoever with red pepper (*Capsicum*). We can thank Christopher Columbus for the misnomer of calling hot peppers, or chiles, "peppers." Columbus was hell-bent on reaching the East Indies and making a fortune from the spices he would bring back with him to Europe, including pepper. Alas, he never quite made it there, but that didn't stop him from assuming that he did and calling the red chiles he found "red pepper." It is also known as cayenne pepper.

## What vegetable do we eat for its leaf stalks?

If you think about this one, it's easy. The answer is celery. Another vegetable (although it's used as a fruit) we grow for its leafstalks (botanists call them petioles) is rhubarb. For many centuries, bitter-tasting wild celery, known as "smallage," was used for medicinal purposes. A native of the Middle East and Mediterranean, the bitterness was bred out of smallage during the seventeenth and eighteenth centuries, resulting in celery. It was then that it started to be used as a seasoning in France and Italy. The variety that is ubiquitous today is called Pascal. It was bred in Michigan, in 1874, by Dutch farmers near Kalamazoo. California (where else?) grows about sixty-five percent of the two billion pounds of celery grown each year in the U.S.; Florida follows with twenty percent.

It is said that celery is so low in calories that you burn more calories eating and digesting it than you actually get from it. Another bit of celery history says that the first stalk was stuck in a Bloody Mary in the 1960s, at the Ambassador East Hotel in Chicago, when someone stirred his drink with it after the bar ran out of swizzle sticks.

## Can you name the eight vegetables in V-8 juice?

Even if you love this stuff, you may be hard-pressed to name the eight vegetables found in V-8. Introduced in 1948, V-8 contains tomato, carrot, celery, beet, parsley, lettuce, watercress, and spinach juices.

# 9

# Amber Waves

### What two grains were originally weeds in wheat and barley fields?

Oats and rye were at first just unwanted weeds in the highly prized wheat and barley plantings of the ancient Middle East. As time passed and grain cultivation moved farther north into the cooler climates of Europe, these pesky weeds followed the wheat and barley northward and began to outperform them. Finally, someone realized that oats and rye could also serve as good food sources in poor soils that didn't support the other grains.

To this day, rye is pretty much ignored around the Mediterranean region. For centuries, it was a staple for the poor peoples of northern Europe, and it still remains popular there.

Oats are more widely grown than rye, but more rye is consumed by humans. About ninety-five percent of the oat crop goes to feed animals. Oats weren't domesticated until some time after Christ and by the fifteenth century had become a major crop in the moist areas of northern Europe. The only grain that requires more water than oats is rice.

Oats have a much higher fat content than wheat and plenty of fat-digesting enzymes, so they will turn rancid if the bran is not removed or steamed. Because of their high fat content, oats are used in some facial soaps. Like barley, oats have no gluten-producing proteins, so they can't be used to make light breads.

### What are grits?

"Grits," for those who aren't from the South, usually refers to "hominy grits," which is coarsely ground corn. Technically, grits is any coarsely ground grain, such as corn, oats, or rice. In the South, grits are boiled in water or milk and served for breakfast with butter or gravy. More grits are eaten in St. George, South Carolina, than anywhere else, or so people there claim. This is why the town hosts the annual World Grits Festival. It is also why St. George is called the "Grits Capital of the World."

### Why is there lye in my grits?

Lye is sodium hydroxide, which is a caustic soda. It will not only dissolve your skin, but it is also used to dissolve clogs in your drain. So what's it doing in your grits? By soaking corn in a diluted lye solution, a strong alkali, hominy processors loosen the hull and remove the oily germ from the kernels. This leaves the starchy endosperm, which, when washed to remove the lye, is sold as hominy. After drying, the hominy can be coarsely ground into hominy grits.

Another alkali used to process corn is lime (calcium oxide). It acts in the same way as lye, but is not as strong. Native peoples have known about lime for years. It is easy to make by heating calcium-rich limestone or seashells. Mexicans still use lime to break down corn kernels in a process similar to that used to make hominy grits. However, they grind the dried corn into masa flour, which they use to make tortillas.

The use of lime in processing corn has the added benefit of enhancing its flavor and nutritional value. A tortilla's unique flavor is owed in part to the use of lime in processing. The lime not only adds calcium to the masa flour, but the alkali also helps to free up amino acids in the corn that otherwise would not be available. More important, lime enables us to absorb more niacin from the corn than if it were untreated.

### Who invented puffed cereals?

For every invention there must be an inventor. In the case of puffed cereal, the man's name is Alexander Anderson. He was the son of Swedish immigrants to Minnesota who earned a PhD and did research at Columbia University and the New York Botanical Garden in 1901. Somehow he got the idea to see if starch granules could be exploded and blasted into a powder much smaller than the starch granules themselves. He took pow-dered starch and sealed it in glass tubes. He heated the tubes to 400°F and shattered them while still hot. The sudden release of pressure caused the starch to come out porous and puffed up. Not the result he expected, but a fortuitous one indeed. He next tried his experiment using whole grains with similar results. A new product was born.

Knowing he had discovered something with great commercial potential, Anderson returned to Minnesota to start the American Cereal Company, which he sold to the Quaker Oats Company in 1902. There he developed a steam-injected puffing gun. Here's how the process works: The grain, or starchy grain dough, is cooked to gelatinize its starch and is then put into a high-pressure chamber where it is heated to over 500°F. When a pressure valve is released, the grain shoots out of a "gun" and its internal water vapor explodes, much like popcorn, producing puffed cereal.

Puffed rice was introduced as a snack food at the 1904 St. Louis World's Fair (as were so many other new foods). A year later, it was sold as a breakfast cereal.

### What classic American cereal used to have a kangaroo as its mascot?

Tony may say "They're grrreat!," but when Kellogg's decided to spray sugar on its Corn Flakes in 1952, Tony had to share the spotlight with a kangaroo. Originally, Tony and Katy the Kanga-roo were both found on boxes of Kellogg's Sugar Frosted Flakes of Corn. Katy and Tony beat out Elmo the Elephant and Newt the Gnu in a mascot contest run by the company. Tony proved to be the more popular of the two and Katy was retired after a year. For a while in the 1970s, Tony had a whole family including his wife Mrs. Tony (Mama Tony), daughter Antoinette, and son—Tony Jr.— who became the trademark of Kellogg's Frosted Rice cereal.

Sugar Frosted Flakes were twenty-nine percent sugar. Kel-logg's dropped the "sugar" part of the name in 1984, leaving us with "Frosted Flakes"; however, they did not drop the sugar from the cereal. They also changed the names of "Sugar Corn Pops" to "Corn Pops" and "Sugar Smacks" to "Smacks," thinking con-sumers would somehow forget that these products are still loaded with sugar. Smacks had a sugar content of a whopping fifty-six percent.

### When did the Chinese start eating rice?

You might assume that the Chinese have always eaten rice, but this is not the case. The people of southern China have been eating rice since around 800 B.C. Rice cultivation did not begin in Japan for another eight hundred years or so. They imported their first rice plants from China.

Ninety-two percent of the world's rice is used in Asia. Amazingly, there are forty thousand varieties. Americans eat about twenty pounds per person per year. While the Asians like their rice sticky, which is good for molding and sushi, Americans like their rice fluffy.

### How do they "convert" rice?

This has nothing to do with the Catholic Church. Rice's conversion is physical, not spiritual. In 1943, English chemist Eric Huzenlaub teamed up with Texas produce broker Gordon Harwell and developed the process for converting rice. The unhulled soaked rice is pressure-cooked to infuse some of the nutrients from the outer bran layers into the kernel's heart. It is then steamed to partially gelatinize the starch and seal in the vitamins. The rice is then vacuum- and air-dried to return it to its original moisture content. It is then hulled and its bran removed. Converted rice has eighty percent of the B vitamins found in rough rice. White rice, or polished rice, has had the husk, bran, and germ removed.

### What was the first trademarked food?

Bread has been regulated for centuries. The English enacted legislation to regulate the size and price of bread in 1202, to keep bakers from reaping too large a profit. In 1266, England enacted the Assize of Bread, which proscribed penalties for bakers who did not comply. The price of a loaf of bread was tied to the price of the wheat and the grade of flour used to bake it. Each baker had to put his own individual mark on his loaves; this way, any underweight or overpriced bread could be readily traced back to its maker. It is believed that the bakers' mark was one of the first trademarks.

## Who were the first professional cooks?

Bread has always been one of the most labor-intensive and time-consuming foods to prepare. Because of this, bakers were the first cooks to earn a living outside the home. The ancient Greek and Roman cultures both supported professional bread bakers. However, bakers are only useful if one has access to them and their breads. Most peoples throughout history have either lived too far from any existing bakeries or were simply too poor to afford professionally made bread.

Home baking became a little easier in the 1840s with the introduction of "saleratus," or baking soda. This leavening agent, though, required the addition of an acid to do its job. In 1856, someone came up with the idea of selling baking soda with cream of tartar added, and baking powder was offered for sale. Another bread-baking convenience appeared in 1868—individually foil-wrapped cakes of yeast.

For much of American history, bread had been baked at home. In 1890, eighty percent was homemade; by 1910, that number dropped to 70 percent. As commercial bread became more available and women started working outside the home, housewives did less and less baking of any kind. This is illustrated by the fact that in 1900, ninety-five percent of the flour produced was purchased for home use, whereas in 1970, that number dropped to fifteen percent.

## When did white bread become popular?

White bread, made from refined wheat flour, has been a sign of status for much of European history. It was costly and only the affluent could afford it. The lower classes were relegated to eating rye or oat breads. White bread did not become available to the American masses until after Delaware shop owner Oliver Evans's invention of an automated process for grinding and sifting flour in 1780. The disabled Evans devised a flour mill that eliminated the need for millers to carry heavy bags of grain up stairways and dump them down chutes to the millstone. His system relied on a water-driven vertical conveyor belt to carry the grain up to the chute and horizontal belts to move the grain, meal, and flour along on the ground level. His process greatly sped up the milling process and dramatically lowered the cost of white bread. However, wheat did not grow well in the East, so most people still ate corn or rye bread. Once wheat was planted west of the Appalachians, in the 1830s and 1840s, white bread became readily available to the masses.

The quality of white wheat flour was greatly improved and the cost further lowered in the 1840s, when the Hungarians invented a roller for milling wheat that replaced the rotary millstone. By rolling the wheat, the inner kernel could be squeezed out of its coat of bran and germ in one step. While wheat germ is very nutritious, it contains oil; flour containing wheat germ can go rancid in a few weeks' time. This did not make it popular with bakers. It had the added drawback of darkening the flour, making it undesirable to housewives. The Hungarians improved upon the roller-milling technique with the introduction of porcelain rollers, in 1870, which yielded an even finer, whiter flour.

Today, there seems to be a reversal of the "white bread for the affluent" trend of the past. It's the more educated and "sophisticated" among us who fancy expensive dark grain breads and the lower classes who prefer white bread. That's very generally speaking, of course.

### Who invented presliced bread?

The invention of presliced bread seems like a no-brainer, but it didn't become commercially available until 1928, and even then it wasn't an immediate hit. We can thank an Iowa-born inventor named Otto Frederick Rohwedder for one of the world's greatest inventions.

Rohwedder knew that people liked to toast bread but found it hard to fit hand-sliced pieces into the slots of early toasters. In 1912, he developed the first crude bread-slicing machine at a workshop in Monmouth, Illinois. Alas, a fire destroyed his workshop and wondrous machine, and the world had to wait fifteen years for him to build another. Bakers were not impressed with his creation. The machine, which cut and wrapped the bread, produced loaves that did not sell because they were sloppy looking.

Enter one Gustav Papendick. The St. Louis baker brought Rohwedder's second machine in 1928 and perfected it. His improved design packaged the sliced loaves in cardboard trays, keeping the bread neat and orderly, and wrapped it in wax paper.

The first commercial bakery to try a bread-slicing machine was the Chillicothe Baking Company in Chillicothe, Missouri. Sales weren't fast and furious, though. Bakeries were skeptical about the public's acceptance of presliced bread. They thought that the drawbacks of having to buy new equipment and having to wrap the bread right away to keep the slices together might not be worth the trouble. After all, what if this presliced bread thing was just a passing fad? Would people really buy bread that would get stale faster just so that they wouldn't have to slice it themselves? Apparently the bakers weren't very farsighted. Presliced bread went national when Wonder introduced it to the country in 1930 and went on to become the "greatest thing since"—well, maybe since bread itself.

### What were some of the consequences of presliced bread?

For one thing, more bread was eaten. When Mom sliced the bread, the slices tended to be thicker, but she usually only cut what was immediately needed and the family ate that amount. With a whole sliced loaf sitting there, the family tended to eat more slices. This meant more spreads were also consumed, such as butter, jams, jellies, and peanut butter. Likewise, the eating of sandwiches took a dramatic upturn.

### When was sliced bread banned?

Americans had to sacrifice a lot during World War II; they even had to give up sliced bread! You wouldn't think slicing bread would be detrimental to the war effort, but apparently it was. On January 18, 1943, it was announced that there would be a ban on sliced bread. The Secretary of Agriculture maintained that sliced bread went stale faster and therefore Americans used more wheat, which was needed to feed the GIs. It was also said that bread-slicing machines that broke down needed metal parts to be fixed. The metal was better used for manufacturing guns, tanks, and ships.

## When did it become mandatory to enrich white bread?

The milling of refined white flour removes B vitamins and iron. White bread baked from this flour is nowhere near as nutritious as whole grain breads. As a result, people who ate only white bread had a greater likelihood of malnutrition and some related diseases. In 1941, South Carolina became the first state to require the enrichment of white bread with vitamins and iron. At the time, only thirty percent of U.S. bread was enriched. Within two years, seventy-five percent of bread was enriched. On January 16, 1944, by order of the War Food Administration, all yeast-raised commercial bakery goods, such as coffee cakes, sticky buns, doughnuts, and crullers, had to be fortified with B vitamins and iron.

## How much wheat does it take to make a loaf of bread?

One sixty-pound bushel of wheat yields forty-two pounds of flour, from which seventy-three one-pound loaves of bread can be baked. That comes out to about eight-tenths of a pound of wheat per loaf.

The leading wheat-growing state is Kansas (just look at the license plate), followed by North Dakota, Oklahoma, Texas, Washington, and Montana.

## What bread company was started by a man allergic to flour?

A descendant of America's most infamous traitor—Benedict Arnold—started Arnold Bread in 1940. Dean Arnold of Stamford, Connecticut, was an employee of Nabisco until he realized that he was allergic to flour. He quit his job and put an old Dhurkopf brick oven into his backyard. He and his wife Betty began baking their own bread. At night, Betty would wrap each loaf by hand with an electric iron; during the day Dean would drive around in his Pierce-Arrow sedan peddling them. There must have been something special about their bread, because they sold it at fifteen cents a loaf while commercial bread sold for ten cents a loaf at the time.

Business was so good that in 1945 the Arnolds got a $1,500 bank loan and moved their operation to Port Chester, New York, where there was a bakery with three unused Dhurkopf ovens. One later addition to their line was Toasting Muffins, the first muffin sized to fit in a toaster. Great success followed and by the mid-1960s they moved to Greenwich, Connecticut, where they opened the world's largest bread and roll bakery under one roof.

### Has the Atkins diet hurt the flour industry?

Apparently it has. Low carbohydrate diets are blamed by American grain farmers for the recent precipitous drop in flour consumption. In 2002, the average person ate less than 139 pounds of flour—the first time in nine years the number has been that low. Meanwhile, consumption of red meat, poultry, and fish are up to 195 pounds per year. That's fifty-seven more pounds than was eaten in the 1950s.

Do carbohydrates really make people obese? Well, if they do, there are also other factors involved. While sixty-four percent of America is overweight, obesity rates in Italy, Germany, and China are lower. People in those countries eat more pasta, bread, or rice than Americans do. Try eating less calories and getting some exercise, and give the poor grain farmers a break!

### How did a train ride lead to the creation of Bisquick?

Bisquick was inspired by a late-night train ride taken by a General Mills salesman in 1931. Carl Smith was on a Southern Pacific train bound for San Francisco one night when he ordered a meal in the dining car. To his surprise, his meal included freshly baked biscuits. He asked the chef how he had biscuit dough ready on short notice at such a late hour. The chef confided that he always kept a mixture of flour, lard, baking powder, and salt in the icebox to accommodate his late diners. Smith brought the idea of a biscuit ready-mix to General Mills chemist Charles Kress. Knowing that the lard would quickly turn rancid in a box, Kress replaced it with sesame-seed oil, and Bisquick was born. The sesame-seed oil would later be replaced by cottonseed oil and/or soybean oil.

Bisquick was an immediate hit; within a year, there were nearly one hundred imitators on the market.

### Why were biscuits such common fare on long voyages?

Whether at sea or on land, travelers on long journeys in the pre-canned-food era always brought rations of biscuits. The advantage of biscuits was that they were so hard and dry that they didn't spoil readily. What made old-time biscuits so dry was that they were twice baked to remove as much moisture as possible. In fact, *bis cuit*, means "twice cooked" in French. *Biscotti* is Italian for "twice baked." A second baking of five minutes makes it very dry and crispy. Biscotti is so hard and durable that it sailed with Columbus on his explorations to the New World.

The first crackers were made in 1801 at a bakery just south of Boston that made ship's biscuits. Retired sea captain Josiah Dent, of Milton, Massachusetts, was behind the bakery's production of the first biscuit to be called a "cracker." The product acquired its name because the water biscuits were made of unsweetened, unleavened dough that was rolled repeatedly to have a fine grain; this made them crisper than ordinary biscuits. They were so crisp that they made a cracking sound when bitten.

### Why do crackers have holes?

Any cracker you buy will have little holes nicely spaced in its surface. While these perforations may be interesting to look at, they serve a useful purpose. Crackers need those holes to be crisp. During manufacture, sheets of dough roll under "docker" pins that punch tiny holes in the crackers-to-be. This allows the cooking steam to escape, keeping the crackers flat and crisp. The spacing of the holes is important. If they are too close together, too much steam escapes, making for a tough cracker. If too far apart, big blisters will form on the surface as trapped steam tries to escape.

## Why are pretzels shiny?

The pretzel's roots go all the way back to the Romans. The ubiquitous twisted loose knot shape did not appear until the seventh century, when monks in southern France baked their stiff leftover bread dough into a shape representing the arms folded in prayer. The three holes represented the Christian Trinity. They used to give these baked treats to children as rewards for learning their prayers.

Early pretzels were not shiny. The shine we associate with our modern pretzel comes from a spray of a one percent solution of lye (sodium hydroxide) or sodium carbonate at about 200°F. This forms a gel with the starch on the surface of the dough. Salt is added, and a quick, very hot, five-minute baking process hardens the gel and creates a shiny finish. It is the alkaline lye, reacting with carbon dioxide, that gives the pretzel its lovely dark brown coloration. A longer baking period at about 200°F finishes the cooking and dries out the pretzel.

America's first pretzel bakery, run by Julius Sturgis, opened in 1861 in Lititz, Pennsylvania. You can take a tour of the original pretzel shop and learn to roll and fold your own pretzels. Here you will also learn that the expression "tying the knot," comes from the tying together of the dough ends when making a pretzel. Apparently the expression goes back to 1614, when royal couples used the knotted pretzel as a symbol of their union during wedding celebrations.

## Who is the largest baker of bagels?

The word "bagel" is from the Yiddish word *beygl*. It was spelled "beigel" until sometime around 1930, when the word "bagel" began to be used.

Good bagels should be chewy. They are traditionally made from an eggless dough, which, since it contains no fat, is chewier than an egg bagel. Bagels are boiled in water before baking to reduce starch and provide a chewy crust.

In 1927, Harry Lender from Lodz, Poland, opened the first bagel bakery outside of New York City, in West Haven, Connecticut. He began by selling to Jewish delis and bakeries in the New Haven area. Later, Harry's sons Marvin and Murray took over the business. In 1955, Lender's became the first bagels to be sold in a supermarket. Lender's also sold the first frozen bagels, in 1962. They went on to become the largest baker of bagels in the country.

### When was the American pasta industry born?

Until the start of World War I, most pasta was imported to the U.S. from Naples, Italy. The war cut off this supply and promoted the establishment of a thriving American pasta industry.

### What part of the country eats the most pasta?

Northeasterners are the pasta-eating champs. Eighty-two percent have at least one pasta meal a week. Southerners are the least likely to eat pasta on a regular basis, with only seventy percent doing so. But pasta is becoming more popular every year down South. In the last five years, pasta consumption there has grown forty-two percent. In the Northeast and the West, one in five people eat pasta three or more times a week.

### What was the first ready-mix food?

Sometimes necessity really *is* the mother of invention. Such was the case with the creation of Aunt Jemima Pancake Mix. Two entrepreneurial friends—Christian Ludwig Rutt and Charles G. Underwood—pooled their resources in 1888 and bought an old flour mill in St. Joseph, Missouri. They were banking on selling products from their mill to the stream of westward settlers that passed through town. Their plan was flawed, as the number of westbound wagon trains was diminishing. Rutt and Underwood spent a year experimenting and ended up with a new product they called Self-Rising Pancake Flour, which was a combination of hard wheat, flour, corn flour, phosphate of lime, soda, and salt. They sold their mix in one-pound bags.

The product was great, but the name wasn't very catchy. Rutt was inspired to rename their pancake mix after seeing a minstrel show where two black-faced comedians did a cakewalk dance to a popular tune of the time, "Aunt Jemima."

Rights to the mix were later purchased by another St. Joseph miller—R. T. Davis—who improved the formula by adding rice flour, corn sugar, and powdered milk, so that it could be made simply by adding water. In 1893, Davis promoted Aunt Jemima Pancake Mix at the Chicago Fair by building a twenty-four-foot flour barrel. It was full of advertising and had a former slave woman—Nancy Green—cooking up pancakes on a griddle outside.

### What baker invented chiffon cake?

Chiffon cake wasn't invented by a baker, but by a Baker—Harry Baker. He was a Los Angeles insurance salesman who liked to bake. In 1927 he tried using salad oil as a shortening in his cake batter, instead of butter or lard. The result was a cake with a spongecake-like texture. Baker sold his cakes at restaurants in the Los Angeles area and later, during World War II, approached General Mills with his creation. They didn't show much interest at the time. Undeterred, Baker made some of his cakes for the General Mills brass in Minneapolis in 1948. As they say, "the proof of the pudding is in the eating." The executives loved his cake and bought the recipe from him. But General Mills did not sell the chiffon cake recipe in a mix, such as Betty Crocker. Instead, they touted the recipe on their Betty Crocker radio show, calling chiffon cake "the cake discovery of the century." General Mills included the recipe in bags of Gold Medal flour and in magazine advertising.

General Mills and Pillsbury introduced prepared cake mixes a year later. The first offerings were chocolate, gold, and white. Duncan Hines cake mix was brought out in 1951, by Nebraska Consolidated Mills of Omaha. It differed from the others in that it didn't have dehydrated eggs (you had to add your own) and was sold in just one flavor—Three Star Special. The name derived from the fact that the one mix could be used to make three different cakes: by adding water and an egg white you got a white cake; by adding water and a whole egg, you got a yellow cake; and by adding water, an egg, and cocoa, you got devil's food cake. Duncan Hines cake mix thumped the others immediately, capturing forty-eight percent of the market in its first three weeks.

Duncan Hines also makes frostings to go with their cakes. The three favorite flavors are milk chocolate, vanilla, and classic chocolate. Three flavors they tried without success were apple, blueberry, and grape. People don't seem to want fruity frostings.

# 10

# Nuts!

### What is a nut?

Botanically speaking, the definition of a nut is very limited. Technically, a nut is a hard, dry, single-seeded fruit. By this definition, only acorns, beechnuts, hazelnuts, and sweet chestnuts are true nuts. The more common definition is any edible kernel with a hard shell.

Most of the foods discussed in this book are native to one particular part of the world. Usually Old World foods had no counterpart in the New World. Nut trees, however, evolved millions of years ago, before the continents began to drift apart. Hence, many kinds of nut trees were known to ancient man on both sides of the Atlantic.

### What's the most popular nut in the world?

The nut champ is the almond. (Technically, it's a kernel of the fruit.) This cousin of the cherry, peach, and plum is native to western India. Mentioned in the Old Testament, the almond is one of the oldest cultivated foods. God shows his approval of Aaron in the book of Numbers by making his rod blossom and bear almonds. Franciscan padres brought almond trees to California from Spain in the mid-1700s. The moist climate of their coastal missions didn't suit almond growing, however. It wasn't until a century later that they were planted inland and began to flourish.

There are two types of almonds—sweet and bitter. You are probably only familiar with the sweet type, as bitter almonds are illegal in the United States. As the name implies, sweet almonds are sweet (duh!) and are used in candies and baked goods. This is the kind you will find in the supermarket.

Bitter almonds are not as delicate in flavor and can be somewhat dangerous. The uncooked almond contains traces of the deadly poison prussic acid. Although the toxicity is destroyed upon heating, the FDA plays it safe and bans these nuts in order to protect uninformed consumers. Processed bitter almonds are used to flavor extracts and liqueurs.

Almonds are harvested by shaking the trees; this loosens the nuts and they fall down. They are left to dry on the ground for five days before being collected.

California grows eighty percent of the world's almond supply. One large almond factory in Sacramento handles two million pounds a day. Forty percent of almonds are used by chocolate companies. Almonds are also used to produce almond oil. It takes one thousand pounds of almonds to yield just one pint of almond oil. Properly stored at 40°F under low humidity, unshelled almonds will keep for three years.

Japanese teens enjoy snacking on almond slivers and dried sardines (yum!).

## What is the difference between dark and light walnuts?

Walnut meat has a natural color range from extra light to amber. There are probably several factors that contribute to the color variation, but interestingly, you will find dark and light walnuts on the same tree. Commercial buyers will specify which color walnut they want. Ice cream makers and some foreign buyers like the darker nuts because of their more intense flavor. Commercial bakeries like the lighter nuts because they look more "beautiful."

## How do you tell if walnuts are fresh?

Biblical legend says walnuts were given to Joseph at the manger by the wise men, and walnuts have had a long association with Christmas, especially among Germanic peoples. The Germans hung walnuts from Christmas trees to ward off evil spirits and have enjoyed inshell walnuts at Christmas feasts for centuries.

The French and Spanish decorated their homes with items believed to be part of the garden of Eden. Walnuts, being one of the earliest tree foods available to mankind, were thus incorporated into this decorating tradition.

The walnut's association with Christmas is partly due to the time it's harvested, which is typically in October. Since in shell walnuts keep so long, they were always fresh and plentiful during the holiday season. Walnuts will keep in their shells for up to a year, at least, and so right before Christmas is a good time to use up old walnuts and buy fresh ones.

To tell if walnuts are still good, smell them. If the scent is something like old paint, they have turned rancid or oxidized; however, they are still edible. Some European people enjoy their walnuts this way, but you may want to buy fresh ones.

The walnut is second only to the almond in "true" nut popularity. The native American walnut is the black walnut, which grows on a tree that is more coveted for its wood than its nuts. The English or Italian walnut came to the United States from Europe. It is the main commercially grown walnut. Production is centered in California, which grows two-thirds of the world's supply. The walnut is the state nut of Missouri.

### What nut was used to paint the Sistine Chapel?

Walnuts are about seventy percent oil. The ancients used walnut oil as a drying agent in paint. In fact, Michelangelo used walnut oil when he painted the Sistine Chapel.

### How do peanuts grow?

Peanuts are not really nuts but are legumes, like peas and beans. Legumes are edible seeds enclosed in pods that split along both sides when ripe. A peanut plant grows from a seed (kernel) into a bush about eighteen inches high. Small yellow flowers develop close to the ground. These flowers pollinate themselves and form an ovary, that sends out a runner (peg) that grows down to the soil. (Hence their nickname "ground nuts.") Upon reaching the ground, the embryo turns horizontally; it matures into a peanut underground.

All legumes provide excellent protein. Peanuts, while legumes, are treated more like nuts in their use in the culinary world.

During the American Civil War, the Confederate troops used peanuts as an inexpensive coffee substitute. Not so well known in the North, the "goober pea," as Yankees call it, went home with the Union Army and became a popular snack food.

## How many kinds of peanuts are there?

To most of us, a peanut is a peanut. They all kind of look the same, but there are three main types of peanuts grown in the U.S.: Virginia, Runners, and Spanish. The type of peanuts most people are familiar with are Virginia, also called cocktail nuts. They are large-kernelled. Medium kernels are called Runners, and small kernels are called Spanish. These peanuts are grown commercially in the Southeast, Texas, and Oklahoma. Domestically, over 2.4 billion pounds of peanuts are grown annually; over half are grown in Georgia alone. Fifty percent are used to make peanut butter. Twenty percent go into chocolate candy.

That's a lot of peanuts but is only a drop in the peanut bucket. About ninety-five percent of peanuts are grown outside the U.S. More than fifty percent of world production is from China and India. However, very little of the world crop is used to make peanut butter. About sixty-five percent go into making peanut oil and twenty percent goes into candy.

## What is the "peanut gallery"?

Initially, the peanut was a food of the poor and blacks. At ball games, spectators in the cheap seats were the ones eating most of the peanuts and this area became known as the "peanut gallery." In an effort to add some class to the peanut and broaden its appeal, Planter's introduced Mr. Peanut in 1916. They held a logo contest that was won by a thirteen-year-old boy named Antonio Gentile, who drew a peanut person with arms and crossed legs. He received the grand prize of $5. A professional artist fine-tuned Mr. Peanut, adding the top hat, monocle, cane, and white gloves to give him more class.

## Who invented peanut butter?

Your immediate response might be Dr. George Washington Carver. While a great peanut researcher, and developer of more than three hundred uses for the peanut, Carver did not, in fact, create peanut butter. Its origins are much earlier.

The peanut is believed to have originated in Brazil or Peru. Portuguese explorers first took it to Africa, where Africans began to grind it into stews as early as the late fifteenth century. Curiously, it came to North America from Africa via the slave trade. The Chinese have also been crushing peanuts into creamy sauces for hundreds of years, and soldiers during the Civil War made "peanut porridge."

The first person to make peanut butter commercially was George A. Bayle, Jr., an owner of a St. Louis food products company. A local doctor suggested Bayle grind peanuts into a nutritious paste that would be easy for people with poor teeth to eat. In 1890, Bayle began selling this paste out of barrels for six cents a pound. It was introduced at the 1904 St. Louis Exposition as a health food for the elderly.

The Kellogg brothers, of cereal fame, also were involved in peanut butter history. Dr. John Harvey Kellogg and his brother W. K. Kellogg patented a "Process of Preparing Nut Meal" in 1895. They served their "nut butter" as a vegetarian source of protein in Dr. John's health sanitorium, in Battle Creek, Michigan. W. K. soon opened the Sanitas Nut Company to supply peanut butter to local grocers. However, there was one problem with their peanut butter—it didn't taste very good. Instead of grinding roasted peanuts they used steamed nuts. The brothers turned away from peanut butter and found their niche in the breakfast cereal business.

In 1922, Joseph L. Rosenfield started selling many brands of an improved peanut butter in California. His product was churned like butter to yield a creamy smooth peanut butter, unlike the grittier peanut butters available at the time. His process also stabilized the peanut butter by replacing much of the natural peanut oil with hydrogenated peanut oil. He got a patent for this shelf-stable peanut butter, which stayed fresh for up to a year because the oil would not separate out. In 1928, Swift & Co. adopted his method, and Peter Pan peanut butter was born. Rosenfield had a dispute with the Peter Pan people in 1932; he started making Skippy on his own the next year. He added a crunchy style shortly thereafter. (The name "Skippy" probably came from a comic strip of the same name.) Jif was introduced by Procter & Gamble in 1955.

Did you know that people on the East Coast prefer creamy style? Folks out West go for crunchy. No one knows why these differences exist. One more thing: about 550 peanuts go into every twelve ounce jar of peanut butter, and we Americans eat about nine jars of the stuff a year.

## Why does peanut butter stick to the roof of your mouth?

Do you have a problem with peanut butter sticking to the roof of your mouth? It happens to most of us occasionally, but it's no big deal, right? Well, there are people who become hysterical when this happens. There is even a scientific name for their condition—arachibutyrophobia. A tall glass of cold milk would seem to be the best cure.

Why does peanut butter stick to the roof of your mouth? Its high protein content draws moisture from your mouth, making it sticky.

## Who invented the peanut butter and jelly sandwich?

Maybe there is no other single food that is as American as the peanut butter and jelly sandwich. Sure, hamburgers and hot dogs are pretty American too, but they have spread to other lands via fast-food franchising. The PBJ is still solidly American and loved by almost every kid and most adults (although many won't admit it). Like the Australian Vegemite sandwich, which no one else "gets," the all-American PBJ is little appreciated by the outside world. This truly unique comfort food is of very recent origin, and its history is somewhat murky.

Jellies and jams have been around a long time, but peanut butter wasn't even created for the first time until around the turn of the twentieth century and wasn't sold commercially until the late 1920s. There is no mention of the PBJ before 1940. So how did this marriage of sweet and salty occur and become a national phenomenon in such a relatively short time?

No one is sure, but it's a good bet that U.S. troops during World War II discovered the ease and joy of combining peanut butter with jelly, as they had both in their rations. Considering the small selection of food they had (they must have experimented mixing them in all combinations), the mixing of these two seemed inevitable. PBJ was probably created countless times by countless GIs. The Peanut Board claims that peanut butter and jelly sandwiches were on the military ration list at some point in the war. Regardless, when the troops returned home, the sales of peanut butter and jelly soared. The PBJ has been an American icon ever since.

Reasons for its popularity, aside from the wonderful sweet-salty taste, are its ease of preparation, low cost, and nutritive value. Parents don't have to feel guilty for whipping up a PBJ in two minutes and giving it to their children with a glass of milk for a quick lunch or snack. This simple meal is more nutritious than a lot of other foods kids like. It is estimated that the average child eats about fifteen hundred peanut butter and jelly sandwiches before he or she leaves high school (and who knows how many more afterward).

## What nut has the highest fat content?

This nut is a native of the Mississippi River valley. A member of the hickory family, the pecan was held in high esteem by Native Americans. *Pecan* is actually an Algonquin word meaning "all nuts requiring a stone to crack." They made an intoxicating drink from pecans called "powcohicora" (this is where the word "hickory" comes from) and were the first to cultivate the tree.

The first European to encounter the pecan was Spanish explorer Álvar Núñez Cabeza de Vaca, in 1528. He was shipwrecked on the Texas coast, where he was taken prisoner by the local people. They would travel great distances to collect pecans for winter storage. The pecan was first cultivated by colonists on Long Island around 1772. Commercial production began in the 1880s.

## *What is the most economically important nut?*

Unless you are really well informed, or really lucky, you probably didn't guess the coconut. The coconut palm is a native of Malaysia and has spread either by humans or nature, to almost all tropical regions of the world. The nuts are capable of floating from one continent to another on the ocean currents. This is how they first came to South America. (Some people believe they originated in South America and floated to the South Pacific.) These trees can live to be seventy years old and will yield thousands of coconuts over this time.

Coconuts are prized for their pulp, milk, oil, fiber, and wood. Adding to their worldwide importance is the ability to grow in poor soils. A coconut is comprised of several layers. A smooth, dark tan outer covering protects it while on the tree. This layer is removed to reveal the hard, dark brown hairy husk we are familiar with in the supermarket. The husk has three indentations on one end that resemble a monkey's face. The coconut derives its name from the Portuguese *coco*, meaning "goblin or monkey." Beneath the husk is a thin brown skin that surrounds the edible white meat. Inside the meat is the sweet coconut milk.

Coconut milk contains coconut fat, which is chemically similar to butterfat. It can be substituted for cow's milk for almost all cooking needs. Indeed, in tropical regions of the world without milk-producing animals, coconut milk *was* their milk. Coconut meat was used as a sweetener before sugar found widespread use. Dried coconut meat, called "copra," is pressed to extract coconut oil. This oil is unique in that it is a non-animal saturated fat. Coconut oil is used in a multitude of products, ranging from candies to cookies and cosmetics.

The coconut tree also supplies a vegetable—palm hearts. These are the terminal buds of the tree.

Another thing coconuts have going for them is that they can be stored for up to six months. Once opened, however, the meat must be refrigerated and will only keep for about four days, although it can be frozen for six months. Over twenty billion coconuts are produced each year.

## Is the Brazil nut really from Brazil?

Yes. It at one time was grown primarily in Brazil. Since 1999, however, Bolivia has been the world's top producer of Brazil nuts. Attempts to cultivate this Amazonian native have met with limited success. In Brazil itself only a few growers have success-ful plantations. Most Brazil nuts are still collected in the wild after they have fallen from the tree. These nuts (actually seeds) grow in five-inch-diameter orb-shaped pods that are very hard and can weigh up to five pounds. Each pod contains between eight to twenty-four nuts. As the trees reach 150 feet in height, falling pods are a hazard to the nut collectors on the ground, and consequently, they use shields to protect themselves from nasty bumps on the head. A typical Brazil nut tree will produce 250 to 500 pounds of nuts a year.

Brazil nuts are sixty-seven percent fat, but it is mostly unsatu-rated. They don't store as well as some other nuts. Unshelled they will keep about two months.

# 11

# Sweet Stuff

*What was the first American sweetener?*

You may not have known this, but honey and sugar were unknown to North America until the white man came along. There were bees but not honey bees. Native Americans relied on maple syrup as their main sweetener, supplemented with wild berries. Like honey, maple syrup is the product of a dilute solution of plant sugars that have been gathered and concentrated by removing water. In the case of honey, bees do the work. In the case of maple syrup, humans do it. Since maple syrup and honey are less refined than cane or beet sugar, they still contain many of the components of the original plant sap or nectar.

The sugar maple (*Acer saccharum*) is the best source of sap for the boiling and concentrating of maple sugar and maple syrup. The Northeast, especially New York, Vermont, and Canada, have abundant sugar maples and the climate is ideal for the best sugar sap production. To get the highest sugar concentration in the spring sap, several conditions must be met. The more sunlight the tree's leaves receive in the summer, the more sugar the tree produces during photosynthesis. Cold winters are needed to freeze the roots. Spring snow cover helps keep the roots cold. Extreme day-night temperature differences also increase sugar production.

Producers today still insert spouts into the tree and hang buckets to catch the sap. Some larger operations attach plastic tubing to the spouts and run a network of them directly into a collection tank. The sap can be collected when it starts to "run," after the first thaw in the spring, which is usually around mid-February. The tapping can continue for four to six weeks until the leaf buds are about to open. Each tree yields between five and sixty gallons of sap. It takes about forty gallons of maple sap to make one gallon of maple syrup or four-and-a-half pounds of maple sugar. Early in the season the sap is richer in sugar and the yields are higher; at the end of the season the yield is lower. Boiling concentrates the sap into maple syrup. Further boiling, until the liquid is almost entirely evaporated, yields maple sugar, which is twice as sweet as cane sugar.

Most maple syrup produced today comes from small operations in the Northeast or Canada. In fact, Canada produces seventy-five percent of the world's maple syrup.

### Why did Northerners use so much maple syrup during the Civil War?

Maple syrup was all the rage in the Union states during the Civil War. Actually, it was used as a form of protest against the South. Most American sugar cane was grown, and molasses produced, in the Southern states. Just prior to and during the war, Northerners boycotted sugar and molasses; instead, they used maple syrup.

### Is there any butter in Mrs. Butterworth's syrup?

There used to be, but not much. Mrs. Butterworth's was introduced by Unilever in 1961. It contained corn syrups, sugar syrups, natural and artificial flavors, caramel coloring, and various preservatives—and 0.4 percent butter. It didn't taste all that bad. The little bit of butter it contained did give it a slight butter note.

Aurora Foods acquired Mrs. Butterworth's in 1996 from Unilever. They reformulated Mrs. Butterworth's, removing the butter. The name, however, did not change. The new syrup has a funny taste, with no hint of the buttery flavor that made the original product a hit.

### What is high-fructose corn syrup?

Whether you realize it or not, you probably ingested some high-fructose corn syrup today. It is found in a multitude of processed food products, including soft drinks, canned fruits, and jams. As the name implies, corn syrups are made from corn. Corn starch is treated with acids and enzymes to produce corn syrups, which contain dextrose and other saccharides. High-fructose corn syrup is made by treating dextrose with enzymes, resulting in a liquid mixture of fructose and dextrose.

The soft drink industry loves this stuff because it is generally cheaper than sugar, comes from a more reliable source, and is easier to work with. It was created in 1967 by Clinton Corn Processing Company, in Clinton, Iowa. Coca-Cola replaced half the sucrose in Coke with high-fructose corn syrup in 1980, when the price of corn tumbled after Jimmy Carter suspended corn sales to the Soviet Union. In 1984, both Coke and Pepsi replaced all the sucrose in their drinks with high-fructose corn syrup. (They haven't tasted the same since.)

### Why do certain food products contain corn syrup instead of sugar?

One good reason is that there isn't enough cane or beet sugar to go around. The United States doesn't grow enough sugar to meet demand. We import most of our sugar from other countries, and the supply isn't always steady and reliable. However, America leads the world in corn production. Happily, we can make sugar (corn syrup) from cornstarch.

Corn kernels contain lots of starch. Starch is made up of molecules of glucose. By cutting up molecules of starch, we end up with single molecules of glucose (a simple sugar known as a monosaccharide), along with glucose molecules that are in pairs (maltose, a disaccharide), and much bigger groupings of glucose (polysaccharides). These polysaccharides don't move freely over one another. This makes the resultant corn syrup thick. Corn starch is broken down into corn syrup using acids or enzymes from bacteria or fungi. The most commonly used enzymes are derived from the fungi *Aspergillus*.

Left like this, corn syrup would be only about sixty percent as sweet as cane sugar (sucrose). To rectify this problem, another enzyme can be used to convert some of the glucose into fructose, which is thirty percent sweeter than sucrose. This gives us high-fructose corn syrup, which is used to sweeten soft drinks, jams, and jellies. However, corn-based sweeteners don't taste exactly the same as pure sucrose, as the different sugars they contain all vary slightly in taste.

## What is sugar?

The simple answer is that sugar is pure carbohydrate. It occurs naturally in every fruit and vegetable we eat. If you remember your high school biology, you will recall that plants use chlorophyll to transform the sun's energy into food—sugar. Two plants in particular are loaded with sugar. They are appropriately named sugar cane and sugar beets.

Sugar cane is a giant tropical grass; its sugar is produced in the plant stem. Sugar beets prefer a temperate climate and store sugar in the white root. The sugar produced in sugar cane is identical to that made in sugar beets, but the refining methods are different.

Sugar cane is refined using the following steps:

1. Grinding the cane to extract the juice
2. Boiling the juice until the syrup thickens and crystallizes
3. Spinning the crystals at high speed to get raw sugar
4. Shipping raw sugar to refinery
5. Washing and filtering raw sugar to remove leftover plant material
6. Crystallizing, drying, and packing pure sugar

Beet sugar is processed in one continuous operation. The beets are washed, sliced, and soaked in hot water to remove the sugar juice. The juice is purified, filtered, concentrated, and dried in a manner like the process for sugar cane. The raw sugar stage is eliminated.

Another bit of sugar trivia: English sugar merchant Henry Tate started cutting sugar into cubes in 1872.

## What is a sugar "loaf"?

Yes, it is a ski resort in Maine, but it is also the way in which sugar was sold in days of old. Three hundred years ago, sugar was purchased in tall, conical loaves that weighed about a pound. This loaf sugar could be sawed into cubes and/or crushed into powder when needed. The powdered sugar was often stored in a sugar castor, which is a container resembling a very large salt shaker.

## Who brought sugar cane to the New World?

Christopher Columbus's mother-in-law is indirectly responsible for his bringing sugar cane to the Caribbean. The mother of his first wife owned a sugar plantation in Madeira. Columbus was transporting sugar in ships between Madeira and Genoa even before he got married. His close association with the crop doubt-less influenced his decision to bring it with him on his second journey to the New World in 1493.

## When did white sugar become popular?

Bread was not the only staple housewives of the nineteenth cen-tury preferred white. Whiteness was coveted in sugar too. No self-respecting woman of the 1800s or early 1900s would put out cheap, coarse brown sugar on her table instead of the more expensive, refined white sugar. What would her guests think? Couldn't she afford white sugar? So prized was white sugar that when it first became available in Europe, it was kept in a special box under lock and key.

The reason white sugar was more expensive than brown was because of the extra processing steps involved in refining it. Its pure whiteness appealed to the ladies, as did its higher cost, making it something of a status symbol. This was fine with the sugar industry, which was more than happy to sell their more costly product. However, brown sugar was still used in cooking. This didn't sit well with the sugar producers.

In order to boost the sales of white sugar even higher, they resorted to a little bit of deception in advertising to put people off brown sugar for good. In 1898 they started a rumor that brown sugar found in Ireland had been infested with some terrible insect. They even sponsored an ad showing the gruesome bugs and their eggs, which lived in brown sugar and carried who knew what kind of diseases. But they assured the public that refined white sugar was always free of this onerous creature and should be used in place of brown sugar. This was the death knell of brown sugar. Curiously, it's making a comeback today. As with brown breads (discussed previously), people who fancy them-selves health conscious or just a little "snobby," are turning away from white sugar and rediscovering brown.

### What is raw sugar?

Raw sugar isn't really raw, it's just less refined. Raw sugar is a coarse, granulated, tan to brown sugar formed after the evaporation of clarified sugar cane juice. It is about ninety-eight percent sucrose and is not sold to consumers. The FDA considers it "unfit for direct use as food or as a food ingredient because of the impurities it ordinarily contains." What is commonly found on restaurant tables as "raw" sugar is in fact "turbinado" sugar. This is raw sugar that has been washed and centrifuged. This removes the surface molasses, but some natural molasses still remains in the crystals.

### What is blended sugar?

In some places dextrose—a corn-derived sweetener—may be added to beet sugar or granulated cane sugar to produce a cheaper sweetener. Dextrose, however, is only about seventy percent as sweet as sugar. It is also more hygroscopic (water-loving). As such, blended sugar may not perform as well in certain recipes.

### Why do they put cornstarch in confectioners' sugar?

Sugar is hygroscopic, meaning it absorbs moisture, at least in its powdered form. Ordinary table sugar is granular, with each grain being an individual pure sugar crystal. Granular sugar isn't adversely affected by air moisture. Confectioners' sugar can absorb moisture in the air and cake up. To prevent this, cornstarch is added. While the cornstarch helps to alleviate caking, it will not dissolve in water, which you may have discovered if you ever tried to put confectioners' sugar in your coffee. The sugar dissolves, but the cornstarch simply gums up and floats on top.

### What is sucralose?

Known by the trade name Splenda, sucralose is a new sweetener that is six hundred times sweeter than sucrose but has no calories. How can this be? Sucralose is modified sucrose. It is produced by chlorinating sugar (replacing three hydroxyl groups in sucrose with three chlorine atoms). Since sucralose doesn't break down that much inside the body, it essentially contains no calories. It is so sweet that it isn't used in its pure form but is cut with a starchy powder (maltodextrin) to reduce its strength.

Sucralose was discovered in 1976 by scientists working with the British sugar refiner Tate & Lyle Ltd. They arranged with Johnson & Johnson to develop it for commercial sale. Canada was the first country to approve of its use in 1991. It was granted FDA approval, in 1998. That year, Diet Rite cola became the American product to use it.

*One important footnote: Diabetics should not use sucralose.

### Why does sugar rot teeth?

People have always had cavities, but with the introduction of widely available sugar, in the 1500s, tooth decay became much more prevalent. The connection with sweets was apparent early on, but the reason why was not. We now know that *Streptococcus* bacteria can live on sugars in the mouth. They release acids that are capable of eating away tooth enamel. It's not just sweets that promote tooth decay but any starchy food that the enzymes in your mouth can break down into sugar.

### What sweetener is also a laxative?

If you eat sugar-free candy, you are probably ingesting something called sorbitol. It is a naturally occurring alcohol-based sweetener found in some fruits and berries. Sorbitol is about fifty percent as sweet as sucrose and, unlike other sweeteners, can retain moisture. Because of this property, it is used to keep certain products moist and smooth. You may find it in processed foods, as well as cosmetics and toothpaste. Its ability to retain water has one drawback. If you ingest too much sorbitol, you may find that it acts as a laxative by retaining water in your bowel. So take it easy on the sugar-free candies, but don't be afraid to brush your teeth afterward.

### What natural sweetener can be used to dress wounds?

Some people today attribute many wonderful properties to honey. Healers have been dressing wounds with it since ancient times and some people today still use honey, claiming that it inhibits infection. There was no scientific proof of this claim until 1963, when it was found that honey's antibacterial properties are due to its production of hydrogen peroxide. It is generated by an enzyme the bees release during honey making. At high concentrations, hydrogen peroxide damages cell tissues and proteins. Honey seems to release the hydrogen peroxide slowly over time as fluids in the wound activate the enzyme, making it a good dressing for a wound.

One kind of honey currently used to dress wounds is called "manuka" honey. It is a single-pollen honey obtained from bees in New Zealand that collect the nectar of the manuka bush (*Leptospermum scoparium*). Manuka honey has the added benefit of an antibacterial chemical derived from the plant. Commercial manuka-honey wound dressings are sold that have been irradiated to kill *Clostridium*, which could theoretically introduce botulism or tetanus into a wound. Any honey used to treat a wound should not be heated to a high temperature in processing, as this will destroy the enzyme that produces the hydrogen peroxide.

## When did honey come to the New World?

Humankind's first sweetener was undoubtedly honey. This natural sweetener was readily available to Old World inhabitants willing to risk the odd bee sting. Ancient drawings show people collecting honey some ten thousand years ago. Honeybee management was practiced by the Egyptians at least forty-five hundred years ago; citizens there used to pay their taxes with it. Hieroglyphs of this period depict people tending bees housed in clay hives. Honey continued to be popular as a sweetener until cane sugar became readily available early in the sixteenth century.

The first residents of the New World never enjoyed the delights of honey. While the New World had its share of bees, it didn't have the honeybee (*Apis mellifera*), which wasn't introduced until the early seventeenth century. These bees quickly escaped from their domestic hives and spread across the country. Native Americans called the bees "white man's fly." The honeybee spread so quickly that frontier settlers found them and thought they were indigenous.

## Who invented the beehive?

Early beekeeping was unsophisticated. American beekeepers used hollowed out logs or grass and sticks fashioned into a home. Boxes were also used. All of these arrangements had one drawback: the hive had to be damaged or destroyed to harvest the honey. In the 1800s, American beekeepers added separate honey chambers that were more easily accessible. Still, the keeper couldn't inspect the hive to see if the bees were healthy or had become queenless. These old hives produced about ten to twenty-five pounds of honey a year.

It was known for years that bees like to build their honeycombs $1\frac{3}{8}$ inches apart. Honeycombs are one inch wide, so this left a $\frac{3}{8}$-inch passageway for the bees between the combs. In 1851, Lorenzo Langstroth devised a hive with frames that hung from the top with a $\frac{3}{8}$-inch gap between all sides. This forced the bees to build their combs within the enclosed space of each hanging frame, which could be easily removed and handled. Modern beehives are variants of Langstroth's design.

To harvest honey, the honeycombs have the caps on their cells removed. They are then centrifuged to remove the honey. Heating the honey to a temperature of 155°F kills any yeasts that could ferment the honey. Straining removes bits of honeycomb and filtering removes pollen grains and air bubbles that would make the honey appear cloudy.

Today there are over 200,000 beekeepers in the U.S., tending over two million colonies. It takes around two million bee trips to a flower to gather nectar to produce one pound of honey.

## Is honey more nutritious than sugar?

Many people who are concerned with their diets avoid sugar. Some like to use honey as a more healthful sweetener. What makes honey different from sugar?

Honey actually is a combination of different sugars. It is derived from flower nectar, which is produced by an enzyme called invertase that is found in the bodies of bees. A typical honey has the following composition: thirty-eight percent fruc-

tose, thirty-one percent glucose, one percent sucrose, nine percent other sugars, seventeen percent water, and 0.17 percent ash.
On an equal weight basis, there is very little nutritional difference
between honey and sugar. Since honey is heavier than sugar,
honey will contain slightly more calories and carbohydrates than
an equal amount of sugar.

Honey was the primary sweetener in Europe until sugar was
introduced by knights returning from the Second Crusade in the
Middle East. Sugar would eventually reduce honey's importance
significantly, especially after the Protestant Reformation put
many of the beekeeping monasteries in northern Europe out of
business in the 1500s. It wouldn't be for another century, however, that sugar would become more than just a luxury item.

## Are any honeys poisonous?

What could be more pure, natural, and healthful than honey?
Not much, unless the honey is poisonous. Some flower nectars
are toxic to humans. The nectar from some species of azaleas and
rhododendron, while harmless to the bee, are poisonous to us.
Their nectars contain grayanotoxin and can cause symptoms of
dizziness, nausea and vomiting, low blood pressure, and heavy
sweating. Most of these species are not found in North America
though, so don't fret. However, the ancient peoples of eastern
Turkey were frequently affected by just such poisonous honey.

A honey is named after the flower whose nectar is gathered by
the bees to produce it. The most common nectars found in American honeys are clover, orange, and sage. Other regional honeys
include buckwheat, dandelion, heather, linden, raspberry, spear-
mint, and thyme. Worldwide, there are hundreds of kinds of honey
available. Generally speaking, the darker the color of the honey,
the stronger its flavor will be.

# 12

# Junk Food

*How did some of our favorite candies get their names?*

*Charleston Chew.* This nut roll of vanilla-flavored nougat covered in milk chocolate was named after the popular dance—the Charleston—in 1922, by the Fox-cross Candy Company of Emeryville, California. As a promotion, they ran contests with prizes such as a live pony or a monkey with a complete set of clothes.

*Kit Kat.* This bar started out as the Chocolate Crisp, in 1935. Made by the English Rowntree Company, the chocolate-covered wafer bar was renamed after London's Kit Kat Club, in 1937.

*Chunky.* A 1¼ ounce chocolate bar, containing Brazil nuts and raisins, which originally sold for two cents. It was created by New York confectionery wholesaler Philip Silverstein in 1936 and was named after his "chunky" baby granddaughter. When Brazil nuts become too expensive, they were omitted from the bar, but the name wasn't changed.

*Welch's Junior Mints.* These get their name from a Broadway play—*Junior Miss*—that James O. Welch attended at New York's Lyceum Theater in 1941. He kept the name in mind until he introduced the miniature chocolate-covered mint patties in 1945.

*Three Musketeers.* This bar was introduced in 1932. Originally, there were three bars of different flavors (chocolate, vanilla, and strawberry) packaged in one wrapper, hence the name.

*Snickers*. Introduced in 1930, it was named for a horse owned by the Mars family. Up until 1935, the candy contained two bars and was called Double Snickers.

*Lollipop*. This candy is named for a racehorse. The biggest producer of lollipops in the world is the Charm's plant in Covington, Tennessee.

*NECCO Wafers*. These chalky, pastel-colored little disks debuted in 1902 and are named for an acronym of their maker, New England Confectionery Company.

*Clark Bar*. This chocolate, peanut butter, and taffy candy bar was first sold on the streets of Pittsburgh by Irish immigrant David Clark in 1886.

*Mounds* and *Almond Joy*. These were both created by the Peter Paul Candy Manufacturing Company, which was started in 1919 in New Haven, Connecticut, by immigrant Peter Paul Halajian and others. Mounds was introduced in 1920 and was named for its shape. Almond Joy, which now outsells Mounds two to one, debuted in 1946.

*Saltwater taffy*. This summer boardwalk favorite was first created in Atlantic City, New Jersey, in the late 1800s. The boardwalk vendors needed a candy that wouldn't melt in the summer heat, and taffy fit the bill. Early saltwater taffy did contain small amounts of saltwater. It is said the seawater was first added to taffy accidentally when extremely high tides drenched one vendor's taffy. Today, taffy is made with sugar, corn syrup, and shortening. As it cools it is stretched and twisted into long pliable strands to give it a supple consistency.

### What are Pop Rocks?

Why would someone sit around and try to invent something as silly as Pop Rocks? In case you don't know, Pop Rocks are powdered sugar candies that snap, crackle, and pop in your mouth. The creator of Pop Rocks—William Mitchell—didn't set out to create a revolutionary new kind of candy—he was actually trying to come up with a carbonated powdered beverage. A research chemist for General Foods, Mitchell found a way to make carbon dioxide solid in 1956. Nothing much happened with this technology until 1974, when General Mills finally found a way to make a profit from this solid carbon dioxide. Powder it, color it, add a little sugar and flavoring, and you come up with one of the most unique candies ever. Pop Rocks were an instant hit with kids and sold 500 million packs in five years.

### What candy bars were dropped out of airplanes over U.S. cities as an advertising stunt?

Otto Schnering, owner of the Curtiss Candy Company of Chicago, chartered an airplane and parachuted Baby Ruth bars over Pittsburgh in 1928. The stunt created chaos on the ground as people scurried around to collect the free candy. He continued to repeat the stunt, dropping Baby Ruth and Butterfinger bars over cities in forty states.

### Is there any Scotch in butterscotch?

No, but there may be a connection with Scotland somewhere in its history. Yes, there is butter in butterscotch. The confection is a blend of butter and brown sugar. Emile Brach introduced butterscotch penny candies in 1904. His Chicago company, called "The Palace of Sweets," grew into Brach's, the biggest sugar-candy maker in the world. Their butterscotches are cooked in milk with 1.5 percent pure butter and plenty of salt.

The candy business was so big in Chicago around the turn of the nineteenth century that the city was dubbed the "Candy Capital of the World."

### What candy was born in Paul Revere's old house?

Those stick-to-your-teeth, pull-out-your-fillings peanut butter and molasses candies—Mary Janes—were first sold by Charles N. Miller, who started a Boston candy company out of Paul Revere's old house in 1915. He named the candy after his favorite aunt.

## What is a Bible Bar?

This is probably the first candy bar inspired by God. Taking the seven foods of the Promised Land in Deuteronomy 8:8—barley, figs, honey, olive oil, pomegranates, raisins, and wheat—a guy named Tom Ciola created this heavenly health food candy bar. It tastes kind of like a Fig Newton and costs $1.95. Sylvester Graham would have approved.

## Are jelly beans made from jelly?

Jelly beans are neither jelly nor beans. They were, however, originally made with jelly, probably thickened with grain starch and coated with sugar. The forerunner of the modern jelly bean was a Middle Eastern confection called Turkish delight—a jellylike candy coated with confectioners' sugar. Jelly beans get their smooth, hard sugar coating by an ancient process known as "panning." Panning involves rolling the candies around in a drum that resembles a cement mixer while a mist of hot liquid sugar is sprayed on them. Each tumble in the drum adds another thin layer of sugar. (Panning can also be used to coat candies with chocolate.)

The first recorded advertisement for jelly beans in the United States is from the Schrafft Company of Boston. In 1861 they promoted sending the treats to soldiers in the Civil War. The jelly bean's association with Easter began in the 1930s. Today, around fifteen billion are sold during the Easter season.

## What popular candy flavor is used to make cigarettes?

Licorice is a feathery-leaved plant that grows wild throughout southern Europe. Spain is the leading licorice grower. An extract taken from the root—glycyrrhizin—is fifty times sweeter than sugar. It is used in small quantities to flavor licorice candies. However, the main flavoring in licorice candy comes from an anise extract called anethole. Ninety percent of the licorice extract used commercially is as a flavoring in cigarettes.

The best-selling "licorice" is red Twizzlers, which is a strawberry—not licorice—flavor. After popcorn, Twizzlers is the number one movie theater snack.

### How many licks does it take to get to the Tootsie Roll center of a Tootsie Pop?

This was the unknowable question first posed by the cartoon owl in the old Tootsie Pop commercials. Another good question is "How do they get the soft Tootsie Roll in the center of the hard candy lollipops?"

Tootsie Pops are made by wrapping a hot strip of sugar that is formed into a cone. Tootsie Roll mix is fed into the cone and a machine turns the sugar candy around to form a ball around the Tootsie; a stick is then inserted. Originally, the hard outer sugar shell was thicker, but management realized that what people really wanted to do was to get to the center as quickly as possible. As a result, the company began to reduce the thickness of the shell. According to recently declassified documents, it takes an average of 252 licks to get through to the Tootsie center.

### Who designed the Whitman Sampler box?

The Whitman Sampler chocolate box was the first candy box to be wrapped in cellophane. Introduced by Whitman Chocolate Company of Philadelphia, in 1912, the box's cover design was taken from an old embroidered sampler sewn by company president Walter B. Sharp's grandmother. The Whitman family had been in the candy business since Stephen F. Whitman started a little candy shop in Philadelphia, in 1842.

Kids may love candy, but adults eat two-thirds of it. If you think Americans are big on candy (we eat twenty-one pounds per person per year) the Dutch are the candy-eating champs of the world. They each consume some sixty-five pounds a year!

### Why are candy canes red and white?

The candy cane is such a holiday staple that it is literally given away by storefront Santas and banks everywhere. The cane is a symbol of the shepherd's crook held by the sheep herders who gathered at the manger to worship the infant Christ.

Legend goes that the choirmaster of the Cologne Cathedral handed out sugar sticks to his young choirboys to keep them quiet during the long Living Creche ceremony in 1670. He had the sticks bent into shepherd's crooks in honor of the event. It wasn't until the early twentieth century that they were made in peppermint and the red and white stripes added. The white body of the cane represents the life that is pure; the red stripes symbolize the Lord's sacrifice for man.

Bob McCormack, from Albany, Georgia, began making candy canes by hand for his family, friends, and local shops, in the 1920s. Bob's brother-in-law, a Catholic priest, invented a candy-cane-making machine in the 1950s; it enabled Bob's Candies to become the largest producer of candy canes in the world.

### How does hard candy differ from soft candy?

There are three basic types of candy: chocolate, hard, and soft. Hard and soft candies start out with the same basic ingredients of sugar, water, and flavoring. Whether the candy turns out to be hard or soft is determined by how much heat is used in its manufacture. A blend of half sugar and half water heated to 240°F becomes soft candy when it cools. If the same blend is heated to 300°F, it will cool into a hard candy.

### How do they make liquid-center chocolates?

Did you ever wonder how they get the liquid inside those soft-centered chocolate candies? There are two ways to do it. The more obvious one is to make a cup-shaped piece of chocolate, fill it, and seal it with a chocolate top. The more creative method involves some simple chemistry. A firm sugar center has a yeast-produced enzyme added to it; this is then coated in chocolate. The enzyme goes to work on the sugar center and softens it to a creamy syrup.

### What is fairy floss?

Originally sold as "Fairy Floss Candy," cotton candy was invented in 1897 when candy makers William Morrison and John C. Wharton from Nashville, Tennessee, invented the cotton candy machine. The electric machine poured crystallized sugar onto a heated spinning plate, then pushed it by centrifugal force through a series of tiny holes. Morrison and Wharton took their fairy floss to the 1904 St. Louis World's Fair and sold 68,655 boxes of the stuff at twenty-five cents each.

By the 1920s, this confection was known as cotton candy, although they still call it candy floss in Britain.

The early cotton candy machines were unreliable. Gold Medal Products of Cincinnati, Ohio, perfected the machines—but not until 1949. To this day, the company makes almost all of the cotton candy machines in America.

Cotton candy is eighty percent air and twenty percent pure sugar. It only contains about one hundred calories per serving and has less sugar than a can of soda. Because sugar is its only ingredient, cotton candy is a good money maker generating ninety cents profit on every dollar sold. Pink and blue are the most popular colors.

## How do they get the fortunes in fortune cookies?

What would a trip to a Chinese restaurant be without the requisite fortune cookie at the end of the meal? Like chop suey, fortune cookies are an American creation. They were dreamt up by Los Angeles noodle-maker David Jung, in 1916. Fortune cookies were inspired by a story about the Chinese putting notes inside of cakes during the Mongolian invasion of the thirteenth century; it was a way to send secret messages. Fortune cookies just reached China recently, where they are called "genuine American fortune cookies."

So how do they get the little papers inside the cookies? The slips of paper are set on a hot dough disk that is folded over and bent before cooling. You don't have to go to a Chinese restaurant anymore to get fortune cookies. They can now be bought in stores, or even better, some companies will custom make them for you with your own personalized messages inside—a great idea for parties or "popping the question!"

## When were S'mores first created?

The recipe for this campfire favorite first appeared in the publication *Tramping and Trailing with the Girl Scouts*, in 1927. This gooey dessert is made by toasting a marshmallow, preferably over a campfire, and sandwiching it between two graham crackers with a thin piece of chocolate. They were called "some mores" up until the 1970s, when the treat name was shortened to "s'mores."

## Who made the first Girl Scout cookies?

American Girl Scouts began baking their own cookies to raise funds shortly after Girl Scouting came to the United States in 1912. During the 1920s and 1930s, Girl Scouts—with the help of their moms—baked sugar cookies, which they then wrapped in wax bags and sold door-to-door for twenty-five to thirty-five cents per dozen. The official "trefoil" cookie cutter was introduced in March 1932.

Girl Scout Troop 127 of Philadelphia is credited with initiating the annual Girl Scout Cookie drive in 1936. They wanted to raise money to go to summer camp and began selling commercially baked cookies in the trefoil shape. That first year the only flavor was shortbread, which is still a big seller today. In 1938, the national organization—Girl Scouts of the USA—contracted with Interbake Foods of Richmond, Virginia, to provide a uniform product for all Girl Scouts to sell. As time went on, many bakeries were licensed to make and package Girl Scout cookies around the country. By 1951, three kinds of cookies were being offered for sale—Sandwich (Peanut Butter), Trefoil Shortbread, and Chocolate Mints (Thin Mints). By the mid-1960s, ten percent of all cookies manufactured in the U.S. were Girl Scout cookies. There are presently three bakers. Each must make the three cookies just mentioned, as well as three other optional types and one Kosher cookie. Annually, close to 200,000 boxes of Girl Scout cookies are sold.

## How do they get the fig filling in the Newton?

Charles Roser was a cookie maker who came up with the recipe for the Fig Newton—a soft cookie shell filled with fig jam. He sold his recipe to the Kennedy Biscuit Works, which later became Nabisco. Coming up with a recipe is one thing; figuring out how to mass produce such a cookie is another.

In 1891, James Henry Mitchell invented a machine that worked like a funnel in a funnel for just such a purpose. The inside funnel extruded fig jam; the outside funnel encased it in dough. As an endless length of filled cookie is extruded, it is cut up into cookie-sized pieces. This process enabled Kennedy Biscuit to market the first Fig Newtons.

You should know that the Fig Newton is not named after Sir Isaac Newton or any other person. It is named for Newton, Mass-achusetts, a town near the Kennedy Biscuit Works. The company had a habit of naming products after surrounding towns near Boston. Originally called Newton, the name was changed to Fig Newton after the fig filling became a hit.

## What former talent agent started his own brand of cookies?

Apparently it doesn't take any special training to make a name for yourself in the cookie business. Look at Debbi Fields. She started her Mrs. Fields Cookies in 1974 when she was a twenty-year-old kid with a baby and grew it into an eight-hundred-store chain. The same is true of Wally Amos.

Amos was a high school dropout who went to secretarial school, did a stint in the Air Force, and worked for Saks Fifth Avenue before taking a job as a mailroom clerk at the William Morris Agency in New York, in the early 1960s. His charismatic personality enabled him to move upstairs and land a job as a talent representative at $30,000 a year. Keeping true to his bohemian ways, Amos moved to Hollywood to start his own agency. Amos wasn't very successful at representing celebrities, but they did seem to like to eat the cookies that he was making on the side. His clients suggested that perhaps he would be more successful at selling cookies than representing them; some were even willing to put up money to launch the enterprise.

Amos was thirty-nine when he borrowed $25,000 from some celebrity friends and got down to some serious baking. During that first year, in 1975, he had sales of $300,000; he peaked at $11 million in 1982. But all was not rosy. Amos had no idea how to run a business. The cookie company went through four owners in three years, and each time Amos had to give up a little bit more of his control. Finally, he had lost all equity in the company and he couldn't get along with the venture capitalists who were running the show, so he just gave it up. His departure from the company he founded was so acrimonious that the new owners got a court order barring Amos from using his own name, Famous Amos, on any future food product.

In 1995, Amos started an association with a low-fat muffin maker. Today, Amos uses his first name to promote the muffins— Uncle Wally's Muffins. The company has a large bakery on Long Island, but Amos lives in Hawaii. He stays out of the day-to-day operation of the business but is very involved in promotion. He makes personal appearances for the company, which is what he is best at anyway.

## What are our favorite cookies?

If we are talking store-bought cookies, it's Oreos hands down; they sell at the rate of twelve billion per year in the United States. But let's talk fresh-baked. According to Mrs. Fields's unofficial statistics, kids under twelve voted the sugar cookie number one. They also love M&M cookies. At Mrs. Fields there is a strict rule that every M&M cookie has at least one blue M&M on top. Why? Kids love blue M&Ms. Ever wonder how Mrs. Fields keeps her cookies so soft and warm? They are kept in heated, humidified cases until you buy them.

Regardless of the kind of cookie you prefer, we Americans are kooky for cookies. The average person will eat 35,000 in his or her lifetime.

## What top-selling snack cake used to have banana filling?

Twinkies were introduced to the world in 1930, by Continental Bakeries of Chicago. The company made strawberry-filled short-cakes during the six-week strawberry season. The rest of the year, the shortcake pans sat idle. Plant manager Jimmy Dewar got the idea to start using banana filling in the shortcakes. A new snack sensation was born. The banana filling remained popular until World War II created a shortage of bananas. The company then switched over to a vanilla filling, which did nothing to hurt the popularity of Twinkies.

## Why do donuts have holes?

Donuts are not a recent creation. Archaeologists in the American Southwest have found "fossilized" fried cakes with holes in their centers dating back to prehistory. Our modern donuts originated in Holland, where the Dutch prepared what they called *olylkoeks*, or oily cakes. These sweet treats were made by frying leftover bits of bread dough in hot oil. It was hard to get the center of these cakes fully cooked so they were usually stuffed with fruits or nuts. Dutch pilgrims brought them to America in the nineteenth century. Early American recipes called for little "knots of dough" or "nuts of dough" to be fried in oil. Hence the name "doughnuts" (now often spelled "donuts").

That explains why they are called donuts. But why do they have holes? As noted above, the oil cakes often did not cook fully, leaving a soggy, oily dough in the middle. There are many spurious accounts of who made the first donut with a hole, but it is almost certain that it was done to help it cook all the way through.

Most accounts trace the first donut with a hole to the town of Rockport, Maine, in 1847. Supposedly, there was a sea captain by the name of Hanson Crockett Gregory (or Hansen Gregory, or Mason Gregory, depending on what source you access) who asked his mother, Elizabeth, to remove the center of the donut before cooking because he didn't like the uncooked center. Other sources say *he* poked out the centers on his own. Still others say that he stuck his mother's donuts on the handles of his ship's wheel to keep his hands free in rough seas, liked the result, and had the ship's cook make them that way from then on. Take your pick.

Don't like any of those explanations? You are not alone. In 1941, one of Gregory's descendants, a Mr. E. F. Crockett, joined the debate, stating that Hanson would have only been fifteen years old in 1847—too young to be a sea captain—but did request his mom to put holes in her donuts. No matter, Hanson is generally credited in some way with the ubiquitous donut hole we have today.

Regardless of the inventor, there is no doubt that donuts with holes were popularized by the Salvation Army during World War I, when they were served to American troops in France. Apparently, the "doughboys" liked them because they could carry several on their gun barrels and keep their hands free.

John Blondel of Thomaston, Maine, patented the first spring-loaded donut hole machine in 1872, but mass production didn't take off until Bavarian immigrant Arnold Levitt introduced his more modern donut-making machine in 1921.

## Why doesn't the sugar on powdered doughnuts melt?

If you've ever bought powdered sugar doughnuts, you may have noticed that on some brands, the sugar melts during warm humid weather, making them quite unappetizing. The way some bakers avoid this problem is by using dextrose with added fat to coat their doughnuts. This prevents the sugar from soaking into the doughnut and making it soggy.

## What is the Smell & Taste Treatment Research Foundation?

If you thought making broad generalizations about someone's personality traits based on the month they were born in is bizarre, there is research being conducted to determine people's personalities by the kind of snack food they prefer. Dr. Alan Hirsch of the Smell & Taste Treatment Research Foundation, in Chicago, revealed the following about the lover of each kind of snack:

- *Cheese curls:* "Formal, conscientious and always proper, cheese curl lovers can be described with one word: integrity. They will always maintain the moral high ground with their family, work, and romantic partners." (Not to mention the orange powder found on their fingertips.)

- *Pretzels:* "Lively and energetic, pretzel fans seek novelty and thrive in the world of abstract concepts. They often lose interest in mundane, day-to-day routines." (And they drink a lot of beer.)

- *Potato chips:* "Potato chip lovers are successful, high achievers who enjoy the rewards and trimmings of their success, both in business and in family life." (It is said Bill Gates can't get enough potato chips.)

- *Tortilla chips:* "Perfectionists in regard to their own actions and to the community at large, people who crave tortilla chips are humanitarians who are often distressed by the inequities and injustices of society." (They are not compatible with pretzel lovers.)

- *Snack crackers:* "Contemplative and thoughtful, people who prefer snack crackers base their decisions on logic rather than emotion." (Unless their crackers run out; then they tend to get a little irrational.)

The study does not seem to indicate what type of snack food lazy, unsuccessful people eat!

### How do they make Pringles?

Pringles are perfect. Well, at least they are perfectly shaped. How do they get such uniformity? In a word (actually two)—potato flakes. Pringles start out as potato flakes, from which pellets of potato dough are made. The dough is rolled out, cut to shape, fried, and salted, but only on one side. The bottom of the saddle-shaped "chip" has no salt.

This production process has pretty much guaranteed a perfect Pringle since the company started making them in 1969. Every time. Potato chip makers that slice potatoes will get a more varied product. (The thickness of an average chip is $55/1000$ of an inch. Ridged chips are four times thicker.) One amazing technology they employ, which Pringles does not need to worry about, is a high-speed sorter that weeds out green or burned chips. They fly through mid-air in a blur and are examined by an electric eye (camera) that "sees" the bad chips and triggers an air blower to shoot them out of the flow. The whole process happens so quickly that you can't even see the chips. Some companies save the burned chips and sell them as such. It seems there is a market for overcooked potato chips out there somewhere.

So, are Pringles really potato chips? After all, they are not fried potato slices (chips). That's what the Potato Chip Institute (didn't know they had one, did you?) said in 1969. They sued Pringles over the use of the name "potato chip" but lost in court.

By the way, it takes one hundred pounds of potatoes to make twenty-five pounds of chips.

### What is the state snack of Utah?

Invented in 1897, Jell-O is an American classic but is virtually unknown in much of the world. Apparently, it is quite well-known in Utah, where it is the official state snack.

Jell-O is eighty percent sugar right out of the box. The original four flavors of Jell-O were lemon, orange, raspberry, and strawberry. Lime was added in 1930. Some flavors of Jell-O that didn't quite go over so well were mixed vegetable, celery, tomato, Italian salad, root beer, red hot cinnamon, Coca-Cola, and cotton candy. Strawberry is still the favorite flavor.

Jell-O has been put to some non-culinary uses. The horse that changed colors in *The Wizard of Oz* was actually six different horses sponged down with Jell-O. Cecil B. DeMille used Jell-O in his 1923 classic silent movie, *The Ten Commandments*, to create the effect of the Red Sea being parted.

Owning a Jell-O mold once was a status symbol. It showed that you were affluent enough to own a refrigerator.

### What is marshmallow?

Marshmallow was originally a medicinal candy reserved for royalty, as far back as Egyptian times, before its culinary properties were appreciated. The candy was first made with sap from the roots of the marsh mallow tree (*Alothea officinalis*), which is a member of the mallow family that includes Rose of Sharon, okra, hollyhock, and the cotton plant. The gooey sap soothed mucous membranes, like those in the throat. It was used as a thickener in medicinal candy until it was replaced by gelatin in modern recipes. The plant is still common in the wetlands of the eastern United States.

### What is Fluff?

What kid doesn't like fluffernutter sandwiches? Fluff is made from egg whites, corn syrup, sugar syrup, and vanilla. Fluff was first whipped up by Archibald Query, of Somerville, Massachusetts, on his kitchen stove. This occurred sometime in the early 1900s. He sold his Fluff door-to-door. Due to the shortage of sugar during World War I, Query gave up on Fluff and sold his "secret" recipe to two fellows named H. Allen Durkee and Fred L. Mower, for five hundred dollars. They called the stuff "Toot Sweet Marshmallow Fluff" and began selling it in 1920. They sold their first three gallons for three dollars to a vacation lodge in New Hampshire.

There is no marshmallow in Fluff, but then there is no marshmallow in marshmallows.

### Who invented corn dogs?

Corn dogs made their debut at the world's largest state fair. What state would that be in? Texas, of course. Along with chili and barbecue, Texas has made one other major contribution to our culinary diet—the corn dog. A guy named Neil Fletcher first put a stick in a hot dog, coated it with cornmeal batter, and deep-fried it, at the 1942 Texas State Fair. They were an instant hit, eventually selling over twenty thousand per day.

Fletcher's concept has been taken to the extreme in recent years, with vendors deep-frying everything from Snickers bars to Twinkies. Americans have come to love deep-fried food. Three-quarters of us eat it at least once a week. Only eight percent of us avoid it. Surveys show that sixty-seven percent of Americans have no guilt about eating fried foods, which you can easily tell by looking at all the pleasantly plump folks waddling around!

Another deep-fried fair/carnival/boardwalk favorite is the funnel cake. It is of Pennsylvania Dutch origin and is a staple at carnivals around the country. Each year 350 million people go to carnivals and many of them indulge in the funnel cake experience. The beauty of the funnel cake is in its simplicity. It is just batter that is poured through a funnel into hot shortening. It cooks in about a minute and is served piping hot and crisp, covered with powdered sugar.

# 13

# Saucy!

### Why is there a salad dressing named Wishbone?

Salad dressings have been around a long time. The Chinese have used soy sauce for five thousand years. The Babylonians were dressing greens with oil and vinegar two thousand years ago. The Romans dressed their grass and herb salads with salt. The French came up with mayonnaise two hundred years ago. King Henry IV of England's favorite salad was boiled potatoes, sardines, and herb dressing. Mary, Queen of Scots, liked boiled celery root, lettuce, truffles, chervil, boiled eggs, and creamy mustard dressing.

Americans were limited to homemade dressings until after the turn-of-the-century, when restaurants began selling their more popular salad dressing to go. In 1925, Kraft Cheese Company bought up several regional mayonnaise makers and the Milani Company, to gain entry into the pourable dressing market. French dressing was their first offering. Since that time, a great variety of dressings have hit the market.

Phillip Sollomi opened a Kansas City, Missouri, restaurant in 1945. Chicken was his specialty and he called the place "The Wishbone." In 1945, Phil asked his mom for the spicy salad dressing recipe she had brought from her native Sicily. He began selling it as "The Kansas City Wishbone Famous Italian Style Dressing." Wishbone Dressing was purchased by Lipton in 1957.

### Is there really a Hidden Valley Ranch?

Today's favorite salad dressing flavor is a fairly recent entrant in the dressing market. Hidden Valley Ranch was a dry dressing created in 1954 by Steve Henson at his dude ranch—Hidden Valley Guest Ranch—in Santa Barbara, California. The dressing, which Henson served to his guests, became so popular that he started selling bottles of it to his customers. When demand got too great, Henson began selling the dry ingredients in envelopes that could be mixed up at home. When he started a mail order business for his dressing, he received so many orders that he was forced to convert the whole ranch into a salad dressing production facility. The Clorox company bought the rights to sell Hidden Valley Ranch Dressing from Henson, in 1972.

Many competitors followed suit, making ranch dressing America's favorite. The next five popular flavors are Italian, creamy Italian, Thousand Island, French, and Caesar.

## How did Paul Newman get into the food business?

Did you ever wonder how Paul Newman's million-dollar smile and twinkling blue eyes came to grace the label on salad dressings? It wasn't really planned that way. Newman and his Westbury, Connecticut, neighbor—author A. E. Hotchner—used to whip up some homemade salad dressing and put it into old wine bottles every Christmas. They would go out caroling with their bottles of dressing in tow to give out as gifts to friends and neighbors. They then had the brainstorm of selling the stuff to the public. In 1982, each man put up $40,000 to found Newman's Own, Inc. Mr. Newman's Famous Oil & Vinegar Salad dressing was their first product. They agreed that all after-tax profits (about eighteen percent of the retail price) would go to charity. From its first year of sales, Paul donated around $1 million in profits from Newman's Own to charity.

The company's product line has since increased to include pasta sauces, salsas, popcorn, lemonade, ice cream, and steak sauce. While the product line has changed, two things have remained constant: Newman's commitment to high quality, all natural foods, and his donation of all after-tax profits to charity. These two commitments have made the company the success it is today, with products in all major food chains across the nation and in foreign countries. The company's motto "Shameless Exploitation in the Pursuit of the Common Good" has been their philosophy from day one. So far, Newman has donated around $125 million. That's a lot of salad dressing!

## How did other salad dressings come by their names?

- *Russian:* The first versions of Russian dressing were made of mayonnaise, pimentos, chives, olives, ketchup, spices, and that most Russian of ingredients—caviar.

- *Green Goddess:* Created at San Francisco's Palace Hotel, this dressing of mayonnaise, anchovies, tarragon vinegar, parsley, scallions, garlic, and spices, was named for twenties actor George Arliss, who starred in *The Green Goddess*, a play that was made into an early movie.

- *Thousand Island:* As the name implies, this dressing— made from bits of green olives, peppers, pickles, onions, hard boiled eggs, and spices—commemorates the Thousand Islands in the Saint Lawrence River.

- *Horseradish:* Neither derived from horses nor radishes, this member of the mustard family is often made into zesty dressings. Originally, this plant grew in coastal regions of Europe. The Germans called it *meerrettich*, or "sea radish." It may be that the English thought it was "mare" radish and changed it to horseradish.

## What is the difference between a sauce and a gravy?

The English word "gravy" is a bastardization of the French word *garné*, which is from the Latin *granatus*, "made with grains, or grainy." A garné was a kind of stew made from meat drippings. The English somehow began spelling the word "grave," which later became "gravy."

Today, a gravy is a sauce made from meat drippings, usually combined with beef or chicken broth, and thickened with flour or corn starch. It may also be just the drippings left in the pan. A sauce is a separate mixture of spices and thickened liquid. They are used to enhance foods and bring out their flavor. Originally, before the age of refrigeration, they were intended to hide the taste of spoiled foods.

The French chef Antonin Carême is credited with developing an elaborate system wherein hundreds of different sauces were classified under one of five "mother sauces," those being— béchamel (basic white sauce), espagnole (brown stock-based), hollandaise and mayonnaise (emulsified sauces), velouté (light stock-based), and vinaigrette (oil and vinegar).

## Who was Béchamel?

Béchamel cream sauce was first created by French financier Louis de Béchamel in 1654. He was Lord Steward to the Royal Household of Louis XIV, an honorary position. Béchamel invested heavily in the fisheries off the coast of Newfoundland before he came to realize that the French don't much care for dried-out cod from the other side of the Atlantic. To make the bland fish more interesting to the French palate, he came up with the milk, butter-flour roux that bears his name.

## What is hollandaise sauce named for?

Hollandaise sauce, a warm sauce made from butter, egg yolks, and lemon juice, is frequently used on eggs Benedict. The name "hollandaise" would be capitalized in English, but it was named after the country of its origin by exiled *French* Huguenots.

## Why can't you buy Hellmann's mayonnaise in the West or Best Foods mayonnaise in the East?

Mayonnaise was created in 1756 by the chef of the Duke de Richelieu. While the Duke was beating the British at Port Mahon, his chef was whipping up a victory feast that was to include a cream and egg sauce. Upon realizing that he was out of cream, the chef substituted olive oil for the cream. A new sauce was born. In honor of the Duke's victory, the sauce was dubbed "Mahonnaise."

Mayonnaise, as it came to be called, was already popular when German immigrant Richard Hellmann came to America in 1903. He opened a New York City delicatessen two years later. Salads sold in his store featured his wife's homemade mayonnaise, which became so popular that Hellmann began selling it separately, in "wooden boats" that were used for weighing butter. He initially sold two versions of her mayonnaise and put a blue ribbon around one to differentiate it from the other. Demand was so great for the blue-ribbon recipe that Hellmann put it in glass jars with a special blue ribbon label in 1912. The great popularity of his mayonnaise is credited with the rise in popularity of cole slaw as a side dish.

While Hellmann's mayonnaise was growing in the East, Best Foods introduced their mayonnaise in California. In 1932, Best Foods Inc. bought out Richard Hellmann Inc., but kept the two products and market territories separate. That is why you can only find Best Foods mayonnaise west of the Rockies, and Hellmann's mayonnaise east of the Rockies, even though they are owned by the same company.

### What North American flower has become a major worldwide crop?

You probably wouldn't have guessed sunflower. The world's second-most important oil crop is indeed the sunflower, right behind the soybean. It gets its name because the flowers somewhat resemble the sun and they are "heliotropic," meaning that they turn on their stems to follow the sun throughout the day.

Native Americans used the sunflower to make bread at least as far back as twelve hundred years ago. In 1510, the sunflower was introduced to Europe where it found popularity as an ornamental flower. It wasn't until the 1700s that its potential for oil production was taken advantage of in France and Bavaria. Sunflower seeds, which are rich in iron, are forty-seven percent fat and twenty-four percent protein. The sunflower oil extracted from the seeds is low in saturated fat and high in polyunsaturated fat.

Today, Russia is the leading sunflower grower and it is that country's national flower. North Dakota leads the U.S. in sunflower growing, although it is more commonly associated with Kansas (the Sunflower State), where it was adopted as the state flower in 1903. The tallest sunflower ever was a 25-foot 5½ inch monster grown in the Netherlands.

## How did the Jewish community help Crisco?

Crisco, the first solid hydrogenated vegetable shortening was not a big hit when Procter & Gamble of Cincinnati first introduced it in 1911. Women were used to cooking with butter or lard and were reluctant to even accept free cans of the product. So the company targeted the Jewish market with pamphlets in Yiddish. The Orthodox Jews took to Crisco right away. It was great for kosher meals because it was neither a dairy product nor a meat. The rest of the country didn't accept Crisco until World War I, when butter and lard became harder to find.

## What is rapeseed oil?

There are certain words we have an aversion to, especially when it comes to marketing a product. This was the problem faced by the rapeseed oil industry. This oil, which is expressed from the seeds of the rape plant, a member of the mustard family, is now marketed as canola oil. We didn't start calling it "canola" until 1979. This is when Canadian geneticists improved the rape plant so its seeds yielded a vegetable oil high in monounsaturated fatty acids and low in euric acid. The name "canola" comes from the words *Can*(ada), *o*(il), *l*(ow), and *a*(cid), a much catchier name than low-acid rape oil.

Canola oil has the lowest saturated-fat content of any vegetable oil—six percent. Compare this to the saturated fat content of other oils:

| | |
|---|---|
| Safflower oil | 9 percent |
| Sunflower oil | 11 percent |
| Corn oil | 13 percent |
| Olive oil | 14 percent |
| Soybean oil | 15 percent |
| Peanut oil | 18 percent |
| Cottonseed | 27 percent |
| Palm oil | 51 percent |

## What is non-stick cooking spray?

Basically, non-stick cooking sprays are just aerosol cans of veg-etable oil. There may also be some alcohol and lecithin mixed in. Grain alcohol from corn is added for clarity. Lecithin, a fatty sub-stance found in soybeans and egg yolks, helps prevent sticking.

So what's so good about the sprays if they are just plain old oil? Well, for one thing, they are very convenient to apply; for another, you can use a much thinner layer than would be possi-ble if you rubbed oil on your pan or melted butter in it. Thus, you can reduce calories by spraying on a thin coat.

According to the FDA, non-stick cooking sprays are "nonfat." Their loose definition of nonfat is any food that has less than 0.5 grams of fat per serving. The average quick-spray products contain around 0.2 grams of fat and are thus nonfat. PAM uses canola oil, which they state on the can "adds a trivial amount of fat."

## How do they extract oil out of corn?

You wouldn't think that you could get much oil out of an ear of corn. Well, you don't. There is very little corn oil in a kernel of corn, but luckily the United States is brimming with corn.

The little bit of oil each kernel of corn contains is found in the germ plasm. Here it will act as an energy source to nourish a new corn seedling if planted. The germ makes up only about eight percent of the kernel's volume and only half of the germ is oil. To get this little bit of oil out, quite a bit of processing is required.

First the corn is soaked in hot water for a couple of days. Next, it is ground up to free the germ from the kernel. The germs are then separated from the kernel pieces by flotation or spinning. After drying, the germ is crushed to squeeze the oil out. It takes three bushels of corn to produce one gallon of corn oil.

In 1911, Mazola became the first corn oil sold to home con-sumers. It was sold by E. T. Bedford's Corn Products Refining Company in Pekin, Illinois.

## *What soy sauce is named for the tortoise shell?*

Soy sauce has been an indispensable part of Chinese and Japanese cooking for centuries and has recently been incorporated into American dishes such as stews, hamburgers, and salads. Soy sauce is made by fermenting boiled soybeans and roasted wheat or barley and adding salt. Perhaps the best-known name in the soy sauce business is Kikkoman.

In the 1630s, the Japanese Mogi and Takanashi families got together and began production of soy sauce along the Edo River in Noda, a small city located near Tokyo. The name "Kikkoman" was chosen for its significance. In Japanese folklore, the tortoise lives for ten thousand years and is a symbol of longevity. Thus, *Kikko*, which means "tortoise" and *man*, which means "ten thousand," were chosen as the trademark for this long-lived company. The company logo—a hexagon—represents a tortoise shell and the Chinese character found within stands for ten thousand.

Kikkoman soy sauce is made with their proprietary starter microorganism, which is added to the wheat and soybeans. This mixture is left to culture for three days and forms a dry mash called *koji*. Salt dissolved in water is then added to form *moromi*, which is then fermented in tanks until the right flavor is reached. The moromi is poured onto cloths that are folded and pressed to squeeze out the raw soy sauce. The raw soy sauce is then refined and pasteurized. The by-products of the pressing are soy sauce, press cake, and oil. The cakes are fed to livestock and the oil is used for machines.

# 14

# Cheers!

### When did humans first start drinking alcohol?

The discovery of alcohol was likely purely accidental. No one knows when, but a lucky prehistoric person chanced upon some honey that had aged a few weeks and they enjoyed the pleasant high of crude honey wine. Early on, other sweet foods, such as dates and palm sap, may also have been allowed to ferment into wine. Later, it was realized that starchy grains could be fermented into beer.

Beer was being made in Egypt by 3000 B.C. The same malting process we use today goes back to this time period. Malting was probably another accidental discovery. Grain seeds were commonly allowed to germinate in water to make sprouts, which were easy to chew. If left in the water too long, they would begin to give off enzymes that would convert their starch into sugar; fermentation would follow.

The knowledge of beer-making would spread from the Middle East to Europe. Beer became the drink of choice in northern Europe because the climate there is not suitable to the growing of wine grapes but does support the growth of many grains. This is still true today. We see wine as the national drink in France, Greece, and Spain, whose Mediterranean climate is perfect for viticulture, while the cooler countries of Germany, England, Belgium, and Holland prefer beer.

### Why are yeasts used for fermentation?

Yeasts are single-celled fungi. There are about 150 species of yeasts, but only a couple members of the *Saccharomyces* genus are of culinary importance. Various strains of the species *Saccharomyces cerevisiae* are used for their ability to ferment carbohydrates, breaking down glucose to produce ethyl alcohol and carbon dioxide. It is indispensable to brewers and vintners for its alcohol production, and to bakers for carbon dioxide. *Cerevisia* is Latin for "beer." *Saccharomyces carlsbergensis* is another yeast, used in brewing.

In wine-making, the numerous naturally occurring yeast strains present on the grape skins are responsible for fermentation, although starter yeasts may be added.

The reason yeasts are the microbes of choice for use in culinary processes is due to the fact that they perform the task of fermentation without producing any undesirable chemicals that might give off a bad odor or a foul taste. They are said to be "clean" microbes.

### How does baker's yeast differ from brewer's yeast?

Baker's yeast differs from brewer's yeast in that the baker needs more carbon dioxide (to raise the bread) and less alcohol. Although baker's yeasts do produce alcohol, most of it is lost during baking. Brewers use two species of yeast—*Saccharomyces cerevisiae* and *Saccharomyces carlsbergensis*. Most American brewers utilize *S. carlsbergensis* in making their bottom-fermented beers. This yeast can function at colder temperatures than *S. cerevisiae*, and so is used to make lager beers, where it falls to the bottom of the tank during fermentation. *S. cerevisiae* prefers a temperature of around 70°F and is used in the top-fermented ales and beers of England.

### Why do beer and wine have such low alcohol contents?

The distillation of hard liquor is a much more recent development than the making of wine or beer. In the process of fermentation, alcohol is produced by yeast with little help from man. The yeast's production of alcohol can only go so far, however. Once the alcohol content gets above fifteen percent, it's too high for the yeasts to continue their biological processes. This is why we don't see beers or wines with alcohol contents higher than this. To make a stronger drink, humans must intervene.

Distillation is the process of separating alcohol from water by heating a fermented liquid to the point of vaporization, cooling the vapor to cause it to condense, and then collecting it. The reason distillation is possible is because the boiling point of alcohol is 173°F, while the boiling point of water is 212°F. When the alcohol-water mixture is heated above 173°F, the alcohol turns into vapors, while much of the water remains liquid. The vapor is then cooled and condensed in coils that allow it to drip into a collection container. The word "distill" is from the Latin *destillare*, meaning "to drip." The distilled alcohol is now devoid of most flavor and is hence called "neutral spirits."

### Why did beer become so popular?

If you had the choice of drinking contaminated water and getting sick, or drinking clean beer and getting a buzz, which would you pick? Thought so. For most of our history, especially in urban areas, the drinking water was suspect. Contamination with sewage or other sources of dangerous bacteria was common. Beer had no such problems. After the malt was soaked in the water, it was boiled before fermentation. The resultant brew had a high sugar content and contained alcohol, both factors that helped inhibit bacterial growth. As beer was generally considered safer than water, alehouses prospered in England well before the turn of the first millennium. Each house was likely to brew its own ale, because there were no large breweries until fairly modern times.

### What is the oldest recorded recipe?

Beer has been important to mankind for a long time. It was so important that the oldest recipe ever found was a six thousand-year-old formula for beer written on a clay cuneiform tablet. The recipe was part of a poem devoted to Ninkasi, the Sumerian goddess of beer.

So just how old is beer? The first crude version of beer was probably discovered accidentally by one of our nomadic hunter-gatherer ancestors who found that rain-soaked grains, when left alone for a while, would yield a beverage that packed a punch.

We have been brewing beer ever since. There are now tens of thousands of kinds of beers brewed worldwide.

## What was the world's first consumer protection law?

Man has been regulating beer for millennia. In fact, the oldest known recorded laws of any kind are found in the Code of Hammurabi, written in Babylonia in 1750 B.C. Parts of the Code contain regulations on the selling of beer. Beer houses were forbidden to water down their brew, under penalty of death. The Babylonians took their beer very seriously, as do the Bavarians.

In Bavaria, beer is considered a staple food. Duke Wilhelm IV enacted the Bavarian beer purity law—the Rheinheitbebot—in 1516. This law mandates that beer can only be made from barley, hops, malt, and water.

## Is drinking alcohol good for you?

There has been some ink in the press lately about one or two drinks of alcohol a day being good for you. The USDA guidelines indicate that men over forty-five and women over fifty-five can reduce the chances of coronary heart disease by drinking in moderation. What is moderation? According to the guidelines, moderate drinking is one drink a day for the ladies and two for the men. You younger folks, of course, should not drink at all.

## How are light beers different than regular beers?

Most American beers are about ninety percent water, four percent alcohol, and the rest carbohydrates. Regular beers have around 140 calories per twelve ounce serving, with about sixty-five percent of the calories coming from the alcohol and thirty-five percent from carbohydrates. Light beers aren't brewed with as much barley, malt, or other grains, resulting in a product with less carbohydrate, less alcohol, and less calories. Where regular beers average around 4.5 percent alcohol, light beers come in at around 3.75 percent. This is not drastically different, but the calorie content is usually under one hundred.

## How did Miller go from being the number seven brewing company to number two?

For many decades in American brewing, beer was beer. There were many brewers, but Anheuser-Busch was by far and away number one. Miller Brewing Company was a distant seventh until new owners came up with a revolutionary new brewing idea in 1974—diet beer! Well it wasn't exactly "diet" beer, but Miller Lite was lower in calories and appealed to a whole new segment of the beer-drinking market. It actually expanded the beer market to many who heretofore eschewed the high calorie content found in beer and catapulted Miller to the number two American brewing company. Anheuser-Busch saw the "lite," introducing Bud Lite in 1982. It became the number two beer in sales, trailing only Budweiser.

## Why don't they print the alcohol content of beer on the label?

This is going to sound kind of wacky, but brewers were prohibited by law from informing their customers, on the label, as to how much alcohol their beers contained. This kooky regulation was a leftover from the days just after Prohibition was repealed.

Two years after Prohibition came to an end, in 1935, the Federal Alcohol Administration Act was passed, barring the alcohol content of a beer from appearing on the label. The rationale behind this measure was to curtail competing breweries from engaging in an alcohol-content war in which they would try to lure customers by making their brews stronger. Ironically, it was the introduction of low-alcohol light beers that spurred major breweries to challenge the Act. They wanted to be able to boast of how *low* their alcohol content was. In 1995, the Supreme Court ruled that the Act was an infringement on the brewers' First Amendment right to free speech.

The Supreme Court ruling prevents the federal government from regulating beer labels, but states are still free to do so. As such, about half of the states still prohibit the listing of alcohol content on the label. Federal law takes precedence over state laws when it comes to wine and distilled spirit labels, however, and alcohol content must be listed on these.

Most American beers have an alcohol content of between three and five percent. "Ice" beers have a five to six percent content, and malt liquors are about seven percent. Some Canadian beers raised their alcohol content above seven percent, but Americans generally don't favor a beer with a high content, as they are considered to taste too harsh for our palate.

### What famous Japanese brewery was started by an American?

That most Japanese of beers—Kirin—had its origin in a brewery started by Norwegian-born American entrepreneur William Copeland and German brewmaster Herman Heckard, in 1870. Copeland discovered water that he found to be perfect for brewing beer in the Yamate district of Yokohama and started the Spring Valley Brewery. He brewed a light German-style beer that the Japanese came to prefer over the more bitter English-style ales and porters of the time. The enterprise shut down in 1884 and was purchased and reopened by Japan Breweries in 1885. The company flourished, becoming Kirin Beer Corporation in 1907.

### How did Oktoberfest get started?

The origins of the world famous Oktoberfest go back to 1810, when a party was thrown by the king of Bavaria—Max Josef—to celebrate the marriage of his son Crown Prince Ludwig to princess Therese of Saxe-Hildburghausen. As a part of the wedding entertainment, a horse race was run for forty thousand enthusiasts from all over Bavaria. The big party not only celebrated the wedding but also gave thanks to God for the past year's bountiful harvest. It was such a success that it became an annual event known as Oktoberfest.

### How much beer do we drink?

Americans have been brewing beer since before we were a country. Founding fathers George Washington and Thomas Jefferson were both brewers. Many German immigrants who came to the U.S. started breweries all over the country, producing pilsner-style beers. The German influence is still felt in the brewing industry. Most major American breweries have a German heritage. The first brewery in North America was established in 1642, in Hoboken, New Jersey. America's oldest existing beer manufacturer—Yuengling Eagle Brewery—was started in 1829 by David G. Yuengling, on Centre Street in Pottsville, Pennsylvania. He matured his beers in caves dug into the side of a hill.

Before Prohibition there were a couple of thousand small American brewers producing a variety of beer types and serving regional markets. Prohibition helped kill off many of these. After Prohibition, home brewing increased and the big brewers got bigger. By 1980, the number of American brewing companies reached a low of just forty-four, all making roughly the same thing—a light, pilsner-style lager beer. One bright spot, however, was when the federal government finally legalized home brewing in 1978; many people rediscovered the joy of a fresh, dark brew. This contributed to the rise of the microbrewery in the past decade and a half. By 2002 there had been phenomenal growth, with more than fifteen hundred microbreweries and brew pubs in operation.

While the growth of small brewers has been great, the giant Anheuser-Busch still has an annual output of around 93,000,000 barrels, out of a total U.S. production of 195,000,000 barrels, and the top ten breweries produce ninety percent of our beer. Annual per capita beer consumption in the U.S. is 23.95 gallons, compared to Germany at 38.67 gallons. America ranks number eleven out of all nations in total beer consumption. Worldwide, beer is the most popular beverage, after tea. In England and Ireland, beer (ale) is the number one beverage.

### *Where were the first American taverns?*

Taverns in early America were not as widespread as you might think. In New England and Pennsylvania, the Puritans and Quakers didn't believe in having fun or drinking. In the South, most people were spread too thin to make taverns profitable. Manhattan was an exception. Its first private brewery was opened by two Dutchmen at its southern tip, in 1612, and by 1622 governor Peter Minuit ordered the first public brewery opened.

Manhattan's first tavern opened in 1642. The oldest operating tavern in the United States is the White Horse Tavern, built in 1673 in Rhode Island.

## What popular expressions and terms derive from our love of beer?

Many modern terms and expressions have origins associated with the beer business. Many of them, as you would assume, began in England.

- *Wet your whistle:* Long ago in England, pub-goers would have a whistle fashioned on the rim of their ceramic baked mugs. When they needed a refill, all they had to do was give a toot to alert the barkeep to "wet their whistle."

- *Honeymoon:* The word "honeymoon" derives from the old practice of drinking honey mead for one month (one lunar cycle) after a couple's wedding. This twenty-eight-day period was called the "honeymonth," and the drinking of mead was thought to promote fertility and the chances of having a son. This period of time came to be called the "honeymoon."

- *Groggy:* When one drinks one tends to get a little "groggy." This term dates to 1740, when British Admiral Vernon had the fleet's rum watered down. In response, the sailors began referring to the Admiral as "Old Grog," after the stiff wool grogram coats he wore. The term "grog" soon came to mean the watered down rum itself. Thus, getting drunk on this drink made you "groggy."

- *Rule of thumb:* There are a couple of possible origins for this phrase. The one relating to beer is that before thermometers were invented, brewers would dip their thumb into the brew mix to determine the right temperature for adding yeast. Too cold and the yeast wouldn't grow; too hot and the yeast would die. This practice came to be known as the "rule of thumb."

- *Mind your Ps and Qs:* In English pubs, ale was ordered
  by pints and quarts. Unruly patrons were admonished
  by the bartender to "mind your pints and quarts" or
  "mind your Ps and Qs."

## Why do the British drink their beer warm?

If you are an American, there's nothing like a nice cold beer on a
hot afternoon. The English prefer a nice warm beer, regardless
of the weather. This would not be as enjoyable to many of us. We
are used to lager beers that are slowly bottom-brewed cold and
served cold. In England the beers are quickly top-brewed
and served warm, at anywhere from 50°F to 65°F.

Another difference between beers in America and England is
that English beer is generally lower in alcohol but has more body
and taste. It's the taste factor that comes into play when serving
a beer warm. Any beer that is drunk cold will have less taste. By
drinking their beers warm, the English get much more of its carefully crafted flavor if not the cool refreshment we are used to in
our mass-produced beers. Bearing in mind our hot summers, it's
not surprising that English-style beer never really caught on in
America. Our brewing industry came to be dominated by the
German immigrants who practiced lagering a light, refreshing
pilsner-style beer and set up shop in Milwaukee and St. Louis.

## Where was the American wine industry founded?

The first wine maker in the United States was a man in Cincinnati
named Nicholas Longworth. He started fermenting Catawba
grapes in the 1820s and had established Ohio as the center of
American wine making within ten years. Soon people in New
York State got into wine making and eclipsed the production of
their fellow vintners in Ohio.

## What is a "varietal" wine?

If you ever read the label on a bottle of French wine, it doesn't list
the types of grapes that went into it, but you can find what region
of France the wine is from. You can usually assume that the
grapes typical of the region were used to make it. California

wines, on the other hand, are "varietal" wines, specifying the dominant type of grape used to make the wine. The region of production is of much less importance. A zinfandel wine will be made from zinfandel grapes. But don't be misled by the varietal name. The grape variety on the label need only make up seventy-five percent of the wine. Other grape varieties are usually blended into the wine to enhance flavor and character. This practice is not confined to varietal California wines but is done with wines around the world, even the French ones.

## What is "ice wine"?

Canada generally is not known for its wine. That is, of course, unless you consider ice wine. By definition, ice wine must be made in very cold climates. This is because the grapes are harvested in the winter, when temperatures have been below 17.6°F for three straight nights.

Ice wine was first made by accident in Germany, in 1794, when the grape crop froze prematurely due to an early cold snap. These rich and flavorful dessert wines are usually made from tough-skinned vidal blanc grapes. Harvested in the dead of winter, these grapes must be pressed before they thaw. Since much of the water in the grapes is frozen, the resulting juice is very high in sugar content, acids, and flavor. This juice produces a wine that is lower in alcohol content, but much sweeter than regular wine.

Ice wines are sold in bottles half the size of regular wine and at prices at least two to three times higher. The main producers of ice wine are Canada, Germany, Austria, and the states in the Pacific Northwest.

## Why aren't there any vintage sherries?

Like Madeira, sherry is a fortified wine. Sherry making originated in the Andalusia region of southern Spain and the best sherries are still made there. The port city of Jerez was a major export point for much of Spain's sherry. English traders Anglicanized the name of the city into the word "sherry," around 1600.

There are no vintage sherries because of the "solera" system, in which old wine is refreshed with the addition of a younger wine that then takes on the chactereistics of the older wine. Essentially, this year's wine is topped off with last year's, resulting in a blended wine.

## What kind of wine was sent on long sea voyages just to age it?

Madeira is a fortified wine to which brandy or other distilled spirits are added to increase its alcohol content. It originated on the Portuguese island of Madeira. Wines were first fortified to help better preserve them on long sea voyages. It was found that by aging these fortified wines in barrels at sea, they were exposed to many varying temperatures and movements that gave them a distinct flavor. So special was this flavor, that ships in the 1800s were loaded with barrels of brandy-fortified wine and sent to the West Indies and back as ballast, just to age them. Nowadays, Madeira is aged by raising its temperature to around 120°F for several months. Then it is aged with the solera system (see previous entry).

While Madeira is now also made in California, and in other countries, none compare to the quality or costliness of the real deal.

## How did Madeira contribute to the start of the American Revolution?

We are all familiar with the fact that a tax on tea led to the Boston Tea Party and helped catalyze the Revolution. Lesser known is the fact that a duty on the colonists' favorite alcoholic drink—Madeira—may have upset as many as the levy on tea. Up until 1764, there was no tariff on Madeira. Then England decided they could make a few shillings for the royal coffers *and* force Americans to drink more port, an English product, at the same time by taxing Madeira at fourteen times the amount levied on port. Instead the colonists increased their consumption of locally produced cider, beer, and rum.

One famous founding father who was accused of bringing illegal Madeira into the colonies was John Hancock. The British had their eye on Hancock's sloop *Liberty*. It was impounded by British customs officials in Boston Harbor in an attempt to frame this contributor to the Sons of Liberty as a smuggler of Madeira. In a situation comparable to the Boston Tea Party, a crowd gathered and threatened the customs officers until both Hancock and *Liberty* were released.

Madeira remained popular in America up until Prohibition. The loss of its major customer, however, severely crippled the economy of the Madeira Islands. After the repeal of Prohibition, sales of port and sherry overtook Madeira and it never really recovered.

### Is Port from Portugal?

As the name implies, port originated in Portugal. Actually the name derives from the fact that these sweet fortified wines are shipped out of the city of Oporto and are labeled Oporto instead of port. The first ports were made in the Douro valley in northern Portugal, and the best ones still come from there. They are made by adding grape alcohol during a part of the fermentation process, when the wine is very sweet and is at about eighteen percent alcohol.

### Why did gin become so popular in England?

National pride and a hatred of the French had a lot to do with it. During the late 1600s, the English turned away from all things French (kind of like America is doing today), including their wines and other drinks. Port, gin, and beer were the local alternatives. However, an increase on the beer tax had the effect of making gin less expensive than beer and its popularity really took off, especially with the lower classes. To this day, the gin and tonic is considered one of the most *English* of drinks.

The word "gin" comes from the Dutch word for juniper—*jenever*. Gin was first distilled in Holland from rye, with juniper berries used for flavor, in the 1500s.

### What was America's favorite alcoholic beverage after the Revolution?

After the Revolution, Americans continued to favor domestically produced alcohols, with hard cider being their favorite. It was made from apples, but there was a pear version known as "perry" and a peach version called "peachy." Cider's popularity stemmed from the fact that it was cheap and easy to make.

## How did moonshine help create the IRS?

American colonists had been making whiskey since the seventeenth century, and it had become very popular by the time of the Revolution. The distillers of whiskey were generally immigrants from Scotland and Ireland who settled in western Pennsylvania and Maryland. Before 1791, there was no tax on whiskey, but in that year Secretary of the Treasury Alexander Hamilton decided to raise funds for the new nation by taxing various commodities, including whiskey.

Whiskey only becomes "moonshine" when it is made illegally, meaning no taxes paid on it. Moonshine got its name from the fact that these early distillers in western Pennsylvania did their work at night—by moonlight—when the smoke from their stills could not be seen by government agents. Moonshine was officially born in 1794 when the irate Pennsylvania distillers refused to pay the levy and George Washington sent in the militia to crush the Whiskey Rebellion. This only served to drive the distillers underground, giving rise to moonshine and bringing about the resignation of Hamilton. Moonshiners spread south out of Pennsylvania and Maryland, into the mountains of states farther south, where many still thrive.

The Office of Internal Revenue was formed in 1862, under the Department of the Treasury, for collection of, among other things, taxes on distilled spirits and tobacco, which continues today.

## How did the cocktail get its provocative name?

Yes, the cocktail may actually be named for a cock's tail. One version of the cocktail story claims that an Elmsford, New York, barmaid named Betsy Flanagan is responsible. In 1777, she worked at a tavern called Halls Corner, where she decorated the bar with the feathers from the poultry that was cooked and served there. A drunken patron is said to have asked Flanagan for "a glass of those cock tails," whereupon she gave him a mixed drink with a cock feather stuck in it. Cute story. But there is another account of how the cocktail got its name.

In 1795, it is said by some, the cocktail was named in a New Orleans apothecary when Antoine-Amadé Peychaud started making mixed drinks in an "egg cup" or *coquetier*.

In any case, the word "cocktail" first appeared in print in a Hudson, New York, newspaper in 1806.

### Who named the martini?

There are various claimants, but the most commonly accepted is a guy named Jerry Thomas. He was a San Francisco bartender who, one day in 1862, was asked to mix up a cool, refreshing drink by a traveler passing through town. Thomas is said to have mixed together a glass of vermouth, an ounce of gin, a dash of bitters, and two dashes of maraschino that he then shook with ice and poured into a glass with a slice of lemon. When Thomas learned the traveler was on his way to Martinez, California, he decided to name his concoction a "martini."

If you don't buy that story, it is also said that the drink derives its name from Martini & Rossi, the famous vermouth company.

There have been many variations on the martini over the years, but the classic formulation calls for gin and vermouth garnished with a green olive or a lemon twist. It can be served straight up or on the rocks. The "drier" a martini is, the less vermouth it will contain. If it is garnished with a small onion it is called a Gibson.

In 1964 James Bond immortalized the drink, when he started ordering vodka martinis, "shaken, not stirred," in the movie *Goldfinger*.

### What does "Mai Tai" mean?

The Mai Tai was first created by Trader Vic Bergeron in 1944 at his Oakland, California, restaurant, when he mixed seventeen-year-old Jamaican rum, fresh lime juice, a little orange curacao from Holland, a dash of rock candy syrup, and a little almond-flavored French Orgeat syrup over shaved ice. The name came from a friend of his from Tahiti who tried it and exclaimed "*Mai Tai—Roa Ae*," meaning "Out of this world—the best." Thousands of Mai Tais are sold every day in the twenty-two Trader Vics, and countless more at bars and restaurants around the world; however, many variations on the original recipe now exist, most with more fruit juice than Vic had intended his drink to have.

## Who was Harvey Wallbanger?

There is a rather dopey story, if it is to be believed, about the origin of the Harvey Wallbanger. It is said that some surfer dude in California, named Harvey, went into a bar and ordered a screwdriver to which he had Galliano added. Harvey proceeded to trip and bump his head on the wall and a new name entered the bartender's guide. No matter how it really got its name, the story was good enough for Galliano. The Italian anise-flavored liqueur company, founded in 1896, used a cartoon surfer to promote their product for quite some time.

## How did various other cocktails get their names?

- *Highball:* This is a generic term for a cocktail—commonly whiskey and soda—served in a tall glass over ice. It is said that it got its name from 1890s St. Louis saloon-keeper John Slaughtery. He served these cocktails in tall glasses that for some reason were known as highballs at the time.

- *Manhattan:* This drink was said to have been created at the request of Sir Winston Churchill's mother—Lady Randolph Churchill—while she was entertaining politician Samuel J. Tilden at the Manhattan Club in 1874. (It should have been called a "Churchill," no?)

- *Margarita:* Those who keep track of such arcanum believe that the margarita was first concocted in 1948 by Dallas socialite Margarita Sames during a Christmas party at her Acapulco vacation home. Margarita liked to play a poolside game with her guests: she would get behind the bar and concoct several drinks on the spot for them to rate. When she mixed together three parts tequila with one part triple sec and one part lime, everyone loved it. Margarita introduced her concoction to the Dallas social scene and from there it traveled to the Hollywood set and then to the rest of the country.

- *Daiquiri:* This rum, lime juice, and sugar cocktail was named for the Cuban town of Daiquiri, near Santiago, by American troops or engineers who arrived there around 1900.

### Is Irish coffee really Irish?

Irish coffee *is* Irish. It was created in 1943 by a chef at the Port of Foynes, located in the County of Limerick, which was a major travel hub between Ireland and the United States. Travel was by flying boats at that time. One particularly stormy night, a flight took off and met up with some rough weather; the plane turned back. Upon landing, the passengers headed to the restaurant at the terminal, where chef Joe Sheridan made them a special coffee drink to warm them up and calm their nerves; it contained a little Irish whiskey, sugar, and cream. One of the passengers asked if it was Brazilian coffee. Sheridan replied, "No, that's Irish coffee!" A new drink was christened.

Irish coffee was promoted in the U.S. by Jack Koeppler, owner of the Buena Vista Cafe in San Francisco. He traveled to Ireland to learn how to make the drink firsthand and featured it at his cafe. The original Irish coffee is still served at Shannon airport, where a plaque has been erected honoring its creator in the Joe Sheridan Cafe Bar.

### How did the Catholic Church help wine survive the Dark Ages?

With the fall of the Roman Empire and the beginning of the Dark Ages, much knowledge was lost. Monasteries saved some knowledge in their little enclaves that otherwise would have been lost to the Western world. Since wine was important to the celebration of Holy Communion, the monks became master vintners. One well-known latter-day vintner monk was the Benedictine Dom Pérignon, who perfected the making of champagne in the seventeenth century. The monks also continued the practice of brewing beer, due to the fact that each monk was allotted a daily beer ration of five quarts.

## What liqueur was created by monks and uses chlorophyll for coloring?

If the monk part didn't give it away, the chlorophyll part should. Originally made by the Carthusian monks in France's La Grande Chartreuse monastery in the 1500s, this aromatic liqueur contains more than 130 different herbs and other plants. The original green Chartreuse uses chlorophyll for coloring and is 110 proof. Yellow Chartreuse, created in 1840, uses saffron for color and is 86 proof.

## Alcohol warms your body, right?

Many people suffer from this misconception. How many old movies have you seen where they drink brandy to get warmed up? Alcohol actually has the opposite effect—it cools you off. The warm sensation, and the reddening of the face, is caused by the dilation of blood vessels and capillaries near the skin's surface. This brings more of the body's warm blood to the skin and makes you feel hot. However, this internal body warmth is quickly lost to evaporation through the skin, having the net result of cooling you down.

If you are ever exposed to the cold for an extended period of time, don't drink alcohol. You may initially feel warmer, but in the long run you greatly increase your chance of hypothermia.

## What's the best cure for a hangover?

There's an old saying about "the hair of the dog that bit you," that suggests having a drink (even the same drink that got you drunk the night before) the morning after may lessen the adverse effects of a hangover. Obviously, the more you drank the night before, the worse you will feel in the morning. A hangover is a mild form of alcohol withdrawal. Like a drug addict who needs another fix to feel better, a little nip the next morning can help postpone the withdrawal or make it more gradual. You shouldn't make a habit of this practice, however, as it can lead to alcoholism.

There are other ways to treat some of the symptoms of a hangover, which include dry mouth, headache, and lethargy. Dry mouth and headache are caused by the dehydrating effect alcohol has on your body; simply drinking water will help lessen these. Your headache is also caused by the constriction of the blood vessels in your head. Thus, a cup of caffeine-rich coffee can dilate your blood vessels and ease the pain. Your feelings of tiredness are due to a drop in your blood sugar levels, so eating something high in carbohydrates can help restore the balance.

None of these remedies are going to help you if you are also too nauseous to keep anything down. In that case, you just have to ride it out.

### How does the body naturally recover from a hangover?

There's no quick way to get alcohol out of your body. Only a small percentage is lost through urination. Alcohol is a food, and like other foods, it must be digested. The problem: only one enzyme—alcohol dehydrogenase (ADH)—can break it down, and we only have a limited amount of this enzyme.

You may wonder why we have an alcohol-digesting enzyme at all. It's not like we evolved with alcohol. Well, actually we did. As part of the normal breakdown of carbohydrates and the microbial action of intestinal bacteria, some alcohol is produced within the body. ADH is really intended to deal with this naturally occurring alcohol. Most of it is found in the liver. One other odd place ADH is found is in the testicles. Apparently there is some alcohol produced in the manufacture of sperm. Some ADH is also present in the retinas.

The limited amount of ADH we possess works slowly. People with average-sized livers can metabolize about seven grams of alcohol in an hour. The alcohol in a mixed drink or beer needs about six hours to be totally removed from our system.

## How do breath tests work?

Since alcohol enters all the tissues in our body freely and passes through cell membranes, it will diffuse into our lungs and be expelled when we breathe. (Ever smell a drunk?) There is a direct correlation between the amount of alcohol in the breath and the amount in the blood. Therefore, the breathalizer is an effective way to determine blood-alcohol content.

## How much alcohol remains in your food after cooking?

It is a common misconception that most of the alcohol added in food preparation is evaporated away during the cooking process. In 1989, the Agricultural Research Service of the USDA published a table outlining the average amount of alcohol left in foods after being prepared in various ways.

### Alcohol left after preparation

| | |
|---|---|
| 100 percent | Immediate consumption |
| 80 percent | Boiling liquid, remove from heat |
| 75 percent | Flamed |
| 70 percent | Overnight storage |

### Baked or simmered

40 percent after 15 minutes
35 percent after 30 minutes
25 percent after 1 hour
20 percent after 1½ hours
10 percent after 2 hours
5 percent after 2½ hours

These figures may surprise you and may even cause you concern if you don't wish to consume alcohol for one reason or another!

# 15

# Thirst Quenchers

*Who invented soda pop?*

Long before Coke and Pepsi appeared on store shelves, soda was sold at drugstore fountains across the country. The first American soda fountain was opened by French-American Elias Magloire Durand in a Philadelphia apothecary shop in 1825; its carbonated water was a big hit. In 1833, an English immigrant to the United States—John Matthews—devised a small carbonation machine at his New York store and started selling bottled carbonated water to merchants. Curiously, neither of these two gentlemen, or anyone else for that matter, had thought to flavor soda water. This did not happen until the late 1830s. It is believed that either Durand finally came up with the idea or another Philadelphia soda fountain operator—Eugène Roussel—did. Either way, flavored sodas were an immediate success.

Soda fountains were confined mainly to pharmacies, and the pharmacists tried concocting herbal remedies by adding things like root and bark extracts to soda water. Root beer, ginger ale, and birch beer were all created by pharmacists, as were Coke and Pepsi later on. Soda pop became so popular that New York had more soda fountains than saloons by 1891. It may be America's greatest food contribution. Perhaps no other American culinary (food) innovation has been so widely accepted around the world as soda pop.

In case you were wondering, the word "pop" became associated with the word "soda" in 1861, as the early caps used to stopper soda bottles made a "popping" sound when opened. In the 1890s, when the crown cap came along, the popping sound was no longer heard, but the name stuck, even though the bottling industry stopped using the term long ago. Depending on where you live, soda pop is known by different names. Folks in the East refer to it as "soda." In parts of the Midwest many people call it "pop." In parts of the South, the word "coke" is used as a generic term for any soda pop. There doesn't appear to be a good reason for these regional differences.

## What was the first soda sold in a can?

Like Coke and Pepsi, RC Cola was invented in a pharmacy in the South. A young pharmacist named Claud A. Hatcher started it all in 1905 with a line of beverages that he called Royal Crown. His first cola drink was "Chero-Cola." Other Royal Crown drinks were Ginger Ale, Strawberry, and Root Beer. This enterprise grew into the Nehi Corporation with the introduction of fruity beverages. In 1933, Chero-Cola was reformulated and became Royal Crown Cola. The success of RC Cola prompted the renaming of Nehi to Royal Crown Cola Company.

In 1954, RC became the first company to distribute soft drinks in a can nationwide and in 1964, the first to use aluminum cans. Other sodas had been test marketed in cans before this, but all were failures. A soda called Clicquot Club Ginger Ale was probably the first, in 1938. It was produced in a cone-top can. The problem was that the citric acid in the soda didn't react well with the metal can. Pepsi learned this lesson the hard way in 1948 when they tried canned soda; the cans leaked and were prone to explode on store shelves. They shelved the idea in 1950.

Once unreactive linings for cans were developed, soda in cans became practical. In 1952, Cantrell & Cochrane (C&C) introduced Super Root Beer and Super Cola in cone-top cans in the New York metro area and Los Angeles. Shasta did likewise with flat-top cans around the same time. But RC Cola was the first to go national with canned soda in 1954. By 1960, they were the biggest seller of canned soda in the country. Coke and Pepsi didn't go national with canned soda until the late 1950s, but RC had the market share by then and they would have to play catch-up.

## What was the first diet soda?

Royal Crown Cola came out with the first sugar-free soda—Diet Rite—in 1958. They replaced the sugar with cyclamate sweetener. Its original limited release was so successful that Diet Rite went national in 1962 and within eighteen months had become the number four cola in the country. Other soft drink bottlers were quick to see the huge potential in catering to the overweight, particularly women. Coca-cola brought out Tab in 1963.

## Why is there phosphoric acid in Coke?

Coke and Pepsi contain phosphoric acid. Why do they need an acid in a cola drink? Acids are sour and they are used to enhance the sweetness of the syrup and provide a little zip to the drink. By the way, phosphoric acid is not the only acid in Coke. The carbonated water used to make the drink is also a weak acid (carbonic acid). The acids found in Coke are strong enough to dissolve rust.

## What's the best-selling whole coffee bean?

Eight O'Clock Coffee is the number one whole-bean coffee in America. It had its origins early on with A&P stores. In 1919, A&P trademarked its whole-bean Brazilian coffee. They came up with the name Eight O'Clock because they felt that 8:00 A.M. and 8:00 P.M. were the times of day most coffee was consumed. (Seventy percent of Americans drink coffee in the morning.)

During the 1920s and 1930s, most of the coffee sold in the United States, was whole bean. Instant coffees started appearing in the 1940s and 1950s. So much vacuum-packed coffee was sold in this time period that most grocery stores abandoned whole-bean coffee. But A&P stuck with its famous brand. One reason: Eight O'Clock Coffee was believed to be the best-selling coffee in the world between the 1920s and 1940s. In the 1930s, with distribution limited to the East Coast and Midwest, one out of every four cups of coffee consumed in America was Eight O'Clock Coffee. Today, it is the number one whole-bean coffee.

## What little company revolutionized the tea industry in 1971?

Celestial Seasonings Herbal Tea came out in 1971. It was the creation of Morris "Mo" Siegel, his wife Peggy, and their two friends Wyck Hay and Lucinda "Celestial" Ziesing. They gathered local herbs in the mountains around Boulder, Colorado, sewed them into muslin bags, and sold them at health food stores. To fund the enterprise they sold a used Volkswagen.

Their herbal tea concept was a unique one and it created a whole new niche in the tea market. One key to the success of Celestial Seasonings was the catchy, offbeat flavor names (much like fellow hippies Ben & Jerry did with their ice creams). Names like Morning Thunder, Red Zinger, and Sleepy Time helped to land their teas in supermarkets and helped them capture ten percent of the American tea market by the early 1980s, when they had over forty flavors.

So great was the success of Celestial Seasonings that tea powerhouses like Lipton's couldn't ignore the company. They were forced to come out with their own herbal teas in response.

## Where does the name Snapple come from?

The name Snapple doesn't seem to make much sense for a company that achieved its success selling iced teas. Snapple began as Unadulterated Food Corporation in 1972; they would later change their name to Snapple Beverage Company.

Snapple is another unlikely success story. Brothers-in-law Leonard Marsh and Hyman Golden ran a window-washing business until they teamed up with a New York health-food-store operator named Arnold Greenberg. One of their first drinks was an apple soda. The drink wasn't such a big hit, but its name— Snapple—stuck. They went on to eventually market almost sixty different flavors of Snapple drinks, although the company's bottled iced tea wasn't introduced until 1987.

Snapple was the first bottled iced tea and is credited with creating a whole new sector in the soft drink industry. Their success would soon be imitated by the big boys in the tea world—Lipton and Nestea—in 1992. (Lipton went on to sell better than either Nestea or Snapple with their Lipton Original in bottles and Lipton Brisk in cans.) Eventually, Snapple would have fourteen different flavors of iced tea alone.

Iced tea isn't the only beverage Snapple sells. In all, they market over thirty flavored drinks. In 2000, their best-sellers were:

1. Lemon Tea
2. Peach Tea
3. Diet Peach Tea
4. Kiwi Strawberry
5. Diet Lemon Tea
6. Raspberry Tea
7. Diet Raspberry Tea
8. Mango Madness
9. Fruit Punch
10. Diet Cranberry Raspberry

Quaker Oats acquired the Snapple Beverage company in 1994. Along with their ownership of Gatorade, Quaker Oats became the third largest seller of soft drinks in America.

### So what is the "Best Stuff on Earth"?

Snapple boasts that their drinks are "Made from the Best Stuff on Earth." But what does that mean? They maintain that all their beverages, save the diets, are made from all-natural ingredients—meaning stuff from the earth, not a laboratory. No artificial flavorings, preservatives, or chemical dyes are to be found in Snapple, and they have used real fruit flavors and real tea since 1972, a claim no other major soft drink producer can make.

This is why the taste of your favorite Snapple drink may not be consistent over time. Since no artificial flavorings are used, there will be variations in taste due to the fluctuations in the fruit.

Growth factors such as sun, rain, and climate may impact the crop flavor.

### Who invented Kool-Aid?

A Hastings, Nebraska, chemist came up with the "formula" for Kool-Aid. As a child, Edwin Perkins loved to experiment with flavoring extracts and perfumes. His childhood curiosity led him to start his own mail-order business—Fruit Smack—a soft drink concentrate that came in heavy bottles that were prone to break during shipping. Perkins hired a chemist to turn his liquid concentrate into a powder in 1927. He had his whole family filling envelopes with the new crystallized concentrate and pounding them flat with a mallet. The product was renamed Kool-Ade and then Kool-Aid. His company became so successful that he moved the operation to Chicago in 1930; he was selling $1.5 million worth of the stuff by 1936.

The seven original Kool-Aid flavors were grape, cherry, raspberry, orange, strawberry, root beer, and lemon-lime. There now are twenty flavors; the top five in popularity are tropical punch, lemonade, cherry, grape, and orange. The newest Kool-Aid flavors are teas—Strawberry Tea, Wildberry Tea, and Lemonade Tea. Based on per capita sales, Kool-Aid is most popular in St. Louis. The other top Kool-Aid cities are (in order) Memphis, San Antonio, New Orleans, and Little Rock. More Kool-Aid is sold the week before and the week after the Fourth of July than any other time of year. Today, one glass of Kool-Aid, which cost a penny back in 1927, is still a bargain, costing less than a nickel; it has beaten the rate of inflation since 1947.

### Who created the happy face on the Kool-Aid pitcher?

To most of us today, the smiling frosted pitcher face is Kool-Aid, but this happy fellow didn't appear on advertising until 1954. It was on a cold winter afternoon in that year that Marvin Potts watched his son drawing pictures on their frozen windowpane. Potts was an art director for the advertising agency Foote, Cone & Belding and was working on concepts to promote the Kool-Aid slogan, "A 5-cent package makes 2 quarts." Watching his son was an inspiration. He first drew a large pitcher to illustrate how much Kool-Aid one package could make. Then he frosted it and added different messages. That first summer, Kool-Aid used three pitcher ads, each with a different look; one was the frosty pitcher with a 5-cent sign; a second had a Cupid-like heart and arrow; and the third was the smiling face. By the end of the summer, the smiling face was determined to be the most popular. While the face has remained unchanged ever since, it took ten years to standardize the pitcher, which at various times went from tall and skinny to round and pumpkin-shaped.

In 1964, when Kool-Aid packages were redesigned with the smiling picture, the company produced and gave away thousands of plastic pitchers as premiums. The pitcher handle was placed on the right side so children could see the face while pouring. The company still gives away thousands of pitchers annually.

## Who invented Yoo-hoo?

Yoo-hoo was the brainchild of Natale Olivieri, a New Jersey fruit-drink maker in the 1920s, who wondered why a chocolate drink could not be preserved in bottles. He had his wife put some bottles of a chocolate drink he had concocted in with the tomatoes she was canning (boiling), and wonder of wonders, half of them remained stable and did not spoil. After some experimenting he found a way to sterilize the drink under pressure and ensure a product that had a long shelf life and required no refrigeration.

Olivieri began selling Yoo-hoo, which was named after a common expression of the time, with limited success. One day his son Albert met Yogi Berra at the White Beeches Country Club in northern New Jersey and after several rounds of golf convinced him to help Mr. Olivieri find investors for Yoo-hoo. Yogi appeared in commercials saying, "Yogi goes Me-hee for Yoo-hoo." Yogi also got other Yankee greats like Mickey Mantle to help pitch the drink and make it a success. Yoo-hoo has gone through several owners since then and is now owned by Cadbury-Schweppes.

## Is Yoo-hoo a dairy product?

Yes and no. Yoo-hoo is America's number one chocolate drink, but it's not really chocolate milk. It does, however, contain certain ingredients from milk—dairy whey and non-fat milk. This is why Yoo-hoo must be refrigerated after opening. Since Yoo-hoo is heated during processing to keep it from spoiling, glass bottles, not plastic, are used. You may have noticed that Yoo-hoo in cans is not filled all the way to the top. The company is not trying to rip you off, they just have to leave some "head room" for product expansion during the heating process. Thus, there are only eleven ounces of Yoo-hoo in a twelve-ounce can.

Yoo-hoo is not considered a soft drink since it is not carbonated. Something else that sets it apart from soft drinks is that it has vitamins added. Yoo-hoo supplies fifteen percent daily value of calcium; ten percent of vitamins A, C, and D, niacin, riboflavin, and phosphorus; and eight percent of iron. There are currently four flavors of Yoo-hoo: Original, Lite Chocolate, Strawberry, and Banana.

## What is spring water?

Bottled water is poised to become the second most popular drink in America. In 2002, we bought over $7 billion worth of the stuff. That's three times the amount we bought ten years ago. At the time of this writing, each American consumes about 21 gallons of bottled water a year, just behind beer (22.6), milk (22.6), and coffee (21.9), but way behind soft drinks (54). Growth in the bottled water market is currently at about ten percent annually, faster than the other categories, so by the time you read this, it might already be America's second favorite beverage.

Such massive growth has led to a great proliferation of brands. It is estimated that there are five to six hundred domestic bottled waters on the market and some two to three hundred imported waters. With so many waters to chose from, how does one make an informed choice? First off, be aware that about twenty-five percent of bottled waters are nothing more than filtered municipal tap water. Two of the biggest sellers—Pepsi's Aquafina and

Coke's Dasani—both fall into this category. Many tap water products try to fool consumers by putting nice pictures of natural settings on their packaging. This is the case with Aquafina, which has a logo depicting mountains and snow to suggest its origin is a mountain stream. Nice try, but you might as well put a filter on your faucet at home and save yourself a few bucks.

If you want water from a spring, look for the words "spring water" on the label. By law, these waters must come from a spring, which is an underground orifice in the Earth from which the water flows naturally. Other key words to watch for on your bottled water label are:

*Glacial.* If a water claims to be "glacial," it must originate from a glacier source.

*Artesian.* If a water claims to be "artesian," it must come from a natural source above the Earth's water table.

*Drinking* or *purified.* If the label claims that the water is "drinking" or "purified," it has been processed in some way. Processing may include deionization, reverse osmosis (forced through a semipermeable membrane), or activated-carbon filtration (kind of like what your at-home tap water filter does). If the bottled water has not been substantially altered, the label must state that it comes from a municipal source.

## Does Poland Spring water come from Poland?

Yes; Poland, Maine that is. The town has an underground aquifer where the cold water (around 45°F) is drawn up through sand and gravel. The family of Hiram Ricker opened an inn at the site in 1793 and many people would come just to drink the water, which was said to have cured Ricker's father of a fever. In 1845, Hiram began bottling the water, which has a high calcium, iron, and magnesium content. As demand increased, the family had to seek out other natural springs in Maine to complement its water supply. In 1988, Poland Spring became the number one bottled water in the U.S.

## Where does Perrier come from?

There is a spring near Nîmes, France, where calcium-rich carbonated water bubbled up out of the ground. It was originally known as Les Bouillens. However, in 1903, Sir St. John Harmsworth, an English aristocrat, bought the spring and renamed it Source Perrier, in honor of the man who first brought it to his attention—a Dr. Perrier.

In 1793, the mayor of Vergeze, France, began touting the exceptional qualities of this spring's water. Its naturally carbonated sparkling water was first bottled in 1863. Perrier had been imported in the U.S. since the turn of the century. In the late 1970s, health-conscious Americans were looking for alternative beverages; one that had "style" was a plus. Within a decade, Perrier sales had reached over $175 million, even though people were found to prefer cheaper brands in blind taste tests. This was a good example of style over substance. Nestlé Waters North America acquired Source Perrier in 1992, and it is the best-selling imported sparkling water.

Nestlé Waters North America also owns several other bottled water brands including Arrowhead, Calistoga, Deer Park, Great Bear, S. Pellegrino, Poland Spring, and Vittel.

## What was the first American city to have running water?

In days gone by, those living in the country were much better off in some ways—think sanitation—than city dwellers. This was especially true when it came to water. Most country folk had their own wells and ready access to clean water. Urban residents, on the other hand, had to make due with getting water from an often less-than-sanitary public pump and lug it home. In 1830, Philadelphia became the first U.S. city to have a public water system.

## How can you tell if you are drinking enough water?

Most people have heard the recommendation that the typical adult of average weight drink at least eight glasses (that's eight ounces or one cup each) of water a day. Who really does this or could even keep track of daily water intake? One way to tell if you are getting enough water is to look at your outflow (urine): it should be clear and of a high volume. In addition, you should be making trips to the bathroom every two to four hours. If not, you may need to drink more.

## Why can't we drink salt water?

History would certainly have been different if humans could drink salt water since most of the planet is covered with it. While it provides us with a bounty of seafood, it is no good for irrigating crops or drinking. This fact means that peoples in many arid regions of the world with access to the sea, but not fresh water, have to desalinate seawater, an expensive process.

Water is considered highly saline if it contains over ten thousand parts per million (ppm) of dissolved salts. Fresh water contains less than one thousand ppm. The reason we can't drink saline water is because it causes us to dehydrate. How does water dehydrate us, you may ask? The kidneys cannot make urine that is saltier than seawater (salt water). In order to get rid of all the excess salt taken in, you would have to urinate more water than you drank, thus dehydrating and killing you.

The ideal amount of salt you should consume is about 500 milligrams per day. However, many of us ingest closer to 3,500 milligrams per day. A teaspoon of salt is about 2,000 milligrams. Our blood is about 0.9 percent salt and salt makes up about 0.25 percent of our total weight.

# 16

# Eating Out

*What is the largest fast-food chain in the U.S. and Canada?*

It's not the one you think! This company was started in 1965, by seventeen-year-old Fred DeLuca in Bridgeport, Connecticut, who needed to make some money over the summer to help pay his college expenses. Fred would need more money to study to become a medical doctor than a job paying $1.25 an hour at the local hardware store would pay. When a family friend—Dr. Peter Buck—invited the DeLuca family over for a July barbecue, Fred decided to hit him up for a loan. What he got was something more valuable—great business advice.

Dr. Buck suggested that Fred open a submarine sandwich shop. The good doctor explained that all one had to do was rent a small store, build a counter, buy some food, and open the door. Customers would come in and put money on the counter and Fred would have enough money for college. Dr. Buck even offered to become Fred's partner, fronting him the money to get started. By the time the cookout was over, Fred had a business plan and a check for $1,000.

So much for medical school! By 1974, the two had opened sixteen Subway shops throughout the state of Connecticut. That's when they decided to franchise. Good decision. There are now more than 17,500 Subway restaurants in seventy-one countries. As a matter of fact, Subway operates more units in the United States and Canada than McDonald's does!

## At what fast-food chain can you order from two million possible food combinations?

The slogan for Burger King used to be "Have it your way." Subway is the chain for which that line is more appropriate. It has been calculated that with the number of breads, meats, cheeses, sauces, and toppings you can choose from to create your own individual sandwich, you could come up with a mind-blowing two million different combinations! Thus far, no one has eaten every kind.

The choices weren't always so numerous. Subway initially offered seven sandwich varieties with five vegetables but not lettuce or turkey. Business improved when they started baking fresh bread at the shops, in the early 1980s, and customer choices increased. People really do like control over the foods they eat, and it shows in Subway sales.

## Where was the world's first pizzeria?

Italian food ranks as the number one ethnic food in America, and pizza makes up a large portion of that food sector. The U.S. pizza business is a $32 billion-a-year industry. The average American consumes some forty-six slices a year, adding up to about three billion pies! At last count, there were around 61,000 pizzerias coast to coast. So where did this popular food get its start?

Yes, pizza did originate in Italy. Modern pizza is an adaptation of an earlier flat dough Italian food—focaccia—which was herb covered and first served as a snack some one thousand years ago. Focaccia evolved into something called *Casa de nanza*, meaning "take out before." Women would pound out dough into a thin crust, top with leftovers, and bake. It was more or less a peasant food, which pizza kind of is today (anyone can afford it). However, true pizza had to wait for the introduction and acceptance of the tomato from the New World in the late 1600s. It was the peasants of Naples who first put the tomato on their round focaccias.

It wasn't until 1830 that the first pizzeria opened. Named Port'Alba, it cooked its pizzas in an oven lined with lava taken from Mt. Vesuvius, a volcano on the nearby Bay of Naples. This first "pizzeria" didn't make what we would recognize today as modern pizza. That would happen in 1889, when Queen Margherita Teresa Giovanni, the consort of Umberto I, king of Italy, came to Naples. In honor of her visit, a tavern owner named Don Raffaele Esposito was asked to create a special dish for the queen. His tavern was called Pietro II Pizzaiolo. What dish would be more appropriate than a variation on the pizza? He created a pizza with tomato, basil, and the up till then never-before-used ingredient, mozzarella cheese. Esposito's inspiration was the Italian flag, which has the three colors he used in his pizza: red, white, and green. He named the pie Margherita Pizza, after the honored guest. The modern pizza was born. The classic thin-crusted tomato and mozzarella pizza is still referred to as a Margherita pie.

The first American pizzeria—Lombardi's Pizzeria Napoletana—was opened by Gennaro Lombardi in 1905, at 53½ Spring Street in New York City. At first, the business was primarily a bakery, making pizza on the side for the working-class Italian immigrants who came to the area in the early 1900s. He soon ended up selling more pizza, at four or five cents a pie, than bread. This New York–style pizza was not as thin as those made in Naples, but thinner than the Chicago deep-dish pizza that was to follow later. Pizza didn't really catch on in mainstream America until the servicemen returning from World War II began craving this Italian food and opening pizzerias. By 1953, there were some 15,000 pizzerias in the United States.

### What did the French Revolution have to do with the birth of the modern restaurant?

The French aristocracy employed all the best chefs. After the French Revolution, in 1789, when their employers lost their heads, many top chefs found themselves unemployed. What to do? They did what they knew best. Many of them opened the first fine restaurants. With all these top chefs competing for business, and to satisfy the vast public instead of just one household, the chefs were forced to expand their repertoire. Many new creations arose during this time of great culinary experimentation.

### Who invented the toothpick?

People have been picking stuff out of their teeth for millennia. Early toothpicks were made from feathers, coarse hairs, porcupine quills, and twigs, among other objects. It wasn't until 1872 that a toothpick manufacturing machine was patented by Silas Noble and J. P. Cooley of Granville, Massachusetts. It is claimed that the "modern" toothpick was first used at the Union Oyster House in Boston. Maine entrepreneur Charles Forster had them imported from South America. To promote their use, he paid Harvard students to eat at the Oyster House and ask for toothpicks. Today, ninety percent of our toothpicks come from Maine.

The Union Oyster House also holds the distinction of being the oldest restaurant in continuous service in the United States. It first opened its doors in 1826.

### What was the first standardized restaurant?

Before Billy Ingrahm and Walter Anderson started White Castle, hamburger sandwiches were only fit for factory workers. They changed all that when they opened the first standardized restaurant in Wichita, Kansas, in 1921. It was a tiny 10 foot x 15 foot cement-block building with five stools. Their burgers, known as "sliders" at the time, were steam cooked with holes in them.

Ingram, a real estate agent/insurance salesman, met Anderson, who was a professional cook, when he sold him a house. Anderson had come up with a new way to cook hamburger sandwiches that involved using thinner patties of meat with bits of onion mashed into them on the griddle. They were cooked with both halves of the bun placed over them to catch the juices, flavor, and aroma. They were small enough that customers could "buy 'em by the sack" as the slogan went.

Ingram and Anderson incorporated as the White Castle System of Eating Houses, in 1924. In 1933, Ingram bought out Anderson's share of the business and prospered. By the mid-1960s, there were about one hundred White Castles located in eleven metropolitan areas. A sack of five burgers to go cost just twenty-five cents. The average White Castle restaurant was forty-five square feet with three grills that could crank out close to 2,000 hamburgers an hour.

## What is the largest drive-in restaurant chain?

Troy Smith had already tried his hand at running two different restaurants, both unsuccessfully, when he opened a steakhouse in Shawnee, Oklahoma, in 1953. In the lot adjacent to his restaurant was a root beer stand called Top Hat Drive-In. Troy had plans of knocking it down to make more parking for the steakhouse. Happily, he waited. The root beer stand, which served hot dogs and hamburgers, actually was generating more profit than the bigger restaurant—about $700 a week. Troy started thinking of ways to improve on the Top Hat.

While on a trip to Louisiana he saw a hamburger stand that had an intercom enabling customers to place their orders from their cars. Troy had a similar system installed as well as awnings for the cars to park under and carhops to deliver the food. The first week after the intercom system was installed, he made $1,750. When Troy went to expand the business, he found that the name "Top Hat" had already been copyrighted, so he opened the dictionary to find a new one. Top Hat's slogan was "Service at the speed of sound." So when he came upon the word "sonic" it seemed a perfect fit. The Stillwater, Oklahoma, Top Hat Drive-in became the first Sonic Drive-In.

Sonic still serves hot dogs, root beer, and Frozen Favorites desserts, but has now grown to 2,600 locations in 30 states.

## Where is the world's biggest drive-in restaurant?

The Varsity in Atlanta is the world's largest drive-in. It began in 1928 as The Yellow Jacket, an Atlanta hot dog stand that catered to Georgia Tech students. Business was good so owner Frank Gordy moved to a larger location at 61 North Avenue and changed the name to The Varsity to attract students from other schools. He also began offering curbside service. You might think a city is an odd setting for a drive-in business, but it wasn't always so.

When first opened his urban fast food place, cars had to park at the curb and a young man would run out to take customers' orders. This worked for a while, until an establishment across the street began sending their own people out to take orders from Frank's customers. Frank bought the lot next to The Varsity to give customers a place to park. As business increased parking became a problem again, so Frank built a parking deck for his drive-in restaurant. It eventually grew to two city blocks and can now accommodate six hundred cars at one time!

The fare at The Varsity includes chili dogs, fried pies, and a special orange drink. When there is a Georgia Tech home football game, The Varsity may serve up to thirty thousand customers in one day! This kind of volume gives the world's largest drive-in the added distinction of serving more Coke in a year than any other single restaurant.

## Where were onion rings invented?

The Varsity may be the biggest drive-in and Sonic may have the most locations, but it all started with the first drive-in joint, a place called the Pig Stand in Dallas, Texas. In 1921, tobacco and candy tycoon Jesse G. Kirby witnessed the national obsession with the automobile and noted that, "People with cars are so lazy they don't want to get out of them to eat." He opened the first drive-in restaurant—the Pig Stand—to capitalize on the car craze. He hired young men who would jump up on the running boards of the Model Ts as they drove in and take orders. Thus the origin of the word "carhop."

The number of Pig Stands increased, and they became famous for their pig sandwiches and Texas toast. These are regional favorites, however. The Pig Stands' real claim to fame is their creation of onion rings, a dish that found wide acceptance.

## What was the first fast-food drive thru?

The first major fast-food chain with a drive thru was Jack in the Box. They started the drive thru in 1951 and it still accounts for eighty-five percent of their business today. Other Jack in the Box firsts were the breakfast sandwich and the portable salad. Jack in the Box serves 500 million guests a year and has one thousand nine hundred locations in seventeen states, mainly in the West and Southwest.

## What restaurant chain was started by a Japanese Olympic wrestler?

Benihana, of course. Hiroaki "Rocky" Aoki was a twenty-one-year-old wrestler on the 1960 Japanese Olympic team. He stopped in New York on his way to the Rome Olympics and had a brainstorm while eating at a short-order hamburger joint. Perhaps, thought he, Americans might go for the kind of sukiyaki restaurants found in Tokyo, where they practiced tabletop cooking. His father was an entertainer and owned a restaurant in Japan called Benihana, meaning "red flower." It was Aoki's idea to combine his father's talents for entertaining and cooking in a new kind of restaurant in America.

Aoki earned a degree in restaurant management at a local community college by night and saved up money by working as an ice cream man in Harlem (where he was mugged three times and stabbed twice) by day. He made $10,000 selling his ice cream. One thing that helped sales was a marketing gimmick in which he put little Japanese umbrellas in the ice cream.

In 1964 he opened Benihana of Tokyo, a four-table Japanese steakhouse at 61 West Fifty-sixth Street in Manhattan. He called what he did at Benihana "eatertainment." Not only did his top-notch chefs prepare the food at hibachi tables in front of the customers, they also entertained them with corny jokes and dazzled them with deft cutlery skills. At first, no one came and family members had to moonlight at other restaurants just to pay the bills. It wasn't until six months later that an enthusiastic review by *New York Herald-Tribune* restaurant critic Clementine Paddleford changed Aoki's fortunes. He soon had a hit on his hands, and America had a new kind of dining experience. He promoted himself and the business with countless publicity stunts. Aoki has gone on to open more than one hundred Benihanas since.

Before Benihana, Japanese cuisine was virtually unknown in America, as was the concept of tabletop cooking. Some credit Aoki with opening the door for America's acceptance of other Japanese foods, such as sushi, and the popularizing of soy sauce.

## What restaurant chain started out as "Danny's Donuts"?

No, it wasn't Dunkin' Donuts. Good guess, though. Danny's Donuts was the precursor to Denny's. The first one was opened in Lakeview, California, in 1953, by a man named Harold Butler. His goal was to serve a good cup of coffee, a good doughnut, and stay open around the clock. He managed to do all three, and made $120,000 in his first year. As he opened more Danny's, the menu grew to include sandwiches, and he changed the name to Danny's Coffee Shops. In 1959, the name was changed to the now familiar Denny's. By 1963, eighty Denny's restaurants were in operation; ironically, none sold doughnuts.

In 1969 Denny's became the first restaurant chain in the country to have no-smoking sections at all locations. They introduced the Grand Slam breakfast in 1977.

## Who started Domino's?

Four-year-old Tom Monaghan and his younger brother Jim were placed in a Catholic orphanage by their mother when their father died. When Tom grew up he entered the seminary and studied to become a priest. Upon being thrown out of the seminary, he headed in an opposite direction, joining the Marines. He then tried getting a degree from the University of Michigan, but dropped out. All this he had accomplished by the age of twenty-three, when, in 1960, he borrowed $500 and bought DomiNick's pizzeria in Ypsilanti, Michigan, with his brother Jim. In one of the worst business moves of the twentieth century, Jim traded his fifty percent share of the enterprise to brother Tom for a Volkswagen Beetle. Tom renamed the pizzeria Domino's in 1965 and started taking phone orders. He guaranteed delivery in thirty minutes or less. Tom finally had found his niche. Today, there are over 7,000 Domino's.

## What is the number one takeout pizza chain?

Mike Ilitch was an aspiring shortstop with the Detroit Tigers' farm team. He dreamed of being a big league shortstop someday, but he also dreamed of pizza. He never was good enough to make the big time in baseball, but he became a pizza superstar. When teammate and fellow shortstop Harvey Kuenn was called up instead of him, Ilitch hung up his glove. He set himself to earn enough money to start his own pizza business.

With the help of his wife, Marian, they socked away $10,000 and borrowed another $15,000, committing to monthly payments of $500 a month for three years, to open their first pizzeria. Mike wanted to call the place Pizza Treat. Marian, who thought of Mike as her "little Caesar," preferred the name Little Caesars Pizza Treat. In 1959, they opened their pizzeria in a strip mall in the Detroit suburb of Garden City. The rest, as they say, is history. There were two thousand Little Caesars by 1988. With a series of ads on national network television featuring the "Pizza, Pizza" guy, they almost doubled sales between 1988 and 1990. Little Caesars is still a family-run and owned business.

## Who was Nathan of Nathan's Famous?

There really was a Nathan behind Nathan's Famous. He was Nathan Handwerker, and in 1916, at the age of twenty-five, he began selling hot dogs from a stand at the corner of Surf and Stillwell Avenues in Coney Island, New York. Handwerker started as a counterman working weekends at Feltman's German Gardens on Surf Avenue. He and his wife, Ida, invested their savings of $300 to open the hot dog stand. They put in eighteen-hour days, selling their hot dogs for five cents each, half the price that his weekend employer at Feltman's was charging. His local competitors spread rumors that five-cent hot dogs could not be of very high quality. To dispel these claims, Handwerker hired college students to hang around and eat his hot dogs dressed in white coats with stethoscopes. People assumed they were doctors from Coney Island Hospital and, therefore, that the dogs *must* be good.

Hot dog carts have been around since the 1860s. A good hot

dog cart today costs about $2,000, but at a choice location, it will pull in between $300 and $500 a day. Summer is prime hot dog season. Americans eat about seven billion hot dogs between Memorial Day and Labor Day!

### Who started Cracker Barrel?

There is a small town off of I-40 in Tennessee called Lebanon. It was there, in the late 1960s, that a fellow by the name of Dan Evins began transforming the family gas station into a place where the weary traveler could also get a decent cooked-to-order meal and enjoy a relaxed country store atmosphere, unlike the hurried fast-food joints that were spreading across the country. With the help of his friend Tommy Lowe, Evins opened the first Cracker Barrel Old Country Store in 1969.

Evins and Lowe put quality ahead of speed. Their maple syrup *was* maple syrup, the kind that comes from trees. Their corn bread was made from corn meal, not mix. People began lining up for Cracker Barrel's turnip greens, biscuits and gravy, and other southern country favorites, not to mention the eclectic folksy antique decor and friendly service. By 1977, Dan had thirteen stores from Tennessee to Georgia. The first stores also had gas pumps, but the oil embargo of the mid-1970s convinced him to get out of that end of the business.

In the 1980s, eighty-four new stores opened. There were 260 by 1996 and today there are 470 Cracker Barrels in forty-one states. To maintain control over quality, Evins never went the franchising route. He owns all the stores and makes sure each conveys a sense of rural values and serves up made-from-scratch mashed potatoes every day.

### What two major food chains both started out in the same town?

Dunkin' Donuts and Howard Johnson's both opened their first stores in Quincy, Massachusetts. Dunkin' Donuts started out as "The Open Kettle," a coffee and doughnut shop in 1950. It is now the largest coffee and baked goods chain, with over five thousand outlets. The first Howard Johnson's also opened in Quincy in 1929. The franchise didn't get big until the first toll road—the Pennsylvania Turnpike—opened in 1940. Howard Johnson's became the number one toll-road restaurant and had over 350 restaurants by 1952, making it the world's largest food chain at the time.

### What pro football player started a fast-food chain?

Do you remember Gino's? It was a hamburger-chicken fast-food chain that reached its peak in the late 1960s. In 1957, three Baltimore Colts football players—Alan Ameche, Joe Campanella, and Louis Fischer—opened several hamburger joints in the Baltimore area. Two years later, they were joined by defensive end Gino Marchetti, and the chain's name was changed to Gino's. They went public in 1960; by 1972, Gino's had 330 franchises in the mid-Atlantic states. One thing that helped the popularity of Gino's was that they were the Kentucky Fried Chicken outlet in the areas in which they operated. Clever advertising, featuring Dom DeLuise as the "Gino's Genie," also helped boost sales.

Gino's opened the Rustler Steakhouse chain in the early 1970s. Rustlers were situated next to Gino's and featured a rustic western facade. There were 147 rustlers by 1978.

Gino's was purchased by Marriott Corporation and merged into Roy Rogers in 1982. The Rustler chain was sold to Collins Food and converted into Sizzler Steak Houses.

### What other Baltimore Colts player started a fast-food chain?

What is it with Baltimore Colts players? A former Colts wide receiver had a hand in starting the Hardee's franchise chain. It all began when Wilbur Hardee opened a charbroiled hamburger stand in Greenville, North Carolina, in 1960, and was making a profit of $1,000 a week. Two businessmen from Rocky Mount, North Carolina, talked Hardee into opening a fast-food restaurant with them in 1961. Their success convinced ex-Colts wide receiver Jerome J. Jerry Richardson and three others to chip in $20,000 to open the first Hardee's franchised restaurant in Spartansburg, South Carolina, in that same year.

## Who opened New York's Russian Tea Room?

A bunch of performers in the Russian Imperial Ballet started the restaurant in 1926. It soon became a gathering spot for Russian artists, musicians, and writers. The restaurant caught on with American celebrities who marveled at its palatial opulence. Sadly, this New York dining landmark closed recently, but you can check out its former splendor on its still operating Web site.

## What are the world's fastest growing food franchises?

While McDonald's may have showed reduced earnings in 2002, they still continued to open new restaurants at a dizzying pace. The following are the top seven food franchise openers in 2002, based on stores opened per day.

| | |
|---|---|
| McDonald's | 5.4 per day |
| Subway | 4.2 per day |
| 7-Eleven | 4.1 per day |
| Taco Bell | 1.7 per day |
| KFC | 1.4 per day |
| Baskin-Robbins | 1.2 per day |
| Quizno's | 1.1 per day |

## When did the first diners appear?

The origins of the diner go back to a pushcart vendor named Walter Scott. In 1872, Scott had the inspiration to sell sandwiches, coffee, and pie to the local factory workers in Providence, Rhode Island. In those days, restaurants closed at around 8:00 P.M., which meant that men working the late shift had to go home hungry after work. Scott's food cart was a welcome sight.

Ten years later, after standing in line on a freezing night waiting for his order, a customer named Sam Jones decided to open a food wagon big enough to seat patrons. He saved up for five years and took to the streets with his walk-in eatery. A new dining trend had started, and by the early 1900s there were so many mobile lunch wagons in New England that cities passed laws limiting their hours of operation from dusk till dawn. To get around these restrictions, clever food vendors simply found a prime location, pulled off their wagon's wheels, hooked up to power, water, and gas and kept their businesses permanently on one spot. The diner was born!

What we consider the modern diner was born in 1919, when P. J. Tierney & Sons Dining Car Company began making dining cars that were designed to be parked. His salesmen called them "diners" for short. These diners were not converted railway cars, but their design was inspired by the railroad dining car. When booths were added, in the 1920s, diners became more family friendly. Soon, many companies were manufacturing diners and they popped up from New Jersey northward. However, some diners became hangouts for seedy individuals and some areas, like Buffalo, New York, and Atlantic City, prohibited them.

By 1937, one million people ate at least one meal a day in a diner, and there were nearly ten thousand of them in the 1940s. Fast-food restaurants have taken their toll on the diner. Today, there are only a couple of thousand left.

### What is the diner capital of the world?

Today, New Jersey is the diner capital of the world. To be a legitimate New Jersey diner, the place has to be open twenty-four hours a day and serve breakfast at all hours. You should be able to sit at the counter or be shown to a table right away, be given an enormous menu, and get your food quickly no matter how busy they are. The menu should run the gamut from moussaka to fries with gravy, and huge homemade pies and cakes should be prominently displayed behind the counter. Takeout orders should be no problem, and it also helps if a Greek family runs the place, as they are the diner masters. If a restaurant doesn't meet most of these strict criteria, they may call themselves a "diner," but they are something less.

### How many restaurants are there in America?

You could eat out every meal in your life and still not make it to all the restaurants in the United States. There are over 650,000. You could probably guess that Saturday is the most popular day of the week to eat out, followed by Friday, then Sunday. The least popular day is Monday (everyone has spent their money eating out on the weekend). About thirty percent of our meals are eaten away from home.

## What city rates restaurant cleanliness and puts their grades in their windows?

Ever wonder how sanitary the restaurants you eat in really are? Sure, they all get some kind of health department inspection, but you never see the report or know what their grade was. Well, Los Angeles has changed that. All eateries must now post in their front windows a letter grade given to them upon surprise visits made by county inspectors.

The L.A. County Department of Health has initiated a grading system for restaurant cleanliness and food-handling practices. It is based on a one hundred-point scale, with ninety to one hundred points being an A, eighty to eighty-nine points a B, and seventy to seventy-nine points a C. The color-coded letters (A-blue, B-green, and C-red) must be prominently posted in all of L.A.'s thirty-seven thousand eateries or the business can be shut down. While the one hundred-point system existed before, no one ever saw the grades. Now people decide what places to frequent and which to avoid based on the colored letter grades in the windows. A survey showed that only twenty-five percent of residents would eat at a place with a B grade, while only three percent would eat at a joint with a C grade.

The system has had the desired effect of improving the cleanliness of restaurants. At first many restaurateurs complained, but now most clean up their act to get a good grade. In 1997, only fifty-seven percent of eateries got an A grade; in 2001, eighty-three percent did. The owners now know how the point system works and what things warrant point deductions; for example, one point is deducted for infractions such as beetles in pasta, hair in food, and chipped dishware. Four points are deducted for food displayed without a sneeze guard, defrosting shrimp in standing water, and consumer food not labeled in English. A six-point deduction is incurred for waiters with dirty fingernails, left-overs heated in steam tables, and cooks not washing hands after sneezing.

You can log on to their Web site at www.lapublichealth.org to learn all about the rating system and find a list of recently closed eateries and the violations they committed.

### Where is "Alice's Restaurant"?

There are two Alices that have become part of our culture, both of whom were immortalized in 1960s protest songs. The one was the already famous Alice in Wonderland, sung about by Grace Slick in Jefferson Airplane's drug song *White Rabbit*. The other was Alice Brock, immortalized in folksinger Arlo Guthrie's 1967 antiwar song *Alice's Restaurant Massacre*, later shortened to *Alice's Restaurant*. Yes, there really was an Alice and you can't turn on a pop music radio station at noon or 6:00 P.M. on Thanksgiving day without hearing this eighteen-minute-plus-long Thanksgiving Day classic.

Alice and Ray Brock were former schoolteachers of Arlo's, who ran a restaurant/commune out of a church in Stockbridge, Mass-achusetts. As the song chronicles, Arlo and his friends took their Thanksgiving Day 1965 garbage to the local dump in a VW microbus, found that the dump was closed, and left their trash on a pile of refuse outside the dump (well they really threw it down a nearby hill on the side of the road). Yes, Arlo was later arrested for littering, had to pick up the garbage, and was actually jailed for refusing to pay the $25 fine. Guthrie wove his experiences with the draft board into the song and ended up with the only real Thanksgiving classic song (although Adam Sandler has tried to horn in with his not-so-classic Thanksgiving song).

### What is a "blue plate special"?

This was the name given to the special low-priced meal of the day offered in many inexpensive restaurants. There is some degree of uncertainty as to the exact origins of the blue plate spe-cial, although it was common in the 1920s. Most of the explana-tions of its origin refer to these bargain meals being served on blue plates. The earliest attributed usage goes back to 1892 and the Fred Harvey restaurants. These eateries were located along the line of the Atchison, Topeka, and Santa Fe Railroad and served quick meals to the traveling public. Fred Harvey is believed to have bought cheap disposable plates that were divided into sections for each part of the meal. The plates were colored blue in an imitation of the famous expensive plates made by Josiah Wedgwood. As the blue plates were cheap and saved on dish washing, they were used to serve the inexpensive daily specials.

### What was the first restaurant credit card?

The Diners Club, the first multipurpose credit card, was founded by Francis X. McNamara in 1950, after an embarrassing incident the year before in a New York City restaurant. McNamara had changed suits before dining at Major's Cabin Grill. When the bill arrived, he realized that he had left his money in the other suit. He decided then and there that people should be able to pay for any meal they could afford, not just a meal they could pay for with the cash in their pockets. With partner Ralph Schneider, he founded the Diners Club Card. For an annual fee of three dollars, the original two hundred members could charge their meals at twenty-seven participating New York eateries. In the first year, more than one million dollars' worth of food was charged. Within a few years the card was accepted across the nation and around the world for meals, lodging, car rentals, and at retail stores.

The card became a craze. Hollywood made a movie named *The Man From the Diners Club*, starring Danny Kaye, and the Ideal Toy company put out a board game called the Diners Club Game. By the mid-1960s, membership had reached 1.3 million, but other companies and banks were beginning to issue their own credit cards. Still, over $35 billion was charged to Diners Club worldwide in 2000.

### What Chinese dishes are really American inventions?

As you probably are aware, many of the ubiquitous dishes served at almost every Chinese restaurant in America aren't authentically Chinese at all. Take chop suey, for example. It is said that it was created by a Chinese immigrant to California in the mid-1800s. There weren't many Chinese vegetables available to early Chinese immigrants. In order to create a dish that would be palatable to both Chinese and American tastes, they took American vegetables and meats of the time, chopped them into small pieces, stir-fried them together, and served them over rice to more or less recreate a dish made from leftovers that was eaten in southern China.

"Chop suey" means "odds and ends" in Chinese. It was probably created in San Francisco and helped to feed the laborers on the transcontinental railroad. Other Chinese-American dishes created in the mid-nineteenth century are egg foo young and fortune cookies.

Chow mein is an American adaptation of a northern Chinese dish—"Ciao mein," which means "fried noodles." The peoples of northern China rely on wheat as their staple, hence the noodle dishes, while southern China is the rice-growing region and rice dishes are eaten there. The earliest Chinese immigrants to the U.S. came from Canton in the south; this is why rice dishes are associated with all of China.

General Tso's Chicken is a dish of dark-meat chicken served with vegetables and red peppers in a sweet-spicy sauce. It originated in New York City during the 1970s, when Szechuan and Hunan cuisine became popular. While there really was a General Tso, no one seems to agree about how his name became associated with this dish.

Early Chinese-American restaurants were located in small "Chinatown" enclaves in big cities and not frequented by other Americans. When Chinese diplomat Li Hung Chang visited New York in 1896, he created a great interest in Chinese food, especially chop suey. Gradually, Chinese restaurants gained a wider audience and by the 1920s many had moved out of Chinatowns and catered to non-Chinese customers.

## Who is Orange Julius?

Yes, there was a guy named Julius behind the Orange Julius chain. The company started as a fresh-squeezed orange juice stand opened by Julius Freed in downtown Los Angeles in 1926. Julius was making about $20 a day when Bill Hamlin, the real estate broker who found him his location, came up with a way to create a smooth, frothy orange drink. Sales shot up to $100 a day and customers started to say "Give me an orange, Julius." Hamlin dumped his real estate career and jumped into the orange drink game with Julius. Within three years the two had opened one hundred Orange Julius stands across the country. Selling nothing but orange drinks at ten cents a pop, they were grossing almost $3 million a year.

Orange Julius was purchased by Dairy Queen in 1987. Other items were added to their menu, like hot dogs, hamburgers, and nachos. By 1993, there were over 700 locations worldwide.

# 17

# It's In There!

### What is flavor?

Without the sense of taste, coupled with the sense of smell, we wouldn't experience much in the way of flavor. Taste is our way of detecting chemical molecules dissolved in water. Smell detects gaseous molecules in the air. Often, we smell a food before we taste it. If we don't like the way it smells, odds are we won't like its taste either.

Have you ever noticed that your sense of taste is greatly diminished when you have a bad head cold. This is because up to eighty percent of our perception of flavor comes from smell. The olfactory receptors in our nose can distinguish between thousands of different smells. Our taste buds, found on the tongue and palate, aren't as highly sensitive. When we chew food, we are releasing a lot of its gaseous odors into our mouths. As a consequence, the odors travel up into the nasal cavity. A vacuum is formed in the nasal cavity when we swallow and gases in our mouth are drawn up over the palate into the cavity. Thus, we taste and smell foods at the same time, and flavor is a combination of the two.

### What is a "natural" flavor?

Probably not what you think. A natural flavor is not necessarily something that naturally occurs in nature in the form in which it is sold to you. As long as the flavor is derived from something that occurs in nature, it doesn't matter how many chemical or other processes are used to isolate it. Basically, as long as it wasn't just whipped up out of chemicals in the laboratory it can be called "natural."

## How does salt preserve meat?

The refrigeration of foods is a rather modern practice. Before the age of refrigerators, ice boxes, or cold cellars, foods were preserved by other means. The main chemical used to preserve meats over the ages has been salt. The ancients didn't understand why, but they realized that meats cured in salty water would last a long time. Today we know that this is because of the process of osmosis.

Nature hates chemical imbalances and tries to restore balance. Bacteria, which are comparatively low in salt content, are sensitive to high concentrations of salt in their surroundings. The bacterial cell membrane is a water-permeable barrier. To restore a chemical balance on both sides of the cell membrane, water will be forced out of the bacteria and salt drawn in. Nature thus makes the strong solution weaker and the weak solution stronger. The net result is that the bacteria dry out, shrivel up, and die. If they don't die, at least they are inhibited from reproducing.

A strong concentration of sugar in water can have the same effect. Hence the use of sugar to preserve fruits and berries, creating preserves. In theory, you could preserve fruits with salt instead of sugar, but no one would eat them. Some meats, like sugar-cured hams, are preserved with salt and sugar as well as other additives, including nitrites.

Ham, bacon, and other pork products have salt added today more for flavoring than preservation. We have come to expect these foods to be salty. They now don't contain enough salt to act as effective preservatives. In the early 1800s, Cincinnati slaughtered and packed so many hogs in brine that it was known as "Porkopolis."

## Why are nitrites used to preserve hams?

Nitrites have gotten a bad reputation in recent years. The most commonly used nitrite in the curing of hams is sodium nitrite, which is a salt. Nitrites have three properties that make them desirable as meat additives. Perhaps the most important of these is nitrites' ability to kill the bacterium *Clostiridium botulinum*. As you can probably guess from its name, this is the organism that causes botulism. A second happy consequence of adding nitrites is improved meat flavor. The third benefit is that they react with the meat's myoglobin to produce nitric oxide myoglobin, which gives the meat its nice pinkish hue during the slow-heat curing process.

The downside of nitrites is that they are changed into nitrosamines in the stomach. These chemicals have been found to cause cancer. So the FDA regulates the amount of nitrites that can be found in meat after curing.

### What is kosher salt?

Kosher salt is used for koshering meat and poultry by coating it with salt. It is a large-grained, irregular salt that can be from a mine or the ocean. It may or may not contain additives—check the label. By virtue of being big-crystalled, and irregular, kosher salt will stick better to meats than will table salt. It is best used by the pinch out of a small bowl.

### What is sea salt?

Basically, salt is salt, chemically speaking anyway. All salt at one time was in the ocean. Salt that is mined from the earth today actually crystallized from the oceans millions of years ago. Be that as it may, some salt is taken from the ocean and some is mined from the ground. You would assume that "sea salt" is taken from the sea, but this might not always be the case. The FDA doesn't require that salt labeled "sea salt" actually has to come from the sea; in fact, it is possible that your sea salt may have come out of a mine somewhere. In any case, it is how your salt is processed that is important, not where it came from.

A recipe may specify sea salt to avoid the inclusion of the additives that are common in granulated table salt. Being cubic, with six flat sides, table salt can tend to stick together, so anticaking additives like calcium silicate are added. Others include calcium carbonate, calcium phosphates, and sodium silicates. The FDA requires that these additives be less than two percent of the total product, and they are usually much less than that. While the anti-caking additives keep the salt flowing freely, they don't dissolve in water. Hence, they impart a cloudy appearance when the salt is added to water. They are, however, totally devoid of any odor or taste.

Sea salt that is really taken from the sea may have some impurities, like traces of algae, which can impart a slightly different flavor. However, the main difference between sea salt and that intended for the shaker is how the salt crystals are formed.

Sea salt crystals are created by slow evaporation of seawater. This process yields large, irregular-shaped crystals. Table salt is quickly vacuum-evaporated to produce the small uniform crystals that flow easily through the shaker holes. It's the larger crystals that give sea salt its culinary pop. The larger, flakier sea salt crystals dissolve quicker on the tongue, giving a more powerful burst of salt flavor; smaller crystals dissolve more slowly. This quality of sea salt is only important when the salt is used on a food that is about to be eaten. Once a salt has dissolved, as when used in a recipe, they all taste the same. So save your money and only use sea salt at the table, not in cooking.

## Why don't bakers like iodized salt?

Iodine was first added to salt to prevent goiter, a swelling of the thyroid gland in the neck. Certain areas of the United States have a low iodine content in the soil and thus iodine-deficient water. One such area is the Great Lakes region. In 1924, forty-seven percent of the people in Michigan had goiter! This was the first state to start adding iodine to salt.

Salt that is iodized contains one-hundredth of one percent of potassium iodide and four-hundredths of one percent of dextrose. The reason the dextrose is added is to keep the unstable potassium iodide from decomposing. Warm, humid environments can cause the oxidation of the iodine to free iodine, which will float off into the air. Dextrose is used as a reducing agent to prevent oxidation. At the high temperatures of baking, however, some of the iodine will still be oxidized. This oxidation gives off an acrid flavor that many bakers don't like in their baked goods. A lot of bakers refuse to use iodized salt in their doughs and batters.

### What are salt substitutes?

Salt is sodium chloride, right? Yes, but NaCl is not the only salt, chemically speaking. Salts are chemicals that result from a reaction of a base and an acid. Sodium chloride is the product of a reaction of hydrochloric acid with sodium hydroxide. There are many other salts of culinary importance, such as sodium nitrate, sodium nitrite, potassium nitrate (saltpeter), potassium iodide, and potassium chloride.

Table salt (sodium chloride) gets a bad rap from the sodium it contains. No one gives a hoot about the chloride component. Therefore, a good table salt substitute should be a salt that doesn't have the sodium. Potassium chloride is the salt of choice; it has no sodium but still tastes salty. It is a different kind of saltiness, though.

A product like Morton's Lite Salt Mixture contains about half sodium chloride and half potassium chloride (as well as some calcium silicate, magnesium carbonate, dextrose, and potassium iodide). Since it has half the sodium of table salt, it retains some of its unique salty taste.

A one hundred percent potassium chloride salt substitute (with additives), like NoSalt, tastes a little off. It is allowed to make the claim of containing no salt because the FDA only considers sodium chloride to be salt, when used on product labeling.

A product called Salt Sense is pure sodium chloride (with additives); however, the maker tries to trick you into thinking that it somehow contains less sodium than table salt. Their claim is that Salt Sense has thirty-three percent less sodium per teaspoon than ordinary table salt. This would be impossible, as there always has to be one atom of sodium for every atom of chloride in sodium chloride. The smoke-and-mirrors trick they play on you is to fluff up the salt, making it more flaky. By doing this, one teaspoon actually contains one-third less salt than granulated table salt crystals would. So you are getting thirty-three percent less sodium per teaspoon because you are getting thirty-three percent less salt. Pretty sneaky.

### What is BHA?

BHA and BHT are two of those food ingredients on food labels that make you scratch your head. They don't tell you what the letters stand for, much less what the stuff is doing in your food. Well, BHA, which was introduced into foods in America commercially in 1947, stands for butylated hydroxyanisole. Does that help? No? It's an antioxidant. Does that help? Okay. It gives food a longer shelf life by retarding spoilage. How does it do this? It prevents polyunsaturated oils from oxidizing and turning rancid. If that's not clear enough, just know that it keeps your food fresh longer.

BHT, the other ubiquitous food additive (the frick to BHA's frack) was introduced in 1954. It's another synthetic antioxidant called butylated hydroxytoluene. It also prevents foods from turning rancid and prevents the breakdown of fatty acids and vitamin C (ascorbic acid). BHT works as well as BHA but is much less expensive to produce.

EDTA (ethylene diaminetetra acetic acid) and TBHQ (tertiary butyl hydroquinone) are also antioxidants that you may come across in your label readings.

### What are all those other chemicals in your food?

Reading the list of ingredients on a food label for something as seemingly simple as a loaf of bread can be a mind-numbing experience. Unless you have a master's degree in chemistry, you are unlikely to know what several of the ingredients are or what they do. But don't be alarmed—food manufacturers don't put crazy chemicals into their products just to harm you. There is a good reason why each is there. Sometimes it's to make a better product; other times it's so they can save a few pennies. Anyhow, here's a list of common food additives.

- *Preservatives:* Benzoic acid, calcium propionate, potassium propionate, sodium benzoate, sodium nitrate, sodium diacetate, and sodium propionate. These keep your bread from getting moldy, and inhibit the growth of other fungi and bacteria. Not a bad thing.

- *Emulsifiers:* Lecithin, mono- and diglycerides, and polysorbates. These help other oil- or fat-containing ingredients to mix into the water base and provide baked goods with a light texture.

- *Leavening agents:* Phosphates (and of course yeast and baking powder). These help baked goods rise.

- *Sequestrants:* Help bind metals to prevent discoloration and also prevent foods from turning rancid.

- *Stabilizers* and *thickeners:* Carrageenan, derived from a seaweed called Irish moss (*Chondrus crispus*) and now more commonly from the tropical red seaweeds *Eucheuma denticulatum* and *Kappaphycus alverezii*; gum arabic; guar gum (obtained from an Indian legume); tragacanth gum; and gelatin. These help maintain emulsions. Locust bean gum gives foods like ice cream smooth, creamy textures and helps prevent ice crystal formation. Xanthan gum comes from corn sugar and is used in dairy products and salad dressings.

- *Humectants:* Glycerine and propylene glycol. These help foods like marshmallows retain moisture.

- *pH Control Agents:* Acetic acid, ammonium alginate, lactic acid, phosphoric acid, sodium citrate, and tartaric acid. These help to change or maintain a food's pH (acidity or alkalinity).

### Why did Gerber add MSG to baby food?

Believe it or not, Gerber added MSG to their baby foods in 1951, not to make them taste better for baby but to make them better tasting to mother. They realized that many mothers tasted baby food before feeding it to their infants. If it tasted good to mothers, they were more likely to buy the food for their babies.

## When did we become concerned with vitamins?

We are a society seemingly consumed with health and nutrition, but a hundred years ago we didn't even know that vitamins existed. It wasn't until the turn of the twentieth century that vitamins started to be discovered. In 1905, Englishman Dr. William Fletcher discovered that when special factors were removed from food, disease occurred. He was studying the causes of the disease beriberi and found that people eating polished rice would get it, those eating unpolished rice did not. Obviously, there was some special nutritive value found within the husk of the rice.

In 1912, Polish researcher Cashmir Funk isolated thiamine from rice husks. This led him to name the special nutritional parts of food "vitamines," after "vita," meaning life, and "amine," for the compounds found in thiamine.They were called vitamines until it was discovered, in 1920, by British biochemist J. C. Drummond, that they are not all amines. He began calling them "vitamins" and named the fat-soluble vitamin "A," the water-soluble vitamin "B," and the antiscorbutic vitamin "C."

Food companies jumped on the vitamin bandwagon as a way to promote the health properties of their products. Fleischmann's, for example, claimed four cakes a day of their vitamin B–rich yeast would rid the body of poisons; cure acne, constipation, indigestion, and fallen stomach; and increase energy. (The Federal Trade Commission enjoined Standard Brands, makers of Fleischmann's yeast from making such claims in 1938.)

In 1922, E. V. McCollum isolated vitamin D. He discovered its use in treating rickets. In 1926, it was learned that sunlight converts the sterol ergosterol into vitamin D and thus explained why children who don't get enough sunlight are susceptible to rickets. (A 1929 survey found that thirty percent of children in Baltimore suffered from the disease.) It was also later found to help add calcium and phosphate to bones. Vitamin D was being added to milk by the 1940s. The dairy industry started calling milk the "perfect food." It was not just for kids anymore, but for the whole family. The effectiveness of their advertising can be seen in the fact that during World War I, coffee was the soldiers' favorite drink. By World War II, milk was the preferred drink of GIs.

## What was the "morale" vitamin?

Between 1939 and 1940, researchers at the Mayo Clinic in Minnesota conducted tests on vitamin B1 (thiamine). They put some teens on a diet high in B1 and some on a low B1 diet. It was found that the teens on the B1-deficient diet were more "surly" and "uncooperative." (Sounds like a normal teen.) This concerned the government because white bread has most of its B1 removed during milling. They ordered millers to restore vitamin B1 to white flour and also add in riboflavin and iron. This would help to strengthen the population in case of an enemy attack during the war.

## How did vitamins hurt the food industry?

"Vita" means "life" and most people thought vitamins would add pep to theirs. If getting a little bit of vitamins in various foods was good, taking strong doses of vitamins in tablet form must be even better. The pharmaceutical industry cashed in on this mentality much to the chagrin of doctors, who thought people would begin to treat themselves. Likewise, the food industry wasn't too pleased, since they couldn't tout the benefits of their product's vitamin content like they used to. They had to advertise the other health benefits of their foods, if any.

The appeal of being able to take a little pill without a prescription, and somehow become more healthy, is very great to many people. By 1989, some sixty million Americans were popping vitamins daily to make up for poor eating habits or to offset the deleterious effects of smoking, drinking, or the stress of daily life.

# 18

# Kitchen Science

### How can two cups of sugar dissolve into one cup of water?

Water is not as dense as you may think—its molecules are not that tightly packed together. There is plenty of room between them to squeeze in other molecules, such as those of sugar. So when sugar dissolves into water, it is filling the spaces in between the water molecules and not really taking up more space. In fact, water is so accommodating of sugar that when heated, it is possible to dissolve up to five cups of sugar into a cup of water.

### What does "partially hydrogenated" mean?

You have probably seen the words "partially hydrogenated oil" if you ever read the label on a tub of margarine. Hydrogenation is the addition, under pressure, of extra hydrogen atoms into an oil. What the extra hydrogen atoms do is to make the oil more saturated. The extra hydrogen bonds thicken the oil somewhat. Without hydrogenation, your margarine would be a liquid and you could pour it onto your toast. If your margarine's oil were fully hydrogenated—crammed with as many hydrogen atoms as will fit—it would turn into a solid. By partially hydrogenating the oil, at about twenty percent, a nice spreadable consistency is achieved.

### Is tomato sauce corrosive?

Tomato sauce contains citric acid, which can act as a corrosive, especially on aluminum. If you cook tomatoes or tomato sauce in an aluminum pot, the tomato acids can dissolve some of the aluminum, giving a metallic taste to your food. This is because aluminum is an "active metal," which is prone to attack by acids.

Another interesting phenomenon involving tomato sauce and aluminum occurs when you cover leftover lasagne that's in a metal container with foil. After a while, the sauce can actually begin to eat holes in the foil. This, however, is not due to corrosion, but because of an electrolytic process. Believe it or not, if the container is made of a metal other than aluminum, the combination of the different metals and the sauce create a crude battery; current will be conducted from one metal to the other, through the sauce. The metal in the container is likely to hold on to its electrons rather tenaciously, while the aluminum in the foil does not. Therefore, a current is formed with electrons from the aluminum flowing to the metal container. Aluminum atoms that have lost electrons are easily dissolved in the sauce. Thus, wherever the foil touches the sauce, it will begin to be dissolved away.

### Why is a marble surface recommended for rolling out pastry dough?

Pastry dough has a high butter (or other shortening) content and should be kept cool while handling, to prevent melting, which can ruin your best efforts to achieve a flaky result. Marble surfaces and rolling pins are recommended for rolling out pastry dough instead of wooden surfaces, because marble is "colder." Well, marble isn't really any colder, but it does feel colder.

Wood is a poor conductor of heat; marble is a much better heat conductor. Touch a piece of wood that is at room temperature and it feels neither hot nor cold. Now touch a piece of marble. It will feel much colder, even though it is at the same actual temperature as the wood. This is because the marble will carry heat away from your skin much faster than the wood can. Likewise, the marble will carry the heat produced by the rolling action away from the dough and prevent the shortening from melting. If you really want to work on a cold kitchen surface, try stainless steel. It is a much better heat conductor than even marble.

## Why aren't microwave ovens good at melting ice?

Microwaves heat foods by agitating their water molecules, causing them to flip back and forth and spin rapidly. This causes the molecules to jostle each other; the bumping around has the effect of speeding up the molecules and creating the heat that cooks the food. In ice, the water molecules are bound tightly together in a crystal matrix. This makes it hard for microwaves to get the molecules spinning.

So how do microwaves defrost dinner? Since they can't really act on the water molecules in your frozen roast, the microwaves act on other molecules in the food. By heating them, the ice crystals begin to melt and the process proceeds from there.

## Why does microwaved food seem to cool off faster?

Does your microwaved food seem to get cold faster than food cooked in a conventional oven? As we discussed above, many times foods cooked in a microwave are not evenly heated. This means there are hot areas and cooler areas. So your food isn't as hot to begin with as it would have been from a conventional oven that heats more evenly throughout. Another reason is that microwaves only heat the food, not the container that holds them, like a conventional oven does. The hot container helps keep the food hot by radiating heat into it even after being removed from the oven.

## Is kettle-boiled water hotter than microwaved water?

Boiling water is boiling water, right? Well, not really. Water boiling in a kettle probably is at 212°F throughout. This is because the water being heated at the bottom rises up, pushing the cooler water at the top downward. This up and down cycle continues, keeping the heat evenly distributed.

In microwave-heated water, things work a little differently. We usually heat water by the cup in a microwave. Since microwaves can only penetrate about one inch into the water, all around the cup, there will be some cooler water at the center when the water begins to boil at the top. The water in the center of the cup is heated more slowly, as the hot water around it raises its temperature. This is why you have to stir many dishes halfway through the cooking process when microwaving.

Maybe you don't care if the water at the center of your cup is at 212°F when you take it out, but it could affect the beverage you are preparing. With instant coffee or cocoa it's no big deal. However, you tea lovers will be losing out on flavor and caffeine if you steep your bag in water that is not as hot as it can possibly be. For the perfect cup of tea, connoisseurs recommend boiling your water in a kettle and pre-heating your cup so it doesn't lower the water temperature too much.

## Why does milk form a skin when heated?

If you've ever boiled milk to make hot chocolate, you know all about this. When milk is boiled it starts to evaporate. The evaporation of water leaves a concentration of protein and calcium at the milk's surface. The protein coagulates, forming the skin. By skimming off the skin you are also removing some valuable nutrients. Try to keep the milk just below a boil to avoid skin formation, or keep stirring the milk or keep it covered, both of which will slow down evaporation.

Another problem with boiling milk is that it is easily scorched. This is because casein and whey proteins will precipitate to the bottom of the pan and burn.

## What are the only two alkalines used in the kitchen?

You probably already knew baking soda was an alkaline, but the other one—egg albumen—may come as a surprise. Before leaving the hen, the albumen has a pH of around 7.7, which is slightly alkaline. However, it begins to rise to near 9.9 shortly after laying. The higher the albumen's pH, the clearer the white part of the egg will be. A cloudy albumen, then, is a good sign of a really fresh egg.

Eggs are washed after being laid at the egg farm. This removes their protective waxy coating and can speed up the pH change. To keep the eggs fresher longer, commercial growers coat the eggs with mineral oil after washing. This slows water loss and extends shelf life.

### Why do apples turn brown when you cut them?

Many fruits and vegetables turn brown when their tissues are broken by cutting or bruising—apples, avocados, bananas, eggplants, mushrooms, pears, and potatoes, to name a few. The browning is the result of a an enzyme that oxidizes phenolic compounds contained in the plant cells. When the plant cells are broken, these two chemicals come together and react to form brown or gray polymers. (A somewhat similar chemical reaction takes place in our skin when we are exposed to direct sunlight.) Citrus fruits and tomatoes do not contain this enzyme so they don't brown quickly when their cells are ruptured.

### How did the browning of fruits lead to the discovery of vitamin C?

In the mid-1920s, a Hungarian biochemist named Albert Szent-Györgyi investigated why people afflicted with adrenal gland disorders turn brown. He wondered if there was any correlation between the browning of patients and the browning of certain cut fruits. His studies led him to discover that the juices of fruits that don't turn brown would prevent the cuts on browning fruits from discoloring. When he isolated the agent that delayed the browning, he had discovered vitamin C.

### Why do bananas turn black in the refrigerator?

There is a general rule of thumb when storing produce: fruits and vegetables from the colder climates like to be stored at cooler temperatures than do their tropical cousins. Vegetables like beets, cabbage, carrots, lettuce, radishes, and spinach, which grow best in cool weather, last better when stored at temperatures just above freezing. Tropical and warm weather produce, like avocados, beans, cucumbers, eggplants, lemons, oranges, pineapples, squash, and tomatoes, are happier kept at around 50°F. Some kinds of produce prefer room temperature.

At refrigerator temperatures, bananas will experience damage to their cell structure. As we mentioned above, this will release enzymes that cause the skin to darken considerably. Avocados and oranges don't fare much better in the fridge and also suffer from discolorization. So how do we meet the particular storage needs of all these kinds of produce? (See next question.)

### Why does your refrigerator have that "crisper" drawer?

All modern refrigerators have that special "crisper" drawer, but what makes it different from the other areas of your fridge? As just mentioned, fruits and vegetables continue to respire in the refrigerator, albeit at a slower rate. If stored in a dry environment, they will experience greater water loss (dehydration) than if kept in a humid chamber, i.e. your crisper drawer. These "breathing" produce also need oxygen. While keeping your produce in a plastic bag will keep the humidity high, it will deprive it of oxygen. In the absence of air, produce will switch over to anaerobic respiration, which will do it no good. Alcohols will be formed that will cause brown spots under the skin of fruits like apples and pears. Best to put them in old-fashioned, low-tech paper bags, which will maintain a high humidity but also allow air in and out.

# 19

# Kitchenware

*When did people start using stoves?*

The first iron cooking stove was patented in 1819 by Vermont inventor John Conant. He had no luck in selling them, as women were so used to cooking at the hearth. President Millard Fillmore had a stove put in the White House kitchen in 1850 and his cooks refused to use it. Experts from the Patent Office had to show them how to control the heat using the dampers before they would give up cooking in the fireplace.

The wood-burning kitchen range was grudgingly accepted by women toward the end of the 1800s. It had the drawback of making the kitchen hard to keep clean and the wood was expensive and took up a lot of storage space in small urban kitchens. By the turn of the century, the coal stove, first patented in 1833, was gaining in popularity. Coal stoves were even dirtier than wood stoves, but coal was cheaper and took up less storage space.

In the 1910s, porcelain-coated stoves with legs were the next big innovation. The porcelain coating saved on hours spent scouring the black soot off of cast iron stoves; in addition, that they were up on legs made cleaning behind and under these new stoves a snap in comparison to those that sat on the floor.

Finally, in the 1920s, most city kitchens were equipped with clean, efficient gas stoves. Electric stoves, first patented in the 1890s, came on the scene in 1910 but didn't catch on until the 1930s. The self-cleaning oven was introduced in 1963.

## What is the difference between a convection oven and an induction oven?

Both ovens are rather expensive. The induction oven is something new, while convection ovens have been around longer. Most chefs like convection ovens and have used them for years. A convection oven has a fan on the back wall that circulates the heat all around the food to cook it evenly and quickly. Cooking times and temperatures are generally reduced by twenty-five percent in convection ovens.

Induction ovens are an entirely new way to heat food. They cook using the magnetic transfer principle, which causes heat to be transferred from the burner to the pot by means of magnetic force. They can boil two quarts of water in one minute and are very safe. You can put a paper towel between the burner and the pot and it won't get hot. You must use metal pots that are magnetic, such as stainless steel; glass and copper will not work. These ovens start at around eight hundred dollars and may be the future of cooking.

## How do water filters work?

The little water filter attached to your faucet or water supply line probably contains a combination of charcoal and ion exchange resins. The charcoal does most of the work in removing the more nasty contaminants. The reason charcoal is so good at filtering out water impurities is that it has the ability to adsorb, or grab a hold of, contaminant molecules like chlorine or pesticides. Charcoal is able to do this because it has an incredible amount of surface area.

Charcoal is made by heating wood in a low oxygen environment, so it doesn't burn but rather decomposes into porous carbon. An ounce of activated charcoal has a microscopic internal surface area of about two thousand square feet. That's a lot of room for unwanted molecules to stick to. Charcoal, however, does not remove positive ions (metals), like cadmium, calcium, copper, magnesium, mercury, and zinc.

Another way to filter water is by using ion exchange resins.

Never heard of them? Well, they remove the metal ions that charcoal can't. These resins are little plasticlike granules. They exchange their loosely bound positive ions of hydrogen or sodium for the positively charged metal ions, which become trapped in the resin. This process not only removes the metals but also keeps your water from becoming negatively charged, which is what would happen if the positive ions were removed without being replaced. Since fluoride is a negatively charged ion, it is not affected by these resins.

### If nothing sticks to Teflon, how does Teflon stick to cookware?

Aside from the microwave oven, the greatest kitchen invention in the last fifty years might be Teflon. Nothing sticks to this stuff, so cooking, and cleaning up pots and pans is much easier than it was in grandma's day. But if it is so slippery, how does it stick to the pan?

Teflon is a trademark of DuPont. It is a plastic material known as polytetrafluoroethylene that was accidentally discovered by chemist Roy Joseph Plunkett while working on refrigerants. The secret to Teflon's slipperiness are the fluorine atoms that encircle its molecules. The fluorine atoms repel almost all other materials, preventing them from sticking to Teflon.

DuPont makes Teflon adhere to pans by a process called "sintering" in which the Teflon is heated to melting and pressed firmly on the cookware surface. To ensure the best possible grip, the side of the Teflon that they want to stick to the pan is bombarded with ions in a vacuum under an electric field (plasma) to break away the fluorine atoms. They can then substitute other atoms, such as oxygen, that adhere strongly to metal surfaces.

### How did people keep food cold before refrigerators?

Before refrigeration, people with access to ice used it to keep perishables fresh a little longer. It was usually those with money who could afford to collect ice from frozen ponds and store it in underground icehouses. The ice was packed in salt and wrapped in hay or sawdust to insulate it for summer use. Most folks, however, didn't have any means of keeping their food chilled until the invention of the icebox.

A Maryland farmer named Thomas Moore patented the first icebox in 1803. It consisted of a wooden box within a wooden box, with charcoal placed between them as insulation. It had an upper tin compartment for the ice and a lower section for food storage, and was in wide use by 1840. Most later iceboxes were wooden boxes lined with tin or zinc and insulated with various materials including cork, sawdust, or seaweed. A drip pan was placed below the icebox and had to be emptied daily. Natural ice was commercially harvested and sold by icemen, whose wagons roamed city streets. To order ice, one put a card in the front window of the house with a number on it, indicating the amount of ice desired. In the mid-1800s, two dollars would buy fifteen pounds of ice a day for a month.

The natural ice industry was big business in the United States and Europe. By 1890, America was exporting twenty-five million tons of lake-cut ice a year. It was even shipped to the Caribbean and used to make ice cream.

## Who invented the refrigerator?

The idea of keeping food cold by using evaporative cooling goes all the way back to the Romans, who used wet terra-cotta pots fanned by slaves to cool their food. In the nineteenth century, several inventors experimented with the cooling properties of various gases when evaporated under pressure. In 1823, Londoner Michael Faraday discovered that certain gases, when kept under constant pressure, will condense until they become cold. This basic principle was the foundation of the development of modern refrigeration.

In 1834, American inventor Jacob Perkins, working in England, came up with a gas compressor. A volatile liquid was allowed to evaporate into a gas by absorbing heat from its surroundings. When the gas was compressed, it would turn back into a liquid, releasing heat back to its surroundings. By having the compressor circulate on and off, alternately compressing a gas back into a liquid, releasing heat, then allowing the liquid to expand back into a gas again, enough heat could be extracted from the expansion area to cool water until it froze. In 1855 the first successfully applied refrigerating compressor was developed in Australia (they don't have much natural ice there) by James Harrison. He wanted to cool beer being brewed. His compressed ether machine was not practical for wide-scale use, however. In 1858, Frenchman Ferdinand Carré invented the first refrigeration machine that used liquid ammonia. He brought it to the 1862 London Exhibition and demonstrated its ice-making capabilities. It had many industrial users.

The first practical and portable refrigeration machine was perfected by a German, Carl von Linde, in the 1870s. The first commercially successful electric refrigerator was made in the U.S. by inventor Fred W. Wolf in 1913. It was designed to be attached to the top of one's ice box. Early refrigerators, such as the Kelvinator, introduced in 1916, and dozens of others that sprang up around the same time, had compressors that were driven by belts attached to motors situated in the basement or an adjoining room. These were more for commercial applications than for home use. Kelvinator had an eighty percent share of the electric refrigerator market in 1923.

The first self-contained electric refrigerator—the "Guardian Frigerator"—was invented in 1915 by Alfred Mellowes, working in a Ft. Wayne, Indiana, backyard wash house. It differed from other early refrigerators in being self-contained, with the compressor situated in the bottom of the cabinet. Mellowes set up shop in Detroit and tried to make a go of it in the refrigerator business. He produced his first unit for sale in 1916, but only managed to make forty in his first two years and faced bankruptcy. In 1918, W. C. Durant, the president of General Motors, bought Mellowes' company for $56,000 and began selling Mellowes' creation as the "Michigan Frigidaire," a name chosen from a contest run by GM. Applying the mass production techniques of the automobile industry allowed General Motors to really crank out refrigerators in a hurry. By 1929, one million Frigidaires had been manufactured and the name had become synonymous with the refrigerator.

Other electric refrigerators were already available, but none of them would find many customers right away. With price tags around $900, they cost as much as a car.

In 1927, the monitor-top refrigerator was brought out by General Electric. It had its motor on top and was maintenance-free. By 1934, the compressor was enclosed within the unit and the modern refrigerator was created. At $600 a pop, it was a tough sell. Mass production helped to lower the price to a more manageable $90 by World War II, but it wasn't until after the war that American prosperity allowed the masses to afford this convenience. By 1956, eighty percent of American homes had refrigerators.

Innovations like automatic defrost and automatic icemakers appeared in the 1950s and 1960s. The through-the-door ice and water dispensers were introduced by General Electric in 1969. Today, the refrigerator is the number one kitchen appliance, found in 99.5 percent of homes.

## How does a refrigerator work?

This one indispensable part of our modern lives is the one we probably take the most for granted. Most of us don't even know the basics of how it works. To understand your refrigerator, it is easier to think of it as a machine that removes heat from the air rather than cooling the air. Modern refrigerators have four main components: a compressor, a condenser, a metering device, and an evaporator.

The compressor is a motor, usually found at the bottom of the refrigerator, that (as its name implies) compresses a gaseous refrigerant from a low-pressure state to a high-pressure state. It turns on and off as the thermostat calls for cooling.

The condenser is a series of tubes with fins, kind of like a radiator. The high-pressure refrigerant gas flows through the condenser and becomes a liquid as it cools. Many refrigerators have the condenser on the back. If it is located elsewhere, there will be a fan that blows air over it to dissipate the heat generated when the refrigerant changes states from a gas to a liquid. Originally, sulfur dioxide, ammonia, and other dangerous gases were used. In 1931, Freon 12 (dichlorodifluoromethane) replaced these gases in Frigidaires and soon thereafter in most other brands. Freon remained the refrigerant of choice until it was discovered that chlorofluorocarbons have an adverse effect on the ozone layer.

The metering device is a tiny copper capillary tube that runs from the condenser to the evaporator. It controls the pressure and flow of the refrigerant as it enters the evaporator.

The evaporator, which is usually found within the freezer compartment, also resembles a radiator with larger tubes than the capillary tube. As the liquid refrigerant leaves the tiny capillary tube and enters the bigger tubes of the evaporator, its pressure drops, allowing it to expand back into the gaseous state, thus absorbing heat. The gaseous refrigerant travels through the evaporator, back out of the refrigerator, and down to the compressor, where the whole process begins anew. Because it absorbs heat, the evaporator becomes very cold. A fan in the freezer compartment circulates the air to maintain a constant temperature in the freezer and refrigerator.

Got all that? It's just a little elementary physics. Well, no matter. All you have to do is plug your fridge in and forget about it.

## How does your ice maker work?

For those of you who are *really* curious about what goes on inside your fridge, read on and learn how ice "cubes" are made automatically. Gone are the days of constantly filling ice cube trays with water at the sink and schleping them over to the fridge, spilling water along the way. Now ice just appears, as if by magic, neatly piled in a plastic bin.

The process begins when the ice-maker unit sends a signal to the water fill valve—on the lower back side of the fridge—to open and allow water to flow into the ice maker's water tray. When the proper amount of water is delivered, the ice maker tells the valve to shut. A small thermostat located near the water tray determines when the water is frozen, usually at about 10 to 15°F.

Then a little heater is activated beneath the tray to warm the ice cubes enough so that they can move freely. A sweep fork then rotates and pushes the cubes up and out of the tray. As the cubes are falling into the storage bin, a metal wire arm (the thing that looks like a coat hanger) moves up and out of the way. After the cubes have fallen, the wire arm moves back down. If the bin is full, the wire cannot move down and the ice maker is turned off. Once enough cubes have been used to allow the arm to lower once again, the process begins anew.

## How do today's freezers self-defrost?

If you are older than thirty-five or forty, you may remember the days when people had to defrost the freezer compartment of their refrigerators. After a time, a thick crust of ice would build up all around the inside of the freezer unit. To get rid of it, you had to turn off the freezer, remove the food, and put in pans of boiling water to help it melt away. Some would simply try chopping it off, although this could damage the freezer. Happily, those days are long gone. Modern freezers magically defrost themselves. How do they do it?

Your freezer has a timer that turns off the cooling system of the refrigerator and turns on the defrost heater about once every six to eight hours. The defrost heater is similar to the burner on an electric stove. It is located just beneath the cooling coils, which are found behind a panel in the freezer compartment. When it heats up, any ice forming near the cooling coils melts. The water from the melted ice drips into a trough that is connected to a tube that runs down to a pan at the bottom of the refrigerator. There it is evaporated by a fan that blows warm air from the compressor motor over the pan and out the front of the refrigerator.

When the temperature of the freezer nears 32°F, a sensor turns off the heater. Thus, the food frozen in your freezer is not really maintained at a constant temperature.

## Who invented the Mason jar?

A guy named Mason, of course. A New York metalworker named John Landis Mason received a patent for the jar bearing his name on November 30, 1858. The glass jar with the threaded top and a zinc lid with a threaded ring sealer was a vast improvement over the other jars of the time, which were sealed with cork and wax. Rural families were able to reduce their dependence on root cellars and smokehouses to survive the winter. Urban families also used Mason jars to put up fruits and vegetables.

Poor John Mason, however, never realized the riches of his invention. His patent expired before he could capitalize on it, and he died destitute. In 1887, the Ball brothers of Muncie, Indiana, realized Mason's dream when they began producing Ball-Mason jars. As a nod to Mason's patent, their glass jars bore the mark "Patented Nov. 30, 1858."

## What female socialite invented the dishwasher?

Fed up with her servants chipping her fine china dishes, socialite Josephine Cochrane started washing them herself. Indignant about having to do such lowly work, she invented a hand-operated dishwashing machine in 1886; it had water jets and a rack to hold the china firmly in place. She unveiled it at the 1893 Columbian Exposition, where it was used in the fair's huge kitchens, but only hotels and restaurants showed an interest. The company she founded would become Kitchenaid in 1940.

The first direct-drive home dishwasher was sold by General Electric in 1927. Its basic operating principle is still in use today. The "modern" electric dishwasher was first offered for sale in 1949 but sales stank. It took several years to really catch on. By the end of the 1960s, however, two million units were in kitchens across America.

## When did the electric mixer first appear?

The first electric mixer was patented by Rufus W. Eastman in 1885. It ran on either electric or water power. In 1911, L. H. Hamilton, Chester Beach, and Fred Osirus patented their mixer. The first truly acceptable home mixer—the Sunbeam Mixmaster—was introduced in 1930. It was not portable, but was a far cry from its ponderous, industrially derived predecessors.

## What woman invented the drip coffeemaker?

In 1907, a housewife in Dresden, Germany—Melitta Bentz—created the first drip coffee filter while trying to brew a perfect cup of coffee with none of the bitterness of over-brewed coffee. She took a brass pot, punched a hole in the bottom, and lined it with her son's school blotter paper. By putting coffee grounds on top of the paper and pouring boiling water over them, she made better-tasting coffee. Her husband, Hugo, got a tinsmith to make tin pots with holes in the bottom and the first drip coffeemakers were born.

In 1909, they sold twelve hundred at the Leipzig Fair. Melitta improved upon her design in 1912, using a cone-shaped pot with conical paper. Their business—the Melitta Bentz Company—made further improvements, patenting and marketing the filter bag in 1937. It didn't reach America until 1964.

Mr. Coffee invented the automatic drip process in 1972. They became the best-selling domestic model, a position they still hold today.

## Who invented the soup ladle?

Some things you wouldn't think would have to be invented, but they do. Before the duc de Montaussier, the French dauphin's governor, invented the soup ladle in 1695, people around the table would just take soup from the tureen using their own spoons, or they would pass around a bowl from which each person would sip. As is also the case with many new ideas that seem so obvious that you wonder why they were not invented before, some French people derided the soup ladle as unnecessary or inappropriate. Silly, yes, but keep in mind this was a time when most folks didn't even own a fork, much less use one. Eating with the fingers from communal dishes was the norm.

## When did we start eating toast for breakfast?

In the early 1900s, many homes were beginning to have electricity. At the same time, many middle-class women were losing their household help to better paying office and factory jobs. For the housewife looking for help in the kitchen, electric appliances were just the thing. Electric grills, skillets, toasters, and waffle irons were all displayed to the public at the 1911 New York Electric Exhibition. The electric companies were keen on promoting as many household uses for their energy as possible. They especially pushed for the use of appliances in the morning, when energy usage was normally low. Most consumers only used power at night, for illumination.

In order to increase morning electricity usage, the companies tried to sell the public on toast for breakfast, although it wasn't considered a breakfast food at the time. When people did toast bread, they used an open flame and a toasting fork, or a toasting rack that was used over a gas flame. Compton and Company of Britain sold the first electric toaster in 1893. General Electric began selling an electric toaster in America in 1908. It had a wire body set on a porcelain base, which held the bread close to bare electric coils. It sold for $1.45 and only toasted one side of the bread at a time. Charles Strite invented the automatic pop-up toaster in 1918. It also only toasted one side of bread at a time, and it was several years before the modern toaster arrived. The chrome Toastmaster Model 1A1, an automatic, one-slice, set-the-button toaster, for home use, hit the market in 1926. It was made by the Waters-Genter Company and sold for $12.50. (Amazingly, you can still buy a toaster for this much.) The first automatic pop-up toaster—the Toastmaster—was sold by McGraw Electric Company of Minneapolis in 1926. Its price was $13.50.

One thing that held back the sale of the early toaster was the fact that it predated the introduction of pre-sliced bread. After Wonder pre-sliced bread revolutionized the world, in 1930, toast became much easier to make.

### When did other kitchen aids first appear?

- *Coffee percolator:* It was invented in 1827 in France and allowed water to continually flow over the coffee grounds.

- *Bakelite:* The world's first polymer was invented by chemist Leo Baekeland in 1909. Bakelite is a plastic made from formaldehyde and phenol that does not transfer heat. It was used to make the handles of pots and pans much safer.

- *Waring blender:* Bandleader Fred Waring started to market this F. J. Osius invention in 1938. He took it on the road with his band and set up minibars at all his stops to demonstrate its usefulness.

- *Waffle iron:* It was patented on August 24, 1869, by Cornelius Swarthout of Troy, New York.

- *Garbage disposal:* This was invented by an architect for his wife in 1927. It took John W. Hammonds ten years to perfect his design. His company was called the In-Sink-Erator Manufacturing Company.

- *Pressure cooker:* In 1679, a French physicist named Denis Papin invented the pressure cooker, an air-tight cooker that steam-cooked food under pressure.

- *Cuisinart food processor:* It was introduced by Carl Sontheimer at the National Housewares Exposition in Chicago in 1973. Sontheimer redesigned Pierre Verdun's industrial-strength food preparation machine to make it more consumer friendly, although a price of $140 wasn't. Sales were flat until he won praises from Julia Child, James Beard, and Craig Claiborne, who wrote a rave review of the Cuisinart in his nationally syndicated column in the *New York Times*.

### What's the difference between a pot and a pan?

This one is easy, if you think about it. A pot has two opposing handles and a lid; a pan has one long handle and may or may not have a lid.

Now that you know what pots and pans are, do you want to know how to safely use them? Here are a few common-sense safety tips on stovetop cooking.

- Never cook while wearing loose-hanging jewelry that can get caught on the aforementioned handles.
- Always turn said handles in toward the stove to avoid accidentally knocking them over.
- Don't wear loose-hanging clothing that may catch fire while cooking on the stovetop.

### How did Pyrex get its name?

Our Pyrex dishes of today had their origin in an early Corning Glass product, used in lantern globes and battery jars, called "Nonex," for "non-expanding." This low-expansion glass was developed in 1908 by Corning scientist Dr. Eugene Sullivan using borosilicate glass. Its cooking potential was realized in 1913 by Dr. Jesse T. Littleton of Corning when he cut down a Nonex battery jar and gave it to his wife Becky to bake a casserole in. It survived the oven temperatures as well as the traditional ceramic cookware of the time. Nonex had its lead content removed and Corning started making cookware out of it. They had their new ovenware tested by Sarah Tyson Rorer, director of the Philadelphia Cooking School and culinary editor of *Ladies Home Journal*.

The first product marketed under the Pyrex name was a nine-inch circular pie plate. Some say the word "Pyrex" comes from the word "pie"; others claim Pyrex is a technical derivative of the Greek word *pyra*, meaning "hearth." The "ex" ending, from Nonex, had valuable brand-name recognition.

### What is Corelle?

Corelle Living Ware was introduced by Corning in 1970. This dinnerware was revolutionary in that it was break-resistant. The company guaranteed to replace, free of charge, any piece that broke in the first two years. Made of two different glass compositions laminated into a three-layer sandwich, Corelle Ware had the look and feel of china. It even "pinged" when you flicked it with your finger. Corelle quickly obliterated the low-cost plastic competition; in the first two years, sales topped sixty million pieces; by 1996, two billion had been sold.

## What kitchenware company has had its products exhibited in the Smithsonian and the Metropolitan Museum of Art?

Sam Faber was inspired to design ergonomic kitchen utensils after his wife developed arthritis. Perhaps the most annoying kitchen gadget of the time was the peeler. The handles on the old ones are ridiculous. They are a simple round swiveling rod with a knife blade for peeling and are extremely uncomfortable and clumsy to use. Made of flimsy metal, they are almost impossible to get a firm grip on. Faber solved this problem, and dozens of others, by sticking user-friendly handles on everyday kitchen tools. His handles are bigger and are coated with Santoprene—a processed rubber used in dishwasher gaskets. Embedded fins on the oversized handles bend to conform to the users hands and make for a sure grip even when wet.

His company—OXO—launched their first fifteen products in 1990. They now sell over 450. Not only are their tools a joy to hold, they are a joy to behold. They have won many awards for design and have been exhibited at these venerable museums.

## Who invented cellophane?

A Swiss chemist named Jacques Brandenberger invented cellophane in 1908 while trying to find a way to make stain-proof tablecloths. He coated them with a film he had concocted, but no one was interested in his table coverings. The viscose film coating had possibilities, though. It took Brandenberger ten years to develop a machine that could make thin sheets of the stuff, which he called "cellophane." The name is a combination of "cello," from cellulose, and "phane," from the French word *diaphane*, which means transparent. In 1927, a waterproof lacquer coating was added, making cellophane ideal for kitchen use. Cellophane-wrapped meat was first offered for sale in 1940 by A&P.

## What indispensable kitchen product was first used to coat airplanes?

Saran polyvinylidene chloride (or Saran) was accidentally discovered by a Dow Chemical lab worker named Ralph Wiley in

1933. Ralph was a college student who was paid to clean up the lab's glassware. One day he happened upon a test tube that was coated with a material that he could not scrub off, try as he might. He gave his find to Dow researchers, who turned it into a greasy, dark green film that they called "Saran." This new substance was impervious to oxygen, moisture, and chemicals, and withstood heating. It was used to coat airplanes during World War II to protect them from salt.

After the war, Dow found consumer uses for Saran. They made it clear and sold it for home use in 1953. S. C. Johnson now markets Saran-brand products. Baggies made their debut in 1957; boiling bags in 1961; Handi Food bags in 1964; and Ziploc storage bags in 1972.

## When did aluminum foil make its way into the kitchen?

The other food wrap in our lives was also born out of World War II. Before the war, aluminum foil was used as a packaging material; during the war, there was a great military demand for aluminum. When the war ended, Reynolds Metals Company was stuck with a surplus. What to do? They pressed it into thin twenty-five-foot rolls and started selling it for home use in 1947.

Aluminum comes from bauxite, an ore rich in aluminum oxide, or alumina. By mixing bauxite with lime and caustic soda and heating, the alumina can be extracted. This white powdery substance is then dissolved in a bath and an electric current is run through it to cause the aluminum to precipitate out.

Reynolds Wrap foil is 98.5 percent aluminum. The balance is primarily iron and silicon, which are added to give the foil strength and puncture resistance.

## Who invented the paper napkin?

Scott Paper introduced the Sani-Towels paper towel in 1907. They were not intended to be used in the kitchen but were designed to help stop the spread of germs in Philadelphia classrooms. Scott finally marketed the paper towel as a boon to kitchen sanitation in 1931. Paper napkins also were brought out in the 1930s.

## Who invented straws?

Before the invention of the soda bottle drinking straws were not really needed. They were invented in 1888. The first one was made by winding a strip of paper around a pencil and holding it together with glue. The same basic technique was used by Marvin C. Stone of Washington, D.C., when he patented the first wax-coated drinking straw. The handmade process gave way to automation when his Stone Straw Company created a straw-winding machine in 1906.

# 20

# Packaging

## Who invented the tin can?

Maybe the one invention of the nineteenth century that had the most dramatic impact on the eating habits of Americans was that of the tin can. Before cans came along, people could only eat perishable fruits and vegetables that were in season and generally only ones grown in their region. People in Maine, for example, never really enjoyed pineapples; folks in Ohio found seafood hard to come by. The advent of the canning industry opened whole new culinary worlds to many Americans.

The genesis of the canning industry began in 1795, with a French confectioner named Nicholas Appert. He was trying to win a prize of twelve thousand francs, which was being offered by Napoleon Bonaparte to whoever could come up with a way of preventing military foods from spoiling. He discovered that heating foods that were sealed in glass bottles helped to preserve them, and he won the prize. Around 1806, the French navy took Appert's experiments and ran real-world trials with meat, vegetables, and fruit.

In 1810, Englishman Peter Durand came along and patented a method of sealing food in airtight tin-plated wrought iron cans. The food in the cans had to be steam-heated at a high enough temperature to kill any microbes, but couldn't require heating for too long, which would reduce the food's flavor and nutrient content. The ideal temperature was between 240°F and 250°F. Different foods are heated for varying lengths of time, depending on their density, acidity, and ability to transfer heat; for example, green beans must be heated longer than tomatoes but not as long as pumpkin or corn. Some meats, like tuna, are cooked before being canned to soften their flesh.

Tin cans were first made by hand in the early nineteenth century by tinsmiths. The making of cans by hand was a time-consuming job. The smith had to cut strips of metal for the sides and circular pieces for the top and bottom; these were then soldered together. A good tinsmith could only make about fifty cans a day. By 1849, inventors had devised machines to punch out the tops and bottoms of cans and a machine to do the soldering. This improved the tinsmith's production to about 750 cans a day. Food companies employed their own smiths to meet their can needs.

When the Civil War erupted, there was a huge increase in demand for canned foods. The soldiers became accustomed to eating unspoiled foods out of cans and out of season. After the war, millions of cans of beans, corn, and tomatoes were sold each year. By the 1880s, the whole process of soldering had been mechanized and companies that specialized in the manufacture of cans replaced the individual tinsmiths working for the food-processing companies.

Today, over 200 billion cans of food are made each year. The top-selling canned fruits, in order, are peaches, applesauce, pineapple, and fruit cocktail. The best-selling canned vegetables are corn, beans, tomatoes, and peas. This list is not at all different from the top-sellers of the late nineteenth century.

### Which came first, the can or the can opener?

You would think that whoever invented the can would have invented a way to open it. Such was not the case. The can was introduced in the early nineteenth century, but there was no easy way to open one. Many resorted to using a hammer and chisel. Not too convenient. In 1858, the first patent for a can opener went to Ezra J. Warner of Waterbury, Connecticut, and it was used during the Civil War.

In the mid-1860s, a new type of steel can that was thinner, with a rim around the top, enabled the invention of the "modern" can opener—a cutting wheel that rolls around the lid. It was patented in 1870 by American William W. Lyman. The Star Can Company of San Francisco improved on Lyman's creation by adding a serrated edge to the wheel. The first electric can opener went on sale in 1931. The key for opening canned meats was introduced, in 1890, by Libby, McNeill & Libby, makers of corned beef sold in rectangular cans.

Another indispensable opening device wasn't patented until 1895. It was in that year that American inventor Samuel Henshell made countless wine drinkers very happy with the debut of his corkscrew. Sometimes the greatest ideas are the simplest ones.

### What were the first canned baked beans?

Native North Americans were making baked beans long before the Europeans arrived. They flavored their beans with bear fat and maple syrup, and baked them in earthenware pots placed in pits and covered with hot rocks. The Pilgrims learned how to bake beans from the Indians, substituting pork and molasses for the bear fat and maple syrup.

In 1876, the first baked beans to be sold in cans were B & M; they were named for the fishing fleet of Burnham & Morill Company, who had the beans canned for use by their fishermen in Portland, Maine.

### Are canned foods less nutritious than fresh foods?

In some ways, canned fruits and vegetables are better than "fresh" foods. They are usually processed immediately after picking, when their nutrient content is highest. As canned foods are cooked in the can, they need no preservatives, although sometimes salt or sugar is added to enhance flavor. A study at the University of Illinois showed that canned foods, once prepared for the table, have a nutritive value that is usually equal to, or greater than, fresh foods. Fruits and vegetables that are immediately canned after picking will retain more of their vitamins than "fresh" ones that are picked prematurely and shipped across the country or around the world, and then sit around in produce bins or home refrigerators for a while. Not only that, canned foods will keep for at least two years. So much for the bum rap on canned foods. One thing to remember with canned foods; many of the nutrients may be in the liquid, which most of us discard. Frozen foods don't suffer from this problem; if picked and frozen immediately, they may be the more nutritive choice.

### When did they start selling milk in bottles?

Milk, before the late nineteenth century, was a somewhat risky food, unless you got it directly from the cow. Milk wasn't sold in bottles until 1879, when Echo Farms Dairy began to deliver them in Brooklyn. Before bottles came on the scene, milk was ladled into pitchers from barrels on the back of milk wagons or in grocery stores. Not very sanitary. Consumers were advised to boil their milk before consumption to kill dangerous bacteria. In 1882, New Jersey became the first state to set up a dairy-inspection system. Two years later, in 1884, the modern milk bottle was invented by Harvey D. Thatcher, in Potsdam, New York. The Borden Company then began delivering milk in bottles.

Bottled milk had its drawbacks. Glass bottles were thick and heavy, making them expensive to transport and easy to break. They had to be collected, washed, and sterilized, involving more costs for the milk company and keeping their distribution localized. Clearly, a more efficient form of packaging was needed.

Paper milk cartons were the answer. There were ten different companies making paper milk cartons by the 1920s, but these cartons were delivered whole and took up a lot of storage space. A toy maker in Toledo, Ohio, named John Van Wormer, was granted a patent for a folding milk carton that could be stored flat, in 1915. His cartons were delivered to the dairy flat, where they were folded, glued together, and filled. He called his company Pure-Pak because the container could be thrown away after one use. It took Van Wormer ten years to invent a machine that could actually fold, glue, and fill his cartons. American Paper Bottle Company bought his patent and the first machines became operational in the early 1930s. In 1934, the Ex-Cell-O Corporation bought the rights to distribute the Pure-Pak system. They introduced the tab on the side of the gable end that could be lifted out for pouring. Before this, cartons had to be cut open with a knife. (Kind of like you still have to do with some "modern" foods, like boxed pancake mix and rice.) Ex-Cell-O Corporation paperboard cartons were dipped in wax to waterproof (milkproof) them, until a laminating process was introduced in 1959.

The public was slow to accept milk in a carton. By 1952, about forty percent of milk was sold in paperboard cartons. That number increased to seventy percent by 1968. The plastic milk carton was introduced commercially in 1964. Today, most milk cartons are made out of polyethylene-laminated boards.

Every-other-day home delivery of milk in bottles began in 1942, as a war conservation measure. The milkman was a common early morning sight for many years after the war, but his popularity gradually fell off as more people bought milk at the store. Before the war, fifty percent of milk was home delivered. By 1965 the percentage was down to twenty-five, and by 1973, only ten percent of Americans still got home milk delivery. By 1995, fewer than one percent were visited by the milkman. (This is one old practice that would be welcomed back by many.)

### When was beer first sold in bottles?

The idea for selling beer in bottles was first conceived in 1869 by English brewer Francis Manning-Needham. The benefits of packaging beer in single-serve, sanitary glass containers was not lost on other English brewers like Bass and Whitbread's, which adopted the concept soon thereafter, delivering bottled beer along with kegs to pubs, inns, and hotels.

The first beer in a can was sold by Krueger Beer of Newark, New Jersey, in 1933. The three-piece wraparound tin-plated steel cans were produced by the American Can Company. Later that year, Pabst became the first major brewer to offer canned beer. An opener was needed to get the beer out. By 1950, twenty-six percent of the packaged beer market was made up of canned beer. That percentage rose to fifty-two by 1970. Part of the rise in popularity of canned beer came from the development of easy-open tops. (See next question.)

Aluminum cans started being used on a limited basis in 1958.

They were not immediately accepted by the public and steel cans continued to be made until 1984. Many people were convinced that food and beverages packaged in aluminum cans tasted different from those packaged in glass containers. Bottles had the added advantage of being reusable. The average returnable soda or beer bottle was used up to fifty times, while early aluminum cans were used once and tossed in the trash. With the advent of widespread recycling, aluminum cans slowly gained in popularity.

### Who invented the pop-top can?

By the late 1950s and early 1960s, the world was entering the space age, but we were still opening canned beverages with a clunky can opener. That was to change when the first pull-tab cans debuted in 1962. The pull ring was invented in 1959 by toolmaker Ermal Fraze of Kettering, Ohio, after he went on a frustrating picnic without a can opener and was forced to somehow open his beer can on a car bumper. This experience convinced Fraze to create an easy-open can. While he did not come up with the idea of a tear strip on the top of a can, he did realize that a ring riveted to it would solve the problem. The pop-top was born.

The first beer to employ this new technology was Pittsburgh's Iron City Beer, which test marketed the idea in Virginia. They were not an immediate success. As with any new idea, there were bugs to be worked out and public perceptions to be changed. The early pull tabs could cut your fingers if you weren't careful and there was an added expense to the brewers. However, the tabs were improved and brewers saw the logic behind spending a little more to package a more convenient product. Schlitz was the company that took pull tabs nationwide, in 1963; soon thereafter, scores of brewers followed suit.

The only remaining problem was that of the countless thousands of pull tabs that littered the country. It seemed that wherever people went, they left their pull tabs. The barefooted had to beware. Continental Can helped clean up this mess with the introduction of non-removable tabs sixteen years later. Coors introduced a can with a two-step opening procedure, in which a protruding button of scored metal was first pressed in to release the pressure from the can and a second, larger button was then depressed into the can to create the drinking hole. Today's lever top is a variation on this theme, where the tear strip remains attached inside the can upon opening. It was introduced in 1975 by Falls Brewing Company of Louisville, Kentucky.

## Who invented the bottle cap?

Although not used much anymore, for close to a century the modern bottle cap was a clamped-on, tin-plated steel cap with a flanged edge and a cork inner seal. They somewhat resembled a crown. A man named William Painter invented the bottle cap in 1892. He went on to found Crown Cork and Seal Company of Baltimore.

These "crown" bottle caps had to be removed with a bottle opener. Any of you who are older will remember when they were the only cap around. The cork lining began to be replaced with plastic or vinyl in the mid-1960s. They went the way of the dodo when the plastic bottle with the plastic twist-off caps appeared.

## Who invented PET soda bottles?

You have probably never heard of the guy who invented the polyethylene terephthalte (PET) bottle, but you most likely are familiar with his father and his brother. They are both famous American artists. Our inventor's name is Nathaniel Wyeth, son of Newel Convers (N.C.) Wyeth and brother of Andrew Wyeth. While his father and brother are extremely well-known, the anonymous Nathaniel has touched our lives in a way few others in history have.

Nathaniel Wyeth was an engineer employed by DuPont Corporation. In 1967 he began work on developing a system to mold plastics so that they would be strong enough to hold a carbonated beverage. Up until that time, plastic bottles would explode from the carbonation. Wyeth came up with the modern plastic soda bottle that is lightweight, clear, resilient, and recyclable. He patented his process in 1973 and in 1977, PET bottles hit the market.

PET products are now one of the most recycled materials. Fifty percent of all modern polyester carpets are made from recycled PET bottles.

### Why do bottles of Coke have "drink by" dates?

In the old days (remember when Coke came in the thick green glass bottles?) sodas didn't have "drink by" dates. Why should they suddenly need to be consumed in a timely manner? Coke doesn't go bad does it? Yes, it kind of does, nowadays. The old glass Coke bottles of yore were pretty solid, and they weren't permeable to much, especially to carbon dioxide. Today's bottles are made of polyethylene terephthalate (PET). It's a lighter material than glass and it doesn't break. However, PET is permeable to carbon dioxide gas over a long period of time. This means your soda may start to lose some of its fizz if it gets too old.

Once you open a bottle of soda, the best way to keep it fizzy is to keep it cold. A cold liquid can hold more carbon dioxide than a warm one. This is why a warm soda is more likely to spray you in the face if opened after being jostled.

### Are cork corks better than plastic corks?

Cork, like the grapes used to make the wine bottled with same, is a renewable resource. Cork is harvested from the bark of evergreen cork oaks (*Quercus suber*), native to the western Mediterranean, and it regrows to be harvested again. One has to be patient in the cork business, however. It takes twenty-five years for a cork tree to reach maturity and bear enough cork for harvesting. Then one has to wait nine years before harvesting again. To get the cork from the tree, circular slits are made in the bark of the trunk and any main branches. It is then peeled off in sheets, which are boiled in water and then flattened. Corks are softened in a mixture of sulfur dioxide and glycerol. If they are too porous to make a good seal, they are also waxed.

What makes cork such a good stopper? It is full of microscopic air cells that make it light and compressible. The cell walls of cork also contain a waxy substance called "suberin" that make it water-resistant and durable.

It is said that French monk Dom Pérignon was the first person to stopper a wine bottle with cork; this occurred in the 1690s. He reportedly got the idea from visiting Spanish monks who used corks in their water jugs. Before this, sparkling wines were impossible because the French used hemp plugs soaked in oil to seal their bottles; any effervescence seeped out.

Corks have been the preferred stopper of wine bottles for hundreds of years. They do a good job, but a small percentage of the wines thus stoppered will become "corked," which means that a fungus will grow on the cork and impart an undesirable musty smell and affect the flavor of the wine. The problem can be alleviated by the use of plastic stoppers.

A couple of hundred wineries now use plastic corks, or synthetic closures as they are known by vintners. They are primarily used on wines that are intended to be drunk young (within six months), as no one has studied the long-term effect of plastic stoppers on wines that are aged for several years. Also, most wine buffs don't expect to see a plastic cork in their expensive vintage wine. It's just not the same somehow. After all, wouldn't you feel rather silly smelling a plastic stopper in a fine restaurant?

## Why are you supposed to smell the cork from a bottle of wine?

Buying a good bottle of wine at a restaurant can be a little intimidating for some of us less refined individuals. There seems to be some sort of expected ritual that must be performed when the wine captain (sommelier) presents you with the bottle and cork. You may be interested to know that there is no good reason for you to smell that little piece of cork you are handed. The practice of inspecting the cork originated for reasons other than smell.

During the 1800s, dishonest establishments sometimes tried to sell cheap wine as a more expensive one. Vintners took to printing their trademark on the corks when bottling to fight these dishonest people. This is why the bottle is traditionally opened in front of you, so you can *look* at the cork for its marking. If you are interested in whether the wine has "corked" (become tainted), you are better advised to smell the wine and then taste it.

Something else you can tell from a quick inspection of the cork is whether or not the bottle has been stored properly. Look for wetness partway up the end. If it is a red wine it should be stained a little way up the end. This will tell you that the bottle was stored tilted down so that the wine has covered the cork bottom ensuring a tight seal.

### How does a thermos bottle keep hot drinks hot and cold drinks cold?

The thermos is an adaptation of the vacuum flask invented by Scottish chemist/physicist James Dewar in 1892. Dewar used vacuum flasks to aid him in his scientific work with liquid gases. The vacuum flask consists of two flasks, one inside the other, separated by a vacuum. The vacuum greatly reduces the transfer of heat. Glass is used because it is a poor conductor of heat and it is lined with a reflective metal coating to reduce the transfer of heat through radiation. Thus cold liquids stay cold and hot ones stay hot.

The thermos bottle was the creation of German glassblower Reinhold Burger. In 1904, he put the whole fragile apparatus on a shock-absorbing spring within a metal casing and manufactured it for home use. The trademark "Thermos" was the winning entry in a contest to rename the vacuum flask. It comes from the Greek word *therme*, meaning "hot," and was submitted by a resident of Munich. Three years later, Burger's company—Thermos GmbH—sold their trademark rights to three independent companies in the United States, Canada, and England.

### What kind of meal cooks itself?

Have you ever heard of Heater Meals? They are able to cook themselves and are convenient for emergency situations or living in the wilderness. Heater Meals are a canned food that comes with a heating pad that contains iron and magnesium. When saltwater is added, an oxidation process occurs, causing an exothermic reaction that raises the temperature to 220°F. In fourteen minutes, you can have a hot meal, no matter where you are.

The heating principle behind Heater Meals was originally developed for the military. Vests filled with the iron and magnesium would help to keep downed navy pilots warm in seawater. The principle is now used in military rations—MREs. (See next question.)

### What are MREs?

If you are in the military, you already know this one. MRE stands for Meal, Ready to Eat. They are a totally self-contained meal in a packet eaten by troops in the field. The vacuum-packed food is sealed in a plastic packet that fits easily into military field clothing pockets and comes in a small paper carton. An ingenious heating element (see previous entry) can be slipped inside and will boil within seconds when water is added to it, effectively turning the box into a little oven that will thoroughly heat the meal in ten to fifteen minutes. Or they can be submerged in boiling water.

MREs are nutritionally balanced. Each one contains 1,250 kilocalories, thirteen percent protein, thirty-six percent fat, and fifty-one percent carbohydrates. There are twenty-four MRE menu selections including Beef Stew, Thai Chicken, Meatloaf, Beefsteak, Black Bean Burrito, and Cheese Tortellini. Powdered drinks include cocoa, iced tea, and grape drink. There are snacks and desserts such as M&Ms and Skittles. As you would expect, there are condiments like Tabasco but, curiously, no ketchup. MREs have a shelf life of about three years.

MREs are also used in humanitarian relief efforts. One packet has enough food to sustain a person for a day. They are distributed to refugees and displaced persons around the world.

Troops generally like these modern field rations. They surely are a cut above earlier field meals, such as K-rations, which fed millions of American troops during World War II.

### When did individually wrapped foods become popular?

Up until the turn of the twentieth century, a great many foods were sold only in bulk. If you wanted cheese, you had a piece cut off a huge cheese wheel; if you wanted milk, it was ladled from a big can. The same went for butter, nuts, beans, sugar, flour, candies, and many other foods. The switch to packaged foods had more to do with economics than with hygiene or customer convenience. Packaging helped to keep foods from being damaged in shipping or going bad.

Some foods were sold in individual packets, but they were not always the most suitable to the product; for instance, salt was sold in little cotton bags. The problem was that as the price of cotton went up and down, the bags might cost more to make than the salt was worth. Also, cotton didn't keep out moisture and the salt often caked up in the bag. Hence, Morton Salt introduced its still famous waxed salt container in the round box, with the slogan "When it rains, it pours."

Tin foil became a popular wrapping for candies. Tea began to be sold in bags. Sugar, however, was one of the last holdouts in the bulk market. Up until 1928, ninety percent of sugar was sold from open sugar barrels.

One problem of early packaging was that while boxes were great once the product was put inside, they took up a lot of storage space while they were still empty. This problem was solved in 1879, when Robert Gair, a New York paper-bag maker, invented cardboard containers with creases that allowed them to be laid flat in storage and quickly folded together for use when needed.

### What was the first prepackaged meal?

The first prepackaged meal is still one of our favorites, especially among college students and bachelors—Kraft Macaroni and Cheese Dinner. National Dairy Products introduced it after one of their salesmen suggested combining grated American cheese with Tenderoni Macaroni in a box; it was a way to sell more cheese. The idea was a hit. It remains one of our most convenient and inexpensive foods. If you think it's cheap now, it sold for only nineteen cents when it first came out in 1937; however, some stores sold it for only ten cents. It was originally packaged in yellow boxes but soon changed to blue. The slogan "A Meal for

Four in Nine Minutes," helped launch this American classic on the Kraft Music Hall radio show. It still sells at a clip of one million boxes a day.

### What was the first penny candy to be individually wrapped?

Leo Hirshfield, an Austrian immigrant, brought the idea for Tootsie Rolls to the United States in 1896. He started production of his little chocolate rolls in a New York City shop. Naming his candy after his five-year-old daughter Clara, whom he called "Tootsie," Hirshfield was the first candy maker to individually wrap his penny candies.

Tootsie rolls are made from a base of sugar, corn syrup, soybean oil, skim milk, and cocoa. Over 49,000,000 are produced each day.

### What was the first individually wrapped snack cake?

Up until 1914, when Tasty Baking Company of Philadelphia had the brainstorm of selling prewrapped individual-size cakes, big slabs of cake were cut up at the store and the pieces sold. There were just three people in the company that year—Pittsburgh baker Philip J. Baur and Boston salesman Herbert C. Morris—the founders, and one employee. Morris came up with the name Tastykake. In a royal blue horse-drawn wagon, he set out with a wicker basket of five cent Tastykakes and began making his pitch to Philadelphia grocers. His first day only netted $28.32 in sales, but by the end of the year sales would top $300,000. As the business grew, more royal blue wagons with gray horses were purchased and they were a common sight in southern New Jersey, central Pennsylvania, and Baltimore. In the 1930s, the Tasty Baking Company came up with a revolutionary baking idea— individually packaged lunchbox-sized pies. The first nickel pie was apple, followed by peach, lemon, and blueberry.

### Who invented the paper bag?

The paper bag had been an indispensable part of American food shopping for almost two hundred years, until it was recently more or less displaced by the plastic shopping bag. However, someone had to invent it. Wrapping paper came first in America, being produced in Delaware in 1815. It took another thirty-seven years until a machine was invented to turn wrapping paper into paper bags. It wasn't until 1870 that the first square-bottomed paper grocery bag was made. An inventor in Springfield, Massachusetts, named Margaret E. Knight, patented a bag-folding machine attachment that made the square bottom. A patent for a machine to make flat-bottomed bags was issued to Luther Childs Crowell in 1872. Eleven years later, this machine would be replaced by a better machine that would make the now familiar square-bottomed paper bag with side pleats. This automatic, or "flick," bag, is self-opening with the flick of the wrist.

The plastic supermarket shopping bag, which appeared in 1977, slowly began to replace this old favorite.

# 21

# Chop Suey
# (Odds and Ends)

### Why did Hunt Foods buy a matchbook company?

In 1945, Hunt Foods had sales of $19 million and a net profit of $530,000. Hunt honcho Norton Simon wanted to do better. To increase name recognition, he decided to start a matchbook advertising campaign. What better way to do it than to buy a match company—the Ohio Match Company? Soon countless match covers were plastered with the slogan "Hunt for the Best," pushing Hunt's Tomato Sauce, among other products.

### What second-place Pillsbury Bake-Off recipe defined an era?

There was a time in the late 1960s and early 1970s that you couldn't go to dinner or a party at someone's house without encountering a bundt cake. The woman responsible for this culinary phenomenon was Ella Helfrich of Houston, Texas. She entered her "Tunnel of Fudge" cake in the seventeenth Pillsbury Bake-Off in 1966. Her recipe was a dryish brownie-type chocolate pound cake baked around a moist fudge center made with Pillsbury Frosting Mix. The good folks at Pillsbury only gave her recipe second place (and $5,000), but the American public voted her bundt cake number one. It introduced mainstream America to the wonders of the bundt pan. Up until that time, the crenallater tube pan was used mainly by ethnic bakers. Ella changed all that.

The sales of bundt-cake pans went through the roof. So high was the demand that Northland Aluminum Products of Minneapolis, Minnesota, the only maker of bundt pans, had to put its factory on round-the-clock production. Like many fads of the 1960s and 1970s, the bundt cake seems to have disappeared from the culinary landscape as quickly as it appeared.

### Why do microwave ovens keep turning on and off as they heat foods?

Did you ever notice that your microwave oven sounds like it is constantly turning itself on and off when used on less than full power? This is because your microwave actually *is* turning on and off. The magnetron that makes the microwaves that cook your food is on constantly when you cook at full power. At lower power levels, the magnetron cycles on and off accordingly to allow short periods for the heat to distribute itself more evenly. The noise that you hear is the cooling fan of the magnetron turning on and off.

Some new microwave ovens use "inverter technology," which produces a constant flow of microwaves, even at lower power levels. Instead of blasting full power on and off, inverter technology delivers the exact power level chosen. If you want sixty percent, you get a constant sixty percent of power.

### What are legumes?

After the grains, the legume family is the most important food group. Legumes have about twice as much protein as do the grains and are high in B vitamins and iron. The Romans held them in such high regard that the four most prominent families in Rome bore names that came from legumes—Cicero after the chick pea (*Cicer arietinum*), Fabius (faba or fava bean), Lentulus (lentil), and Piso (pea).

Navy beans got their name from the fact that many navies used them as a staple.

### Why do beans give you gas?

Most of you know about the consequences of eating beans first-hand, although some of you are more susceptible than others.

Many factors affect the gas produced when one eats beans. The quantity of gas and its type of odor depend on a number of variables, such as what food was eaten, how it was prepared, and what type of bacteria are present in the intestine.

The problem with legumes, and beans in particular, is their fiber content and oligosaccharides (complex sugars). Our digestive tracts do not have the specific enzymes required to break these sugars down. In the case of beans, the complex sugar involved is raffinose. Lima beans and navy beans are the worst offenders. Oligosaccharides are also the culprits in other gas-producing vegetables like broccoli, Brussels sprouts, cabbage, and cauliflower.

Since these complex sugars are not digested in the upper intestine, they enter the lower intestine whole, where bacteria do the job. The bacteria give off gases like carbon dioxide, methane, nitrogen, oxygen, and others, when they metabolize the sugars, causing flatulence. This bean intolerance is analogous to lactose intolerance, where a digestive enzyme is lacking, resulting in bacterial fermentation and gas. The kind of gases the bacteria give off during this fermentation and the type of residual proteins and fats in your colon will combine to give your gas its own distinctive aroma. Nuff said.

## How can you reduce flatulence?

Some people are more prone to flatulence than others. What can you do to minimize this problem? People who eat a lot of gas-producing foods seem to develop more of a tolerance for them. Gradually increasing your intake could help. Soaking your beans in water and rinsing them before cooking will also help. Some "experts" recommend adding ⅛ teaspoon of baking soda to the soaking water. After cooking, rinse the beans again.

If flatulence is really a problem for you try Beano. This over-the-counter product supplies the missing enzyme—beta-galactosidase—needed to break down the complex sugars, robbing the bacteria of the chance to do their nasty work. Don't add it to the beans, just take it when you are eating them. Other pills that are marketed for gas distress, like Flatulex, contain activated charcoal that will absorb some of the offending odors.

Making lifestyle changes (you must really have gas trouble to be this concerned) would be to cut back on other gas-producing activities, such as chewing gum, eating or drinking too fast, or drinking carbonated beverages, all of which can cause you to swallow air and contribute to your gassiness later. Or you could just eat something else.

Abstinence or Beano may be the best solution for gas among those who are going to fly. The decreased air pressure during flights can significantly aggravate your gas woes and add to the woes of your fellow passengers. Don't laugh. This problem was thought to be so serious that after World War II the government studied the effects of flatulence on high-altitude pilots and later NASA did likewise for astronauts. The volume of a gas increases as the pressure around it decreases. In an unpressurized cabin this could cause pilots great discomfort. Some were even concerned that a high gas level in an enclosed cockpit or cabin would be detrimental to the crew!

### When did people start eating tofu?

Tofu is made from curdled soybean milk. The soy milk is extracted from ground, cooked soybeans. The curds are then drained and pressed. The Chinese came up with tofu during the Han dynasty, sometime around the second century B.C. They originally added sea salt to bean milk to preserve it but found the coagulated curd to their liking. Japan didn't start eating soybean curd until the eighth century and Buddhist monks ate it as a meat and dairy substitute. It wasn't until the 1300s that the general population took to eating tofu.

### Why is mustard yellow?

Mustard was first used as a food seasoning by the Egyptians. Instead of grinding it into a powder or paste, they simply popped a couple of mustard seeds into their mouths while chewing meat to give it extra flavor. Mustard paste become very popular in medieval Europe, to improve on the taste of their foods. One fourteenth-century pope—John XII of Avignon—was said to be so fond of mustard that he had it put in every dish. The books of one thirteenth-century household lists expenses for seven to ten gallons of mustard a month!

Americans failed to acquire a taste for this spicy condiment until 1904, when George French toned down the European brown mustard to please the American palate; he created his French's Cream Salad Mustard. It quickly became the best-selling mustard in the country. European mustards are made from brown mustard seeds, which are zesty and very flavorful. American-style mustard is made from the less pungent white mustard seed, flavored with sugar, vinegar, and turmeric. It's the turmeric that makes American mustard yellow. Curiously, French Dijon mustard is made primarily from seeds grown in Canada and the United States. Canada supplies ninety percent of the world mustard-seed market.

Today, there are around one thousand kinds of mustard available and 700 million gallons of the stuff are consumed each year worldwide. There is even a mustard museum in Mt. Horeb, Wisconsin, which has over three thousand jars of different mustards from around the world.

### Why is vanilla extract so expensive?

The Aztecs were the first people to savor the taste and aroma of vanilla. They used it to flavor their chocolate drinks and were the ones who introduced it to the Spaniards. Of all the twenty thousand and some-odd orchid species in the world, the tropical American vinelike vanilla (*Vanilla plantifolia*), which can grow to 350 feet in length, is the only one that produces anything of culinary interest.

This orchid's yellow-white flower only opens one day out of the year, only for a few hours, and it must be fertilized on that day. The only natural pollinators are one species of bee and one species of hummingbird. Leaving nothing to chance, growers hand fertilize vanilla with a little wooden needle. If all goes well, a vanilla-bean pod is produced six weeks later and takes nine more months to reach maturity. The still green pods are picked by hand and boiled to halt the maturation process. The beans at this stage are devoid of taste or aroma. They must be cured by warming in the sun during the day and being wrapped up at night to "sweat." This is done for three weeks. Then they are left to dry in the sun for up to six months. It is during this drying time that fermentation occurs; this gives vanilla beans their delightful aroma and flavor. The beans have now shrunk to one-quarter of their original size and have turned dark brown. Better quality beans also become coated with vanillin, a whitish powder (see next entry). The beans are macerated in an alcohol-water solution and left to age for several months.

All in all, that's a lot of time and effort spent just so your French toast will taste a little better.

Today, vanilla is grown in three main regions of the world—Madagascar, Mexico, and Tahiti. Madagascar produces seventy-five percent of the world crop and its vanilla is considered to be of the best quality. It is also the most expensive. Federal law mandates that vanilla extract contain not less than 13.35 ounces of vanilla beans per gallon and be thirty-five percent alcohol.

### What is vanillin?

Vanillin is the chemical most responsible for giving vanilla beans their wonderful aroma and flavor. It can be produced artificially for much less expense than is incurred when extracting it from vanilla beans. Synthetic vanillin, which was patented by a German chemist in 1875, is identical to natural vanillin, and it is used in imitation vanilla extract. However, vanillin is not the only chemical found in natural vanilla extract. There are also some 250 other chemicals extracted from the beans that impart the special complex aroma and flavor that can only be found in natural extract.

Artificial vanillin was made from clove oils between 1875 and 1925. Today it is made from paper industry wood-pulp by-products (lignin). It is about half the price of real vanilla extract, but you need to use twice as much. So do yourself a favor and buy the real thing.

### Why does vanilla extract smell so good and taste so bad?

Vanilla extract, as mentioned previously, is thirty-five percent alcohol, which is quite strong. Many whiskeys are forty percent alcohol. However, whiskeys are lovingly distilled and aged to produce a smooth-drinking alcohol. Vanilla extract doesn't receive this consideration, as it is to be diluted into other baking ingredients and not sipped straight.

Many people think the flavor of vanilla is plain and boring because it is so widely used. Nothing could be further from the truth. In fact, vanilla is one of the most versatile and complex of flavorings.

All in all, vanilla is one of our favorite flavors, at least when it comes to ice cream. Baskin Robbins, for instance, offers thirty-one flavors of ice cream, and yet twenty-five percent of their sales are for "plain" old vanilla. In supermarkets, vanilla outsells chocolate three to one and strawberry is a distant third. Most consumers judge the quality of an entire line of ice cream by its vanilla. If they skimp there, the rest of their products are probably also sub-par. If your ice cream brand says "vanilla ice cream," it must be made with only pure vanilla extract or vanilla beans. If it says "vanilla-flavored ice cream," it can be made with fifty percent imitation flavoring.

## Where did chili con carne originate?

Chili con carne is a dish of ground beef with chiles or chili powder. True chili con carne, found deep in the heart of Texas, doesn't have any beans, although they are added to the dish in most other places.

The name *chili con carne* is Spanish for "chili with meat." Chili con carne, however, has nothing to do with Spain. The Spanish didn't encounter a chile until they conquered Mexico. The Mexicans, likewise, did not come up with chili con carne. In fact, they detest the stuff and don't appreciate being associated with it. The Texans are responsible for the creation of this hot dish and its popularity. San Antonio is credited with having given birth to chili con carne shortly after the Civil War.

## What state has the best farmland?

Iowa has been exceptionally blessed when it comes to growing crops. Nearly ninety-one percent of its land is agricultural and it has more Grade A land (agronomists say) than any other state. All this great farmland makes Iowa the number one soybean- and corn-producing state. Most of this corn is fed to pigs, making Iowa the number one pig-raising state. It is number two in red meat production and number one in total livestock value. Iowa is also the number one egg-producing state. There shouldn't be anyone going hungry in Iowa.

### What popular drink began as an emergency food?

In 1863, George Wander, a Swiss scientist, created a sweet malt extract that was combined with milk, eggs, and cocoa to make an easily digestible, wholesome, nutrient-rich drink/food that could be used in an emergency situation where normal food was not appropriate. He called his food Wander's Ovomaltine but changed it to Ovaltine when he applied for a British trademark.

George's son Albert went on to perfect the beverage powder, making it with malt extract, evaporated milk, powdered eggs, and powdered cocoa. Introduced in 1905, it was prescribed by doctors to patients convalescing and to those with wasting disease.

### What is Vegemite?

If you listened to pop radio in the 1980s, you undoubtedly heard the song "Land Down Under" by Men at Work and its reference to something called a Vegemite sandwich. If you are not Aus- tralian, you probably don't know what the heck Vegemite is. Well, Vegemite is a paste that is made from brown yeast extract. It is a breakfast favorite on toast in the Land Down Under. Loaded with B vitamins and folate, Vegemite is also enjoyed with butter between two slices of bread and is used to flavor soups and stews. It is said to taste yeasty and salty. Don't try to under- stand it, it's an Australian thing.

### In what state is it legal to eat your roadkill?

This may not even be an issue in many states. Most people leave any animals they hit while driving to the local scavengers or the highway department. In many states it is illegal to take your roadkill home with you. This is not a problem in West Virginia, though. They passed a law in 1998 allowing drivers to keep their roadkill so they can take it home and eat it; they just need to report their windfall to the state within twelve hours. The law is supposed to save the Highway Division money, since it no longer has to pick up all the dead critters. Several states save this money by letting the carcasses simply rot away on the shoulder.

### How much dirt will you eat in your lifetime?

Over the course of your life, you will probably eat several pounds of dirt! It may sound like a lot, but stretched out over seventy or eighty years, it's not that much, although you could grow a nice potted plant in it. So what's the nutritional value of dirt? When it's on the surface of the Earth it's called soil and is highly nutritive to the plants growing in it. We, however, are not plants. When soil is on your skin or in your food, it's called dirt and is of no nutritional value, not even for its mineral content. Common dirt isn't bad for you, but you may be surprised to learn about some other unsavory things found in your food.

The Food and Drug (Bug) Administration allows certain amounts of dirt and other "foreign matter" to be present in foods; for instance, they allow one or more whole insects or fifty insect fragments, two or more rodent hairs, and one or more rodent excreta in every fifty grams of cornmeal. Three percent of canned peaches can be moldy or wormy. Twenty or more maggots are allowed in one hundred grams of canned mushrooms. This may sound disgusting, but bugs and worms won't hurt you and they are a good source of protein! Many of these beasties are killed during processing. It's one thing to eat a dead worm you can't see but another to eat the live critter.

### Why did Gerber have a hard time selling baby food in Africa?

In marketing, it pays to know your audience—especially a foreign one. Gerber did not heed this advice when they first marketed their baby foods in Africa. They didn't realize that for Africans, the picture on the label is usually what's in the package. In the case of Gerber that would be a cute, white baby. Shoppers were either amused or befuddled.

Another silly advertising gaffe was committed by Kentucky Fried Chicken (that's KFC for you younger readers). Their motto "finger lickin' good" became "lick your fingers off," when translated into Chinese.

## Why is airplane food so bad?

Granted, a lot of airlines don't put much effort into making your flight a memorable dining experience. But the the less-than-tasty food they serve is not entirely of their own doing. Airline food is less flavorful in flight because altitude and cabin pressure have a dulling effect on the taste buds. Pan Am began serving the first hot in-flight meals in 1946.

The amount of money each carrier spends on its food can also make a difference. The following is a recent survey of what various airlines spend per food serving:

| | |
|---|---|
| USAir | $3.00 |
| TWA | $3.40 |
| Delta | $4.10 |
| Continental | $4.80 |
| Northwest | $4.85 |
| United | $7.50 |
| American | $10.00 |

## Do the cooks on "Iron Chef" know the ingredients beforehand?

If you ever watch the popular Food Network television show "Iron Chef," you are probably amazed that the Iron Chef and the challenger can both come up with such a diversity of dishes, using the theme ingredient, in such a short period of time. The pretext of the show is that two chefs are given a mystery ingredient at the beginning of the hour and are each supposed to cook several different dishes using that main ingredient. Not only do they not appear to think much before starting to cook, some chefs actually write a menu of what they are going to make at the outset.

The reason the chefs have no problem coming up with the dishes, as well as any specialized and offbeat ingredients they need, is that they are kind of briefed beforehand regarding the theme food of the show. The challenger and the Iron Chef are given a list of ingredient categories. Together, they narrow the list down to between five and seven categories from which the show's producers pick the main ingredient. This way, the chefs have a good idea what to expect and can get right down to cooking.

### On "Iron Chef" what does that guy who always interrupts the announcer say?

This bit of information may seem trivial if you don't watch the show, but will be quite enlightening to those who follow "Iron Chef." This Japanese cooking game show is covered like a sporting event in something called Kitchen Stadium. All the participants speak in Japanese. The shows are dubbed for airing in the U.S. During the cooking part of "Iron Chef," there is a seated commentator, named Fukui, who kind of gives a play-by-play of what the chefs are doing. At the same time, there is a reporter, named Shinichiro Ohta, down in the kitchen area who is talking to the chefs. Occasionally, the announcer will say something like "What's the Iron Chef doing now?" He will be interrupted by the reporter yelling out some word that is hard to understand (sounds like "kwisan"). What he actually says is "Fukui-san!" He is shouting the announcer's name to get his attention and says the "san" part as a term of respect. The announcer then says, "Ohta, go!" and Ohta describes what the chef is doing.

"Iron Chef" has a fanatical following in Japan, where each Iron Chef has devoted fans who root him on. The country follows the show like a soap opera and results are even covered by the Japanese newspapers.

### When did deep-dish pizza become popular?

During the Depression and World War II, Americans ate a lot of one-dish meals, or casseroles. The deep-dish pizza fit in nicely with this trend. People were looking for meals that could stretch their budget and not use many ration coupons during the war. You could load whatever you wanted into a deep-dish pizza and have a complete, satisfying meal. Deep-dish pizza is also easier to make than thin crust. There is no need to stretch and toss the dough. Not only is the dough thicker than a New York–style pizza, the mozzarella cheese is at the bottom and the other ingredients are on top.

### In what week is the most pizza consumed?

You could probably guess this one if you really thought about it. Pizza is a great party food and one of the biggest parties of the year is Super Bowl Sunday! More pizza is eaten the week of the big game than any other. And what kind of pizza do we prefer? Regular thin crust pizza makes up sixty-one percent of sales; thick-crust and deep-dish follow with fourteen percent each. Only fourteen percent are extra thin.

### What is the number one pizza topping?

Sixty-two percent of Americans like toppings on their pie. Pepperoni is America's favorite topping. It is ordered on thirty-six percent of pizzas. We eat about 251,770,000 pounds of it per year. Anchovies are the least ordered topping. Women are twice as likely as men to order vegetable toppings. No surprises here, but wait till you see what they like to top pizza with in other parts of the world.

In Pakistan, curry is a big hit. The Japanese like eel and squid. In Russia, red herring is number one, and Australians love shrimp and pineapple, or eggs. Costa Ricans like coconut. Chileans choose mussels and clams. You can put almost anything on top of a pizza. Is this a versatile food or what?

### When did soup gain popularity in America?

America wasn't very keen on soup before the twentieth century. For one thing, it was a pain to make and took a long time; for another, Americans traditionally have viewed themselves as individualists and spurned the communal soup pot of the Old

World. That was to change with the help of one Dr. John Thomas Dorrance.

Dorrance earned a doctorate degree in Germany and became a big soup eater. He worked in some Paris restaurants to study the proper flavoring of soup. As fate would have it, his uncle, Arthur Dorrance, was president of the Joseph Campbell Preserve Company, purveyors of canned tomatoes, vegetables, soup, jams, jellies, condiments, and mince meats. There were only two major canned soup makers at the end of the nineteenth century and neither was very successful. Campbell's only soup at the time, introduced in 1895, was ready-to-serve beefsteak tomato. John Dorrance realized that this was because the soup cans they were selling were much too heavy to transport economically and too cumbersome for women to handle in the kitchen. What to do? Make the product lighter. That was his goal when he returned from Europe and took the position of research chemist at his uncle's company. He was only paid $7.50 per week and had to buy his own laboratory equipment.

In 1897, at the young age of twenty-four, John came up with the idea of a double-strength condensed soup that had most of the water removed, allowing the cans to be much smaller and lighter. This lowered the cost of packaging, shipping, and storage and the company was able to offer a ten-ounce can of condensed soup for the price of ten cents. A typical ready-to-serve soup of the time came in a thirty-two-ounce can and cost thirty-five cents. The first five Campbell's Condensed Soups, were vegetable, chicken, consommé, beefsteak tomato, and oxtail. Their tomato soup still ranks in the top ten dry grocery items sold today.

Creating a new kind of soup was one thing but getting women to buy it was another. John took to the road giving taste tests to wary housewives. Instead of trying to convince them that his soups were as good as homemade, he pushed them as something slightly different with a taste all their own. He was successful in his endeavors and sales began to rise. In 1898, the company showed a profit for the first time in several years and John got a raise to $9 a week! By 1902, the soup line was expanded to twenty-one varieties and, in 1904, sixteen million cans were sold.

To increase interest in soups, Campbell's came up with a new marketing ploy in 1914. Instead of just pushing them as a meal by themselves, their potential as an ingredient in other food preparations was encouraged. The real boon to soup being used as an ingredient came in 1952, with the publication of the Campbell's *Cooking With Condensed Soup* cookbook, which encouraged its use in casseroles. Not only did the use of condensed soup skyrocket, so did the making of casserole dishes. One million cans a day went into casseroles. Campbell's still sells 200 million cans of Cream of Mushroom soup a year.

Campbell's Chunky Soups hit the shelves on the West Coast in 1969.

## *When you cook with alcohol, is any left in the final dish?*

To most of us, the question isn't really that important, but there are some people who, for one reason or another, don't wish to have any alcohol in their diet. One common misconception that seems to be fairly prevalent is that cooking a food makes any alcohol added in the preparation disappear.

It is true that pure alcohol evaporates at a lower temperature than water—173°F—but alcohol is no longer pure when used in a recipe. The alcohol interacts with any water (moisture) in the dish. The actual evaporation temperature of the liquid ingredients will fall somewhere between 173°F and 212°F, which is the boiling point of pure water. If there is more water than alcohol, the temperature will be closer to 212°F, if there is more alcohol, it will be closer to 173°F.

It is hard to say how much alcohol will be left in the dish when you serve it, but there will be some. Alcohol in a mixture with water evaporates rather slowly. Studies have shown a wide range of alcohol content in finished dishes with alcohol. There may be from five to fifty percent alcohol remaining (see chart on p. 182).

If you think that's high, flaming dishes like bananas flambé and cherries jubilee only lose about twenty percent of their alcohol content from the spectacular flames we so admire. Remember, only high-proof alcohols have enough alcohol in their vapor to burn; you can't ignite a beer, for example. You can see that once the flames bring the alcohol level in the vapors down to a critical level, they will go out, but there is still plenty of unburned alcohol left over.

### Are mushrooms really grown in manure?

You bet! Mushrooms just love decayed organic matter. They are grown in beds not filled with nice topsoil but with mixtures containing farm debris; this includes old corn cobs, hay, chicken manure, and the droppings cleaned from stables. Doesn't sound to appetizing, does it? While this mushroom growth medium may not enhance your enjoyment of eating a mushroom, bear in mind that it is perfectly safe. All mushroom growth substrates are composted for a few weeks before seeding the fungal spores. The composting raises the heat level of the medium to a temperature high enough to ensure sterilization of any nasty microorganisms.

So is that brown stuff sticking to your mushrooms manure? Calm yourself; it's probably just some harmless peat moss. The growers cover their mushrooms with peat moss after seeding the spores, to keep them moist. It is the moss that the mushroom caps grow through before picking. Just rinse it off.

Pennsylvania grows half of the nation's mushroom crop. In fact, Kennett Square, Pennsylvania, calls itself the "Mushroom Capital of the World."

### What do mushrooms have in common with insects?

For every little mushroom you see growing in your yard, there is an extensive underground network of filaments (hyphae) that supply it with moisture and nutrients. Unlike plants, fungi contain no chlorophyll and are not dependent on sunlight for growth. Instead, they are saprophytic, taking their nutrients from decomposing organic material. The mushroom that we eat is the fungi's fruiting body, which contains its spores in the gills under the cap. These spores are like its seeds; they disperse in the wind and start new hyphal colonies elsewhere.

Another difference between fungi and plants is the fact that fungi do not have cellulose in their cell walls. Instead they have chitin, which is a tough polysaccharide that also makes up the exoskeleton (outer body) of insects.

### What are portobello mushrooms?

They are just really big regular mushrooms. The ubiquitous little white mushrooms sold wrapped in plastic in every supermarket across the country are *Agaricus bisporus*. They are harvested before their caps open much and they are still whitish brown. If allowed to mature, they get a lot bigger, their caps open wide, and they darken in color. They are now called portobellos.

### What's the difference between barbecuing and grilling?

The terms grilling and barbecuing are often used synonymously, but they are not exactly the same thing. Grilling is like broiling. It is a way of cooking small pieces of meat quickly over a hot open flame that sears the meat and seals in juices. Barbecuing is more like roasting. It can also be done on your grill, and involves adding sauce and smoking the meat during the slow, moist, covered-cooking process, over indirect heat.

Kansas City is the barbecue capital of the world. The first BBQ joint opened there in 1908 and today there are over one hundred in that city.

### Who invented the modern grill?

The modern covered grill with a lid was created in 1952 by George Stephen, a Chicago metal worker who didn't care for the open grills of the time. Fashioning a metal grill with a lid from a buoy he cut in half, Stephen began selling them to friends. Their response was so positive that he purchased the barbecue division of the Weber Brothers Metal Works and started his own company—Weber-Stephen Products—offering the Weber Kettle grill at $49.95. The grill worked so well because the dome-shaped lid reflected the heat back down on the food evenly.

Today, seventy-six million Americans own grills—forty-eight percent own gas, twenty-nine percent own charcoal, and fourteen percent own both.

### How do you get your charcoal just right?

Traditional grilling involves charcoal briquettes. They have never been easy to light, but many people still prefer them to gas for grilling. The trick is to get the heat even and at the right temperature. As a general rule, the coals should be spread in an even layer about four to six inches below the food grate. When about three-quarters of them are white, you can begin grilling. You can hold your hand over the food grate to determine if you have the proper cooking temperature. If you can only keep your hand there for two seconds, the coals are considered hot; three seconds indicates medium-hot; four seconds is medium; and five seconds is low heat. Of course, if you don't want to put your hand over a hot grill and time it, just throw your meat on, like most people, and check it every few minutes.

As you might suspect, surveys show that in sixty-six percent of families it is Dad who does the grilling.

### Who invented the charcoal briquette?

This long-time staple of backyard barbecuing was not commercially available until the 1920s. You wouldn't think something this basic needed to be invented, but it took two of America's greatest inventors to do so. The ever-frugal Henry Ford hated waste. He was determined to come up with a use for the leftover scraps of wood and sawdust generated at his automobile plants. With the help of none other than Thomas Edison, he invented charcoal briquettes in 1920.

Ford had a large sawmill built on 313,447 acres of land in the Upper Peninsula of Michigan that year. He was helped with the purchase of the land by the husband of his cousin—Edward G. Kingsford—who was a real estate agent and owned a Ford dealership in the area. The mill employed thousands of people and a small village known as Kingsford sprung up around it. In 1924, Ford had a chemical plant built in Kingsford to reclaim the waste wood from the mill. For each ton of scrap wood, 610 pounds of charcoal briquettes were produced. They were sold as Ford Charcoal Briquettes.

Henry Ford II closed down the sawmill in 1951 and sold the chemical operation to a group of local business interests that formed an enterprise known as the Kingsford Chemical Company. They continued making charcoal briquettes under the Kingsford name. The charcoal plant moved to Kentucky in 1961, but the City of Kingsford remains.

### How do they make charcoal?

Waste wood scraps are ground into mulch that is then roasted at temperatures as high as 1,800°F. This turns the wood mulch into a black carbon substance known as "char." The char is mixed with coal to create charcoal, which is formed into briquettes in molds and dried.

### How do they flambé desserts without setting the bottle on fire?

By pouring the liqueur directly from the bottle onto the food, a most dramatic fireball effect is achieved. The trick to safety during the flambé technique is to use a full bottle of liqueur. If the bottle is half empty, the vapors in the bottle can ignite first and severe burns can result!

### What athlete invented the PowerBar?

The PowerBar was concocted in 1986 by Canadian Olympic marathon runner Brian Maxwell and his wife in their Berkeley, California, kitchen. He was inspired to create a low-fat and long-lasting energy food after running out of steam near the end of a marathon race. It took three years of testing and tweaking to find the right balance of carbohydrates, vitamins, minerals, fiber, and protein for the bar. Maxwell came up with the name when friends began asking him for those "powerful bars." The first three flavors were malt, nut, and chocolate. Today, vanilla crisp is the most popular.

## Who invented the Heimlich maneuver?

A Dr. Heimlich, of course. It's not every doctor who gets a "maneuver" named after him, but Heimlich's maneuver has saved thousands of lives. Cincinnati surgeon Henry Jay Heimlich first described his technique in the June 1974 issue of *Emergency Medicine*. Heimlich said it was easy to tell choking, which he referred to as a "café coronary," from real heart attacks. A choker cannot talk, will turn blue, and will pass out. It is important to treat a choker as such. Administering mouth-to-mouth resuscitation will just push the trapped food farther down. To save someone from choking, he suggested approaching the choker from behind, placing the heel of one hand on the abdomen just above the navel and using the other hand to apply sharp upward thrusts to dislodge the food.

## What American had the most voracious appetite?

While no studies have been done, or hard data collected, American financier Diamond Jim Brady (1856–1917) is definitely up there in the eating department. For breakfast this guy would have breads, muffins, grits, pancakes, home fries, eggs, chops, and steaks washed down with a gallon of orange juice. To hold him over until lunch, he had a mid-morning snack of two or three dozen oysters. By lunch, he was ravenous, eating clams, crabs, lobsters, oysters, meat, pie, and orange juice. Dinner was his big meal of the day, consisting of dozens more oysters, six or seven lobsters, a dozen crabs, steak, terrapin, green turtle soup, two canvasback ducks, pastries, and more orange juice, followed by two pounds of chocolate. After the theater, he had a supper consisting of game birds, wild fowl, and shorebirds, with, of course, more orange juice. Wow! New York restaurateur George Rector called him "the best twenty-five customers I ever had."

As you can imagine his stomach was quite large. At his death, the autopsy revealed a stomach six times larger than that of an average man. His friend and eating companion, Lillian Russell, star of the stage, could also pack it away. It was said that she could match Brady bite for bite. Her rotund figure—she weighed in at 200 pounds—was the ideal of female beauty at the time. This was in the day when weight-gain products outsold weight-loss products.

## Who came up with the idea for Green Stamps?

There was a time, not so long ago, when you would get S&H Green Stamps with many purchases that you made, especially at the grocery store. If you saved enough of these things you could redeem them for a multitude of items. People saved them in special books. Catalogs were issued showing the merchandise available at redemption. At one point they had become so popular that S&H was printing three times as many stamps as the United States Post Office and its catalog was the single largest publication in the country. In the 1960s, S&H was the single biggest buyer of consumer products in the world. How did this phenomenon get started?

In 1896, two gentlemen—Thomas A. Sperry and Shelley B. Hutchinson—founded Sperry & Hutchinson (S&H) Company and issued their first stamps. One stamp was issued for every ten cents a customer spent at participating stores. After collecting enough stamps, one could go to "premium parlors" to redeem them. The largest store chain to get involved in the plan was A&P. Green stamps went out of vogue for a while, but made a comeback in 1951, when the Denver grocery chain King Sooper reintroduced them. By the end of the decade, 200,000 American retail stores offered green stamps, with S&H being the leader.

## What man invented Dexatrim and started Slim Fast?

Fat people are a gold mine for many an entrepreneur. One such person who preyed upon the portly was S. Daniel Abraham. Not only did he introduce the diet pill Dexatrim to the world in 1976 but he also brought out Slim Fast meal replacement powder a year later.

## Who is Salmonella named for?

It may be an honor to have a species named after you, but of all organisms, *Salmonella* must be one of the worst to be remembered for. This bacteria associated with food poisoning is named in honor of Daniel Elmer Salmon. In 1885, while working for the Bureau of Animal Husbandry at the USDA, he described this bacteria, which causes gastroenteritis and fever when ingested with bad food.